D1037269

CONTEMPORARY GLASS SCULPTURES AND PANELS

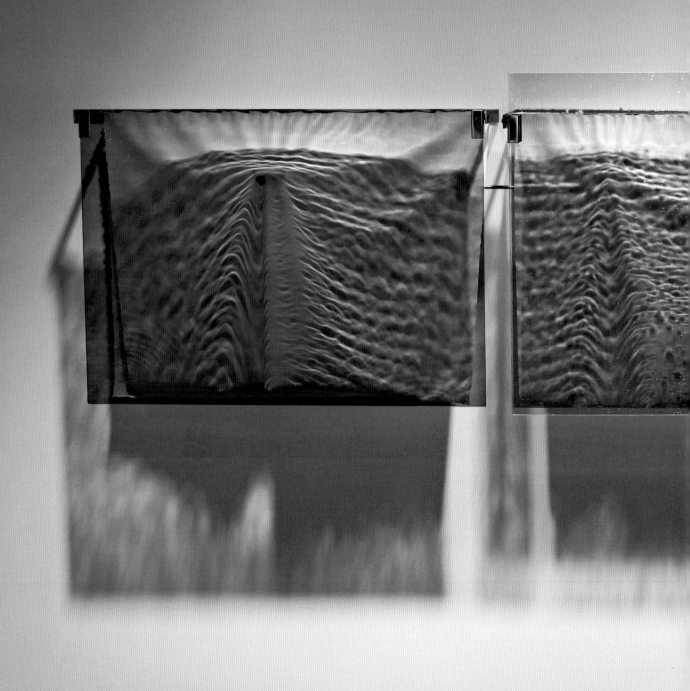

CONTEMPORARY GLASS SCULPTURES AND PANELS
SELECTIONS FROM THE CORNING MUSEUM OF GLASS

Tina Oldknow

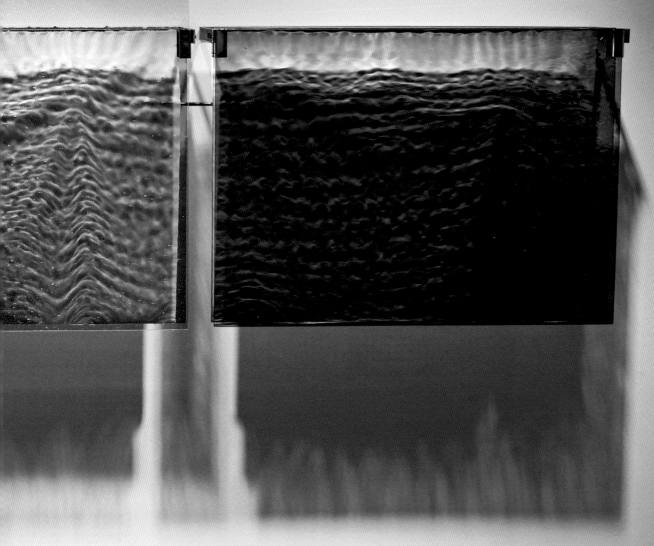

THE CORNING MUSEUM OF GLASS, CORNING, NEW YORK
In association with Hudson Hills Press, Manchester and New York

Editor: Richard W. Price
Design and Typography: Jacolyn S. Saunders
Photographic Supervisor: Nicholas L. Williams
Proofreader: Mary B. Chervenak
Reference Librarian: Gail P. Bardhan
Research Assistant: Laura A. Cotton
Rights and Reproductions: Jill Thomas-Clark

All of the photographs in this book are by
The Corning Museum of Glass (Nicholas L.
Williams and Andrew M. Fortune), unless
otherwise stated.

Copyright © 2008
The Corning Museum of Glass
Corning, New York 14830-2253

Published by The Corning Museum of Glass
in association with Hudson Hills Press LLC
3556 Main Street
Manchester, Vermont 05254

Distributed in the United States, its territories and possessions,
and Canada by National Book Network Inc. Distributed
outside North America by Antique Collectors' Club Ltd.

Publisher and Executive Director: Leslie Pell van Breen
Founding Publisher: Paul Anbinder

All rights reserved. No part of this publication may be reproduced,
stored in a retrieval system, or transmitted in any form or by any
means, whether electronic or mechanical, including photocopying,
recording, or otherwise, without the prior permission in writing of
the publisher.

ISBN 13: 978-0-87290-168-1
ISBN: 0-87290-168-8
Library of Congress Control Number: 2007936244

Library of Congress cataloguing-in-publication data is available
from the publisher upon request.

Cover: Dale Chihuly and James Carpenter.
The Corning Wall, 1974 (plate 27).

Frontispiece: Thérèse Lahaie. *Silver Gray
Nocturne Triptych,* 2005 (plate 80).

Contents

Contemporary Sculptures and Stained and Painted Glass in The Corning Museum of Glass

An Overview

Glass is a unique material for sculpture, and it is a contemporary material. It is unique because no other medium has its ability to change color, texture, and, seemingly, mass. As glass moves from transparency to translucency to opacity, its volume is understood in completely different ways. Its most distinctive characteristics are its transparency, which is both visible and invisible, and its ability to hold light as well as to reflect it. Glass is contemporary because only recently, since World War II, have artists truly learned how to use it sculpturally. It has shifted from being a material of function to a material of metaphor.

Stained glass has long been appreciated for its functional and symbolic qualities, and its ability to transform space. Anyone who has ever stood inside a dark church that has suddenly been lighted by the sun knows what this means. Transparent windows allow light and sight, but colored windows create mood and emotion, and they serve as a vehicle for narrative. From the turn of the 20th century, stained glass has been used as a material for architecture as well as a material for two-dimensional representations, or painting, in glass.

This book is a selection of glass sculptures and panels, dating from the late 1950s to 2007, from the collection of The Corning Museum of Glass. At 81 objects, it is by no means comprehensive. The sculpture, for example, does not include vessel-based work. Functional, nonfunctional, symbolic, and sculptural vessels will be the subject of a second volume of selections from the Museum's collection of contemporary glass. The stained glass chosen for this book focuses on the glass panel as painting, although a couple of examples of architectural glass are included.

What I have tried to do in these pages is to show the work of a range of artists who use glass as their primary material. In some cases, I have selected more than one piece by an artist when there are several important examples of his or her work in the Museum's collection. I have also included objects by artists who work in multiple media, and by those who come to glass from outside the glass world.

Some artists use glass because they have ideas that are most appropriately expressed in it. For others, the work is about developing new ways in which glass may be expressed. The artists selected here do not represent all or even most of the individuals who have worked in new ways with glass. What these artists share, however, is an experimental approach to glass that has encouraged its development—throughout the late 20th century and into the early years of the 21st—as a medium for sculpture and painting.

Historical glass panels and sculpture

Glass panels, unlike glass sculpture, have a long and well-known history. The glass window dates back to ancient Roman times. Some of the finer houses

Photo by Frank J. Borkowski.

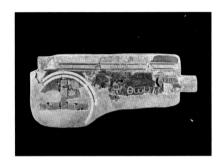

1   Fragment of Panel with Thomas
    Second half of the fourth century A.D.
    Roman Empire, eastern Mediterranean
    Glass mosaic
    L. 79 cm
    86.1.1

2   *Christ on the Road to Calvary*
    About 1570–1580
    Probably Austria, Hall or Innsbruck
    Reverse-painted glass, gilded
    H. 45.4 cm, W. 44.7 cm, D. 4.6 cm
    2002.3.5

3   Louis Comfort Tiffany
    Window with Hudson River Landscape
    1905
    United States, Corona, New York, Tiffany Studios
    Colored and opalescent sheet glass, cut,
    assembled; lead came, wood frame
    H. 346.2 cm, W. 330 cm
    76.4.22

in Pompeii, for example, were outfitted with glass windows that were most likely translucent rather than transparent, but they allowed light to pass through them. Medieval European stained glass, in conjunction with stone, created transformational spaces for sacred architecture, with soaring elevations of color and light. Glass also served historically as a medium for murals and painting. Two examples in the Museum's collection are a fragmentary fourth-century Roman glass mosaic (Fig. 1) and a late 16th-century reverse-painted glass panel, *Christ on the Road to Calvary* (Fig. 2). The stained glass of Louis Comfort Tiffany (American, 1848–1933; Fig. 3), whose landscapes were inspired by those of the plein-air painters, encouraged the development of a close relationship between glass and painting in secular stained glass.

Before the 1930s, the use of glass for sculpture, outside of the manufacture of small figurines, was rare. Highlights of the history of early glass

sculpture in the Museum's collection include the diminutive portrait of an Egyptian king (possibly Amenhotep II), which is also one of the earliest examples of glass in the Museum (Fig. 4). This head, cast of dark blue glass weathered to a brownish white, may have come from a representation of the Pharaoh as a sphinx. Another exceptional object, made about 1790 of a fashionably opaque white glass imitating porcelain, depicts the French queen Marie Antoinette (1755–1793; Fig. 5). Desperate to appear in support of the new regime (while planning her escape from France), she is shown as having sacrificed the heart of the nobility on the altar of the republic.

In the early 20th century, the making of small figural sculptures in glass was popularized in France by individuals such as Amalric Walter (1870–1959), Georges Despret (1862–1952; Fig. 6), and, later, René Lalique (1860–1945). In the 1930s, glass sculptures were designed in Italy by Napoleone

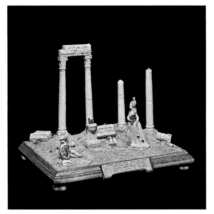

4 Portrait of an Egyptian
King
Late 18th Dynasty,
about 1450–1400 B.C.
Egypt
Cast glass
H. 4 cm
79.1.4

5 Pierre Haly
*Marie Antoinette Sacrifices the Heart
of the Nobility on the Altar of the
French Republic*
About 1790
France, Nevers
Lampworked glass; gilded wood base
H. 22.5 cm, W. 28.2 cm, D. 21.2 cm
2003.3.35

6 Georges Despret
Bust of a Woman
About 1905
France, Jeumont
Pâte de verre
H. 11.9 cm, W. 6.5 cm
79.3.146, gift of Lillian
Nassau Ltd.

7 Sidney Waugh
Atlantica
1938–1939
United States, Corning,
New York, Steuben Glass
Cast glass, cut, ground
H. 94.5 cm, W. 57.9 cm
72.4.222

Martinuzzi (1892–1977), Guido Balsamo Stella (1882–1941), and Flavio Poli (1900–1984). At this time, too, there were artists working in Czechoslovakia, including Jaroslav Brychta (1895–1971); Zdeněk Pešánek (1896–1965), who made large experimental sculpture in glass and mixed media; and Jaroslav Horejc (1886–1983), who designed monumental, architecturally scaled glass reliefs.[1] The Czechs' new, very large scale was mirrored in the United States with the creation of *Atlantica*, a 300-pound solid glass sculpture depicting a mermaid (Fig. 7). It was designed by Sidney Waugh (American, 1904–1963) and executed by Steuben Glass for the 1939 world's fair in New York City.[2]

The major catalyst for the creation of large-scale sculpture in glass occurred in Czechoslovakia, in tandem with the development of new uses for glass in architecture. The figurine maker Jaroslav Brychta, who was famous for his prize-winning mise-en-scènes of subjects such as aquatic life

and the circus, founded the important department of glass in architecture at the Železný Brod glassworks in northern Bohemia. In the course of developing glass for architectural purposes, his daughter, the sculptor Jaroslava Brychtová (Czech, b. 1924), would lead the way in the 1950s for the making of large-scale glass sculpture with another

1. For images of works by Pešánek and Horejc, and an account of the development of glass sculpture in Czechoslovakia, see Susanne K. Frantz, "Twentieth-Century Bohemian Art in Glass: The Artistic and Historical Background," in *Czech Glass, 1945–1980: Design in an Age of Adversity*, ed. Helmut Ricke, Stuttgart: Arnoldsche Art Publishers, and Düsseldorf: Museum Kunst Palast, 2005, pp. 14–35.
2. Steuben Glass never attempted another sculpture on the scale of *Atlantica*. The founder of Steuben, Frederick Carder (American, b. England, 1863–1963), made sculptural architectural decorations during the 1930s. In the 1940s and 1950s, after his retirement, he created many *pâte de verre* sculptures that he cast himself. See Paul V. Gardner, *The Glass of Frederick Carder*, Atglen, Pennsylvania: Schiffer Publishing, 2000, pp. 125–132.

remarkable artist: her husband, Stanislav Libenský (Czech, 1921–2002).

Postwar glass sculpture

Stanislav Libenský and Jaroslava Brychtová's iconic *Head I* (Fig. 8), in which the influences of the painter Amedeo Modigliani (Italian, 1884–1920) and African tribal art may be appreciated, represents a turning point in 20th-century glass sculpture. Libenský and Brychtová created a new direction for sculpture in glass by using a larger scale and an abstract, modernist approach, rather than the traditional, tabletop-sized, classicizing representations that were so pervasive in the decorative arts up to that time.

After World War II, the main European centers for glass production in Italy, Czechoslovakia, and the relative newcomer Scandinavia preserved their craft traditions by integrating art into industry. Artists were invited into factories to design product lines as well as one-off and limited-edition objects. In Czechoslovakia's unique situation, the communist government supplied studio space for artists inside the factories. Thus, postwar Czech artists using glass, such as Libenský, Brychtová, and René Roubíček (Czech, b. 1922), had access to factory facilities where their designs could be realized.

While the Czechs were exploring abstraction in large-scale glass painting (stained glass) and sculpture created for Expo '58 in Brussels, Belgium, the Italians navigated their own way in sculpture. In 1961, the contemporary art collector and art dealer Peggy Guggenheim (American, 1898–1979) worked with Egidio Costantini (Italian, b. 1912), the owner of a small glassworks on Murano called the Fucina degli Angeli, in commissioning sculptures, reliefs, and vessels by internationally recognized artists. Among the artists who created work for Costantini were Pablo Picasso (Spanish, 1881–1973), Marc Chagall (French, b. Russia, 1887–1985),

8 Stanislav Libenský
and Jaroslava Brychtová
Head I
1957–1958
(Plate 1)

9 Jean Cocteau
King Athamas
1957
France, Nancy, Cristallerie Daum
Pâte de verre, gilded
H. 24.9 cm, W. 26.1 cm, D. 15.4 cm
2006.3.34

Jean Cocteau (French, 1889–1963), and Guggenheim's husband, Max Ernst (German, 1891–1976).[3] A pitcher from the Museum's collection, designed by Cocteau for the French glassworks Cristallerie Daum, is typical of the kind of experimentation that was going on at that time (Fig. 9).

3. A complete set of Picasso's glass nymphs and fauns, made at the Fucina degli Angeli in 1964, is in the collection of the Albright-Knox Art Gallery in Buffalo, New York. For more information on the Fucina, see *Egidio Costantini e i suoi artisti. Sculture in vetro della Fucina degli Angeli: Da Picasso a Fontana, 1954–1996 = Egidio Costantini and His Artists. Sculptures in Glass from the Fucina degli Angeli: From Picasso to Fontana, 1954–1996*, ed. Gianmaria Prati and Emanuela Tinelli Piatti, [Piacenza]: Fattidarte. [1996]. Steuben Glass also executed a series with artists that was initiated by Henri Matisse, a friend of Steuben's design director, John Monteith Gates (American, 1905–1979). The series, "27 Contemporary Artists," was completed in 1940. It included vases and bowls engraved with designs by Thomas Hart Benton (American, 1889–1975), Jean Cocteau, Salvador Dali (Spanish, 1904–1989), Giorgio de Chirico (Italian, b. Greece, 1888–1978), André Derain (French, 1880–1954), Raoul Dufy (French, 1877–1953), Marie Laurencin (French, 1885–1956), Aristide Maillol (French, 1861–1944), Isamu Noguchi (American, b. Japan, 1904–1988), Georgia O'Keeffe (American, 1887–1986), and Grant Wood (American, 1891–1942).

10 Robert Willson
Ranch Doll
1984
(Plate 28)

11 Edris Eckhardt
Archangel
1956
United States, Cleveland, Ohio
Pâte de verre
H. 22 cm, W. 10 cm
61.4.64

12 Harvey K. Littleton
Torso
1942
United States, Corning, New York
Slip-cast Vycor glass, fused
H. 28.6 cm, W. 12.8 cm
78.4.38, gift of Dr. and Mrs. Fred A. Bickford

By 1956, the sculptor Robert Willson (American, 1912–2000) had begun to travel to Italy every year to produce his work. Willson was one of the few American artists who recognized the potential of hot glass as a material for sculpture. Lacking the technical resources to attempt such a project in the United States, he enlisted the help of the accomplished Venetian glass sculptor and designer Alfredo Barbini (Italian, 1912–2007).[4] The sculptures of Willson, a Texan who had spent several years traveling in Mexico, were inspired by ancient and Native American art, modern Mexican art, and the landscapes of Texas. *Ranch Doll*, a monolithic figure based on the ancient Toltec stone guardians at the Mexican site of Tula, illustrates Willson's distinctive syncretistic style (Fig. 10).

4. While Barbini was Willson's closest collaborator, Willson also worked with other well-known Muranese glass sculptors, including Pino Signoretto (Italian, b. 1944) and Loredano Rosin (Italian, 1936–1991).

Glass in the studio

In the late 1950s, artists working in glass in Europe and the United States began to realize, independently of one another but at the same time, how compelling a material for sculpture glass might become. The designer-craftsmen Edris Eckhardt (American, 1910–1998) and Harvey Littleton (American, b. 1922) were among the few American artists drawn to glass as a sculptural material. The small, cast *Archangel* in the Museum's collection, which recalls the figures of Marc Chagall, reflects Eckhardt's interest in modern art (Fig. 11). The Museum is also fortunate to have a couple of early experimental sculptures by Littleton, created in Corning in 1942. They are from a series of female torsos made of fused Vycor, an industrial, heat-resistant glass with a high silica content (Fig. 12).

After 1945, glass and other materials associated with the applied arts and studio craft, such as ceramics and textiles, expanded from a functional, decorative arts and design core into the peripheral areas of the fine arts. This migration has been documented in many texts about postwar studio craft. Glass, however, is a technically demanding material that had its own medium-specific challenges in its adaptation for use in the artist's studio. Cold glass processes such as cutting and assembling stained glass, as well as the so-called warm processes such as slumping, fusing, and certain types of casting that may be executed in a simple kiln, do not require elaborate equipment or highly specialized technical knowledge. These are the kinds of glassworking techniques that were commonly practiced by artists in their studios in the first decade after World War II. For hot glass processes such as glassblowing and large-scale casting in which glass is worked in a molten state, the opposite is true. These processes require specialized equipment as well as a technical knowledge of the material that can take years to acquire. It should come as no surprise, then, that for most of its history, the working of molten glass has been confined to the glasshouse or glass factory, just as molten metals have been traditionally restricted to the foundry.

In 1962, a group of young American artists attending two workshops at The Toledo Museum of Art—led by Harvey Littleton and the glass research scientist Dominick Labino (American, 1910–1987)—were introduced to the idea of exploring hot glass as a material for art.[5] One year after these historic workshops, which were made possible by Labino's development of a glass-melting furnace suitable for studio use, Littleton established a glass program at the University of Wisconsin in Madison. He encouraged his students, many of whom came from ceramics, to work with glass sculpturally. The aim, Littleton said, was to "investigate the material, like the painters were investigating paint; not with the thought of making anything."[6]

While Littleton and his first group of students—which included Marvin Lipofsky (American, b. 1938) and Dale Chihuly (American, b. 1941)—pursued hot glass, a handful of New York sculptors were also drawn to the material, in the form of commercial plate and mirror glass. In the late 1960s, Lucas Samaras (American, b. Greece, 1936) made mirrored rooms that exploited the material's capability to reflect and disorient, while mirror constructions and piles of earth and broken glass by Robert Smithson (American, 1938–1973) examined properties such as reflection, illusion, and transparency. The well-known glass boxes and sculptures by Larry Bell (American, b. 1939), which also date to the late 1960s, were made of industrial plate glass, as were sculptures by Christopher Wilmarth (American, 1943–1987), which often combined glass and metal.

The reflective and illusionistic surfaces of Bell's early boxes reappear in *Window Bkd #6*, a wall piece that utilizes the same kind of highly reflective plate glass that has been vacuum-coated with vaporized metals (Fig. 13). An early sculpture by Wilmarth in the Museum's collection, titled *Gyes Arcade*, dates to 1969 (Fig. 14). The composed elements—flat and curved plate glass that was

5. In this essay, the history of 20th-century glass sculpture can be only briefly treated. For full accounts of the beginnings of the American Studio Glass movement, see Susanne K. Frantz, *Contemporary Glass: A World Survey from The Corning Museum of Glass*, New York: Harry N. Abrams, 1989; and Martha Drexler Lynn, *American Studio Glass, 1960–1990: An Interpretive Study*, New York: Hudson Hills Press, 2004. Researching the potential for studio glassblowing in the late 1950s, Littleton visited some of the small factories (*fornaci*) on Murano, near Venice, and the glassblower Jean Sala (French, 1895–1976) at his

Montparnasse glass studio in Paris. As a glassblower who worked in a private studio, outside a factory, Sala was in a unique situation.

6. Joan Falconer Byrd, interview with Harvey K. Littleton, March 15, 2001, Nanette L. Laitman Documentation Project for Craft and Decorative Arts in America, Archives of American Art, Smithsonian Institution. A glass program at Alfred University in Alfred, New York, was also established in 1963 by Andre Billeci (American, b. 1933), and many others soon followed.

13 Larry Bell
Window Bkd #6
1993
(Plate 45)

14 Christopher Wilmarth
Gyes Arcade
1969
(Plate 5)

15 Marvin Lipofsky
California Loop Series 1969, #29
1969
(Plate 4)

commercially cut and slumped, and then acid-etched, stacked, and balanced by Wilmarth—form an abstract floor composition that both reflects light (clear elements) and absorbs it (etched elements). For Wilmarth, as for Bell, the behavior of reflected and absorbed light is the subject of the art work.

While artists such as Bell and Wilmarth were unaware, until later, of what was going on in studio glass, studio glassblowers interested in sculpture and installation were well aware of them. Studio glass artists appreciated the new and radical uses for glass that Bell and Wilmarth were investigating, but their aim was to learn to work the material themselves, and to work it in new ways. In a 1971 video that records Dale Chihuly demonstrating glassblowing with James Carpenter (American, b. 1949), Chihuly says: "We probably spend most of our time developing the techniques and figuring out how to make [the objects]. Generally, once

we've made a series of something and are able to finish it, we usually drop it and go on to something else, because as you are working with the material, you are always discovering new possibilities."[7]

As essential as it was for studio glassblowers to learn technique, the focus on the execution of artistic ideas in glass was just as important. An early sculpture by Marvin Lipofsky illustrates how studio glass artists searched for ways to subvert the traditional associations between blown glass and functionality by developing sculptural forms (Fig. 15). This sculpture is blown, sandblasted, and flocked, illustrating the new emphasis on unconventional forms and materials. Other ways of working hot

7. Dale Chihuly and James Carpenter, *Glass Blowing*, videotape (b/w, 13 minutes, narrated by Chihuly) by Bob Hanson for the American Craft Council, made at Haystack Mountain School of Crafts, Deer Isle, Maine, 1971. Rakow Research Library, The Corning Museum of Glass.

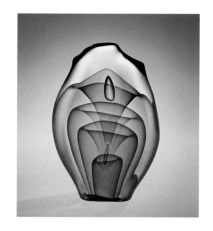

16　Harvey K. Littleton
Upward Undulation
1974
United States, Verona, Wisconsin
Slumped sheet glass; aluminum base
H. 161.5 cm, W. (base) 60.9 cm
79.4.145, purchased with the aid
of funds from the National
Endowment for the Arts

17　Harvey K. Littleton
*Gold and Green Implied
Movement*
1987
(Plate 35)

18　Dominick Labino
Emergence Four-Stage
1975
(Plate 11)

glass sculpturally in this period are seen in Harvey Littleton's pieces about movement and stasis, which look at the paradoxical nature of a material that is fluid when molten and rigid when cooled. The sculpture *Upward Undulation* (1974) shows where Littleton was headed with this idea (Fig. 16), while a mature realization of the concept can be seen in *Gold and Green Implied Movement,* made 13 years later (Fig. 17). Yet another direction is illustrated by Dominick Labino's well-known study in color and transparency, *Emergence Four-Stage,* made in 1975 (Fig. 18). Labino's air traps create a diaphanous veiling within the glass, heightening the transparency by creating a sense of depth and volume.

Although their work was not well known outside Czechoslovakia—a Soviet-bloc country cut off from the West—Czech artists such as Stanislav Libenský, Jaroslava Brychtová, and René Roubíček were investigating glass as a material for sculpture in the late 1950s, as is demonstrated by the remarkable

sculptures and installations created for Expo '58 in Brussels. For American studio glass artists who visited the Czechoslovak Pavilion at Expo 67 in Montreal, Canada—including Harvey Littleton, Marvin Lipofsky, and Dale Chihuly—the large-scale sculpture in glass was a revelation.[8] The cast lead glass *Disk* in the Museum's collection, by Václav Cigler (Czech, b. 1929), dates from this period (Fig. 19).

8. A new relationship between painting, sculpture, and glass was pioneered in Czechoslovakia in the 1950s and 1960s, and the development of abstraction in glass was a key component of this relationship. While abstract painting and sculpture were vigorously suppressed by the communist regime that controlled Czechoslovakia after 1948, glass was not considered a fine art. It was deemed a material for functional and ornamental objects, and thus artists could be much freer in what they chose to do with it. Glass designers were encouraged, and even supported, in their experimentation with styles and approaches to content that were forbidden in painting and sculpture. See Tina Oldknow, "Painting and Sculpture in Glass: Czech Design Drawings from the 1950s and 1960s in The Corning Museum of Glass," in *Czech Glass, 1945–1980* [note 1], pp. 58–73.

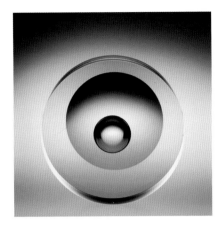

19 Václav Cigler
Disk
About 1966–1971
(Plate 2)

20 René Roubíček
Untitled
1971
(Plate 6)

Throughout his career, Cigler has investigated the mechanics of transparency and reflection. His sculptures are not meant to be displayed in neutral contexts, such as a white-painted gallery, but to interpret the world around them. (Cigler had his sculptures photographed outdoors, for example, and in architectural spaces.) An untitled sculptural form by René Roubíček, made in 1971, is a three-dimensional interpretation of an abstract drawing (Fig. 20). This object was once owned by Harvey Littleton, who collected early 20th-century and contemporary glass in order to show his students

firsthand the many different approaches to the material.[9]

Studio stained glass and architectural glass

Unlike glassblowing, the working of stained glass has always been associated with the artist's studio. While its popularity rose and fell throughout the 20th century, stained glass has been of ongoing interest to artists from outside the glass world, such as Marc Chagall, Josef Albers (German, 1888–1976), Henri Matisse (French, 1869–1954), Diego Rivera (Mexican, 1886–1957), and, most recently, Wim Delvoye (Belgian, b. 1965). Typically, it is difficult for artists working in stained glass to have their work recognized outside their field. Many artists make a living as restorers in addition to creating personal work, a practice quite different from that of artists working in other glass-forming techniques. Stained glass and its successor, the broad and diverse field

9. This sculpture was purchased by Littleton from Ray and Lee Grover. Littleton believes that because glass is transparent, it hides nothing, and thus one can always see how it is made. In an interview, Littleton said: "There are no secrets. In the first place, glass is transparent. If you understand how it's made, every piece has its history right there for you to read. . . . All the technique is there for us to see. . . . It's transparent to a trained mind." Harvey K. Littleton [note 6].

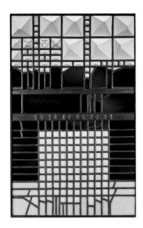 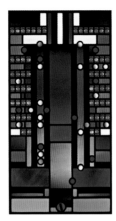 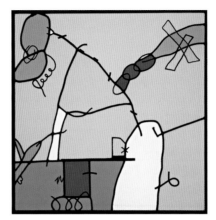 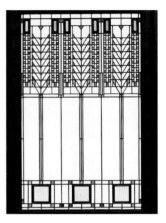

21 Ludwig Schaffrath
Untitled
1968
Germany, Alsdorf
Cut glass; lead came
H. 90.4 cm, W. 58.2 cm
90.3.44, bequest of Robert
Sowers in memory of
Theresa Obermayr Sowers

22 Robert Sowers
Turkish Delight
1972
(Plate 7)

23 Robert Kehlmann
Composition XXXI
1976
(Plate 13)

24 Frank Lloyd Wright
Window, *Tree of Life*
1904
United States, from the Darwin D.
Martin House, Buffalo, New York
Cut glass, iridized; gold leaf,
lead came
H. 100.9 cm
92.4.175, Clara S. Peck Endowment

of architectural glass, have their own history, which intersects with that of the American Studio Glass movement but is not limited to it.[10]

After World War II, stained glass, along with other craft media, experienced a resurgence of interest in the United States. In the 1950s, Robert Sowers (American, 1923–1990) introduced the influential modernist work of German stained glass artists such as Ludwig Schaffrath (German, b. 1924; Fig. 21) to an American audience. It was the Germans who freed stained glass from architecture, in the form of the autonomous panel, which could then be approached like painting. This paved the way in the United States for artists such as Sowers (Fig. 22) and, later, Robert Kehlmann (American, b. 1942; Fig. 23) to experiment with abstraction in glass. In this endeavor, they were undoubtedly influenced by the early 20th-century stained glass of the architect Frank Lloyd Wright (American, 1867–1959; Fig. 24).

Pioneering work with abstraction in stained glass was being realized in Czechoslovakia in the late 1950s by artists such as Vladimír Kopecký (Czech, b. 1931) and Jan Kotík (Czech, 1916–2002). These artists made monumental pieces for Expo '58 in Brussels and for Expo 67 in Montreal that were unparalleled.[11] In Italy, Paolo Venini (Italian, 1895–1959) designed experimental fused glass panes for international exhibitions. One example is the Museum's *mosaico tessuto* (woven mosaic) panel designed for the 1957 Milan Triennale (Fig. 25).

During the late 1960s and early 1970s, stained glass was more popular in the United States than

10. For recent publications on the history of 20th-century stained glass, see, for example, Virginia Chieffo Raguin, *The History of Stained Glass: The Art of Light, Medieval to Contemporary*, London: Thames & Hudson, 2003; and Robert Kehlmann, *20th-Century Stained Glass: A New Definition*, Kyoto: Kyoto Shoin, 1992.

11. For more information on Czech glass at the world's fairs, see Verena Wasmuth, "Czech Glass in the Limelight: The Great Exhibitions Abroad," in *Czech Glass, 1945–1980* [note 1], pp. 86–103.

25 Paolo Venini
Mosaic Panel
1957
Italy, Murano, Venini Glass
Mosaico tessuto (woven
mosaic), hot-worked
canes, assembled, fused
H. 150 cm, W. 75.1 cm
2001.3.59

26 Narcissus Quagliata
Melancholia
1981–1982
United States, Oakland, California
Cut glass, painted; lead came
H. 139.7 cm, W. 142.2 cm
87.4.17, gift in part of John Hauberg, Anne
and Ronald Abramson, and the artist

27 Dale Chihuly
and James Carpenter
The Corning Wall
1974
(Plate 9)

at any time since the turn of the century. American studio glass artists appreciated the artistic potential of stained glass, which was soon adopted by painters and glass artists unfamiliar with the medium. Because the new work went beyond conventional stained glass techniques, materials, and concepts, this category of two-dimensional glassworking became known as "flat" glass. Robert Kehlmann and other pioneering northern California artists, such as Paul Marioni (American, b. 1941) and Narcissus Quagliata (American, b. Italy, 1942; Fig. 26), found autonomous flat glass to be an exciting new format for abstraction and contemporary narrative. Artists still create autonomous panels using stained glass, reverse painting on glass, and other techniques. However, the popularity of this kind of work has diminished since the late 1980s.

The once avid interest in stained glass has shifted, in recent decades, to the field of large-scale architectural glass, in which stained glass is only one of many techniques available to artists. One of the pioneering artists working in architectural glass is James Carpenter, whose work is represented in the Museum's collection by an early panel he made with Dale Chihuly in 1974 (Fig. 27). *The Corning Wall* is an excellent example of how historical methods of working and using glass were redefined by studio glass artists. Instead of putting together a traditional stained glass window, Chihuly and Carpenter blew multiple elements that were then cut, assembled, and leaded. The combination of cold (cutting and assembling) and hot (blowing) processes and the integration of sculptural (three-dimensional) elements into a flat (two-dimensional) panel were considered forward-thinking at the time. The initials "F.L.," signifying "Flood Line," refer to the devastating 1972 flood that swept through the city of Corning. The thick white line beneath the letters marks the height to which the floodwaters rose inside the Museum.

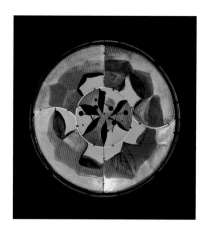

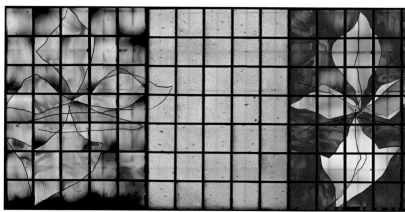

28   Dominick Labino
      Ionic Structure of Glass
      1979
      (Plate 18)

29   Brian Clarke
      The Glass Wall
      1998
      (Page 6 and Plate 59)

A significantly larger scale in studio flat glass was achieved by Dominick Labino, whose special commission for the Museum, *Ionic Structure of Glass* (Fig. 28), is composed of five large and colorful fused glass sections. The scale, as well as the technique, was still experimental in the United States in 1979.[12] The shift from studio flat glass to architecturally scaled studio glass is demonstrated in the groundbreaking work of Brian Clarke (British, b. 1953). His window in the Museum, titled *The Glass Wall* (page 6 and Fig. 29), has an area of more than 1,000 square feet, and it was fabricated at Franz Mayer Inc. in Munich. It is not meant to be understood as a window, as is historical stained glass, or even as part of the architecture. It is, rather, a large mural or painting.[13]

Glass in the late 20th and 21st centuries

During the 1980s, American studio glassworking experienced an exponential growth. In 1979, it was not difficult to know the names of all of the

12. Another architectural panel was made by Labino in the same technique for The Toledo Museum of Art. For an image, see Jutta-Annette Page, ed., *The Art of Glass: Toledo Museum of Art*, Toledo, Ohio: the museum in association with D. Giles, 2006, frontispiece. A related technique was developed by Stanislav Libenský and Jaroslava Brychtová for the cast windows they created in 1964–1968 for the chapel of St. Wenceslas at St. Vitus Cathedral, Prague. For an image, see Milena Klasová, *Stanislav Libenský, Jaroslava Brychtová*, Prague: Gallery, 2002, pp. 65–67.

13. The piece is dedicated to the late Linda McCartney, wife of the musician Sir Paul McCartney. The repeating fleur-de-lis motif—"sketched" with aluminum came on top of the glass—is based on the lily, a flower that for centuries has served as a symbol of royalty. This theme was chosen by Clarke as a tribute to his friend Linda McCartney's love for the flower, and as a reflection of his own interest in the colors and symbolism of British heraldry. Developments in glass technology by architectural glass fabricators, such as Franz Mayer and Derix in Germany, have enabled studio artists to create a range of work, in very large scale, with techniques new to glass in architecture.

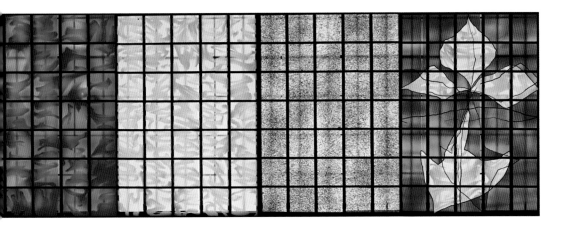

American artists working in studio glass. By 1989, it was impossible. Artists from Europe came to the United States throughout the 1980s to teach, and American artists went to Europe, Australia, and Japan. Studio glass became global, with exhibitions held in galleries and museums around the world. It seemed as if new techniques were being developed every month, and previously underutilized glassworking methods, such as casting, fusing, and flameworking, were enthusiastically taken up.

When looking at American studio glass made in the 1970s versus that made in the 1980s, the most obvious changes are the widespread technical improvements that resulted in more sophisticated-looking work, the increase in colors available to artists, and the dramatic growth in the size of objects that artists were able to make. European studio glass, which has its own history quite different from that of American glass, did not experience the same changes. What Europeans took from

Americans was not knowledge of how to work glass, but the inspiration of how to be free with it, of how to break with established traditions. Internationally, glass was increasingly used as a vehicle for sculpture and painting.

One of the biggest changes in American studio glass in the last 15 years is not how it is used—that is, how it is employed in the service of craft, design, or art—but how it is accessed. In the early years of the American Studio Glass movement, many artists believed (and some still do) that it was essential for the artist to make his or her own work. By the 1990s, however, even die-hard glassblowers were willing to work with other glass artists, better at certain techniques, to make their objects.

The phenomenon of artists coming to glass from outside the glass world began to increase significantly during the 1990s. This signaled an important shift. In general, throughout the 20th century, it was not easy for American artists to gain access to glass. Harvey Littleton introduced it into the private studio and into university and art-school curriculums, but it was still a complicated matter for artists who did not want to invest time in learning how to work the material. A new access to glass was enabled by, and quickly gained momentum with, the development of public-access studios across the country and the availability of glassblowers for hire. Suddenly, glass artists and studios became available—for the first time in the United States—to any artist. Sculptors who had ideas for glass could use a glass studio like a bronze foundry. They could rent facilities and engage artists to work with them to produce blown, cast, hot-sculpted, and flameworked objects in glass.[14]

In the 2000s, glass has increasingly been used as a material for sculpture by artists from outside the glass world, as well as by artists for whom glass is a primary material. Glass is intersecting with the worlds of design and contemporary art in multiple directions, and the American Studio Glass movement, as it was defined from the 1960s through the 1980s, no longer exists. Although the international studio glass community has always been, and remains, strong and cohesive, glass has become a material available to all. It has become inclusive rather than exclusive. The methods of working it, and how it may be accessed, have become truly open and transparent.

Subjects of contemporary glass

In content and meaning, the contemporary glass panels and sculptures discussed in this book address the same large and complex subjects traditional to the fine arts. These subjects include history, narra-

30 William Morris
Standing Stone
1982
(Plate 26)

31 Howard Ben Tré
Dedicant 8
1987
(Plate 33)

tive, the figure, and observations on the natural world. Sometimes the subject is the material itself, and the qualities that set it apart from other media.

In a general survey such as this one, it makes the most sense to discuss the content of contemporary works in thematic, rather than chronological, groupings. The glass sculptures and panels that I have chosen give form to certain ideas, and the ability to compare and contrast how these ideas have been realized is meaningful. In the plates section of this book, however, the objects are organized chronologically. In both cases, the information communicated is important for the understanding of how glass has developed in recent decades as a medium for art.[15]

14. Although glassworkers and factory owners on Murano, for example, have been involved in this kind of service for decades (and still are), many American artists cannot afford to work there, or they prefer to work closer to home.

15. For information on glassmaking terms and processes, which are not discussed in this essay, go to the Museum's Web site at www.cmog.org. Under "Glass Resources," there are glassworking videos (see "A Video Guide to Glassworking Processes and Glass Properties"), a glass dictionary, and a general resource on glass.

32　Howard Ben Tré
From Jack J
1980
(Plate 22)

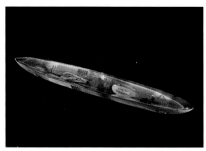

33　Bertil Vallien
*Unknown
Destination II*
1986
(Plate 32)

Narrative, history, and time

In general, narrative in art addresses memories, stories, and histories, which range from those of an individual, a family, and an institution to those of a community and a nation. A narrative implies a past and a future, which introduces the element of time. Narratives in the Museum's collection of contemporary glass cover historical, legendary, personal, political, documentary, and symbolic topics. These include sculptures and panels by Michael Aschenbrenner (American, b. 1949), Howard Ben Tré (American, b. 1949), György Buczkó (Hungarian, b. 1950), Robert Kehlmann, Vladimír Kopecký, Silvia Levenson (Argentinean, b. 1957), Paul Marioni, Josiah McElheny (American, b. 1966), William Morris (American, b. 1957), Richard Posner (American, b. 1948), Robert Rauschenberg (American, 1925–2008), Gerhard Ribka (German, b. 1955), Ginny Ruffner (American, b. 1952), Judith Schaechter

(American, b. 1961), Joyce Scott (American, b. 1948), and Bertil Vallien (Swedish, b. 1938).

Archeology, with its record of the remote human past, is a subject that is well expressed in glass. Glass is an ancient material, and in its fragility and luminosity, it gives the impression of transcending time. Inspired by the Neolithic monuments found on Scotland's Orkney Islands, William Morris's *Standing Stone* (Fig. 30) is a heavy, hollow chunk of mold-blown glass that represents an impressive technical achievement: in 1982, it was the largest blown form to be attempted by an American artist. The muted colors and striations in the glass recall the ancient Scottish stones, stained with lichens, that stand in grassy fields dotted with wildflowers and heather. A sense of the remote past also pervades Howard Ben Tré's monolith: the massive sand-cast *Dedicant 8* (Fig. 31), which was also unusually large when it was made in 1987. A traditionally delicate and fragile material, glass is not generally expected to assume huge proportions, and the attempt to shift it into an architectural scale here is significant. A decade later, the heroic size of these objects was not exactly common, but it was no longer extraordinary.

Like all of Ben Tré's sculptures, *Dedicant 8* and *From Jack J* (Fig. 32) are inspired by elements of architecture and industry, such as columns, heavy stone fragments, ancient monoliths, and machine parts. A sense of passing time is evoked in these pieces, which may refer to sacred or industrial architectural remains. The theme of the journey from past to present, and from present to future, is given form in the symbolic boat *Unknown Destination II*, sand-cast by Bertil Vallien (Fig. 33). This sculpture is mysterious in aim and somewhat claustrophobic in feeling, with its inclusions of small human figures frozen in suspended animation. The rough, sandy texture of the glass adds to the object's air of great age: the vessel appears as if it had been pulled out of the ground. This is also the case

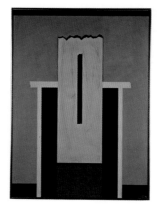

34 György Buczkó
Ti
1991
(Plate 40)

35 Robert Kehlmann
Entombment, Station 14
1982
(Plate 25)

36 Gerhard Ribka
St. Anastasius
1992
(Plate 43)

in *Ti* (Fig. 34), György Buczkó's mysterious hiero-glyph, whose dark and roughened surface is sug-gestive of an ancient relic.

In glass, the most effective vehicle for narra-tive has traditionally been stained glass, which for centuries represented religious scenes such as the Passion of Christ, the lives of the saints, and other, often violent, Christian accounts. Two panels by Robert Kehlmann and Gerhard Ribka illustrate Christian subjects, which especially benefit from the dimension of light (symbolizing divinity) that stained glass brings to images. Kehlmann's abstract panel, from a series on the Stations of the Cross, depicts the 14th station, the entombment of Christ (Fig. 35). This station, which symbolizes death and rebirth, has been depicted for centuries in Western art. Kehlmann's imagery is simple and stripped down, consisting of a post-and-lintel outline of a tomb with a slab of jagged stone placed above it. The colors are muted and light-absorbing, with the

opaque black giving the composition an air of sadness and solemnity. The denouement of the martyrdom of Saint Anastasius, a Persian soldier who converted to Christianity and became a monk, is the subject of Ribka's panel (Fig. 36). While trav-eling in Turkey, Anastasius was captured by his countrymen, and because he refused to renounce his Christianity, he was strangled and his body was thrown to the dogs. The dogs did not touch the body, and on this basis, Anastasius was granted sainthood. The simple figures and awkward com-position relate this work to that of painters such as Paul Klee (Swiss, 1879–1940) who were inspired by children's art.

The dramas depicted in historical stained glass and painting are updated by artists such as Judith Schaechter, who creates images inspired by con-temporary life. Like many images of events in the news, the natural disaster depicted in Schaechter's *Caught in a Flood* has both literal and symbolic

37 Judith Schaechter
Caught in a Flood
1990
(Plate 39)

38 Judith Schaechter
Nedotykompectomy
1986
(Plate 30)

39 Josiah McElheny
Untitled (White)
2000
(Plate 68)

meaning (Fig. 37). This panel is about loss and being lost—disappearing into the deep—but it also refers to tragic events seen in great historical paintings, such as *The Raft of the Medusa* (1819) by Théodore Géricault (French, 1791–1824). Throughout her work, Schaechter depicts characters experiencing suffering, loss, and redemption. *Nedotykompectomy* (Fig. 38) was directly inspired by Hieronymus Bosch's famous painting *The Cure of Folly* (about 1475–1480), which shows a patient undergoing a lobotomy. In Schaechter's panel, a bound, bleeding individual has a small figure plucked from its forehead by a disembodied hand descending from above, much as the hand of God is depicted in early European painting.[16] The Punk/ Gothic style of Schaechter's characters recalls the anxious but beautiful figures of medieval art, as well as modern German Expressionist painting.

The long and rich history of glassmaking, as a topic for contemporary glass, is most literally expressed in the reproduction and reinterpretation of older forms. Josiah McElheny looks at the recent past of glass in an installation that pays tribute to Modernism and the history of 20th-century glass design (Fig. 39).[17] An accomplished glassblower, McElheny creates installations of glass vessels that are based on real and imagined art and glass histories, and he often uses a specific anecdote as a point of departure. In this work, Untitled (White),

16. Schaechter's title, a made-up word, refers to an impish being, the "Nedotykomka," that lives in the head of the protagonist of *The Petty Demon*, a novel by the Russian Symbolist author Fyodor Sologub, published in 1907.

17. Although sculptural vessels will be the subject of a second volume, McElheny's concept for and presentation of this piece—as a symbolic arrangement of objects inside a display box that is as important as its contents—influenced its placement here. Unless otherwise indicated, all of the interpretations of works in the Museum's collection are based on conversations with the artists and/or on notes in files at The Corning Museum of Glass.

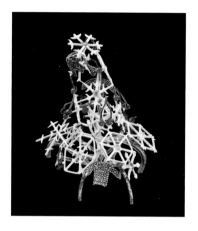

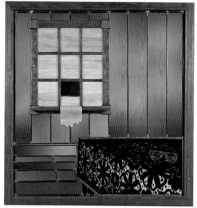

40 Ginny Ruffner
*Shirts, Cherries, and
Snowflakes, Of Course*
1993
(Plate 49)

41 Paul Marioni
The Conversationalist
1974
(Plate 10)

McElheny's choice of color—a brilliant white—and purposeful lack of title refer to Modernist concepts of purity, spareness, and simplicity. The objects are displayed in a 1950s International Style cabinet, and they reproduce the work of famous 20th-century glass designers who have inspired McElheny. These include Oswald Haerdtl (Austrian, 1812–1886), Josef Hoffmann (Austrian, 1870–1956), Gunnel Nyman (Finnish, 1909–1948), Paolo Venini, Tapio Wirkkala (Finnish, 1915–1985), and Vittorio Zecchin (Italian, 1878–1947).

Life experience and the life of the mind are fertile sources for narrative, especially when the interpretation is suggestive and mysterious, rather than literal. Ginny Ruffner's distinctive sculptures are inspired by the randomness of dream imagery and by the Surrealists' unusual juxtapositions of everyday objects. Ruffner turns these elements into a personal vocabulary of symbols that refer to events in her life (Fig. 40). Paul Marioni's stained

glass images, also drawn from experience, can be darker, with intimations of drug-induced hallucination. Although the setting is comfortably normal in *The Conversationalist*—a wood-paneled room, a patterned tablecloth, a pair of glasses laid down— there is the quiet, alarming or absorbing event (depending on your state of mind) of the sky sliding out of one of the panes of the framed window (Fig. 41).

While themes drawn from personal experience appear throughout contemporary narratives in glass, political and social commentaries generally do not. In contrast to painting and graphic design, which are the best-known tools of irony and protest in art, glass, being easily pretty and transparent, may seem shallow. Yet some artists have succeeded in using the material's beauty to communicate a pointed message. Glass is used as a symbol of beauty, treachery, and the potential for violence in the work of Silvia Levenson. As a young woman

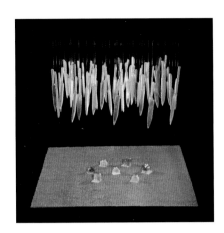

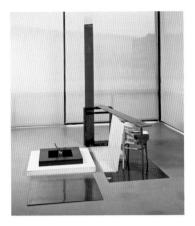

42 Silvia Levenson
It's Raining Knives
1996–2004
(Plate 54)

43 Joyce J. Scott
*Three Graces Oblivious
While Los Angeles Burns*
1992
(Plate 44)

44 Vladimír Kopecký
Drepung
1992
(Plate 41)

in Buenos Aires, she protested and then fled the military dictatorship of Jorge Rafaél Videla, moving to Italy with her husband and young children in 1981. Under General Videla's rule, thousands of Argentineans were imprisoned, tortured, and murdered, including members of Levenson's family.[18] Conceived in response to this turbulent period in the artist's life, the installation *It's Raining Knives* (Fig. 42) has since served—in post-9/11 America—as a thoughtful commentary on the threat of terrorism in general. Much of Levenson's art is an attempt to resolve the difficulties of living with threats of violence, both political and domestic, that are out of our control.

Joyce Scott uses glass beads to address topics such as sexuality, violence, and civil rights. *Three Graces Oblivious While Los Angeles Burns* (Fig. 43) was created in the wake of the beating of Rodney King by police officers in Los Angeles, and the city-wide rioting that followed their acquittal in 1992.[19]

Beneath the head of an African-American, representing the victimized King, the three Graces—who symbolize gracefulness, peace, and happiness—turn their backs on a burning city skyline. For Scott, the choice of beads is intentional. Beadworking is traditionally regarded as a woman's pursuit, and it is usually associated with jewelry and other decorative applications, especially in ethnographic and folk art. In Scott's hands, the bead regains its currency, but it is a value that is symbolic rather than monetary.

Drepung by Vladimír Kopecký is abstract and enigmatic (Fig. 44), and unlike most of his work, it

18. General Videla staged a coup d'état in 1976, deposing Isabel Perón. A junta composed of the commanders of the army, navy, and air force (the most repressive regime ever experienced in Argentina) ruled the country until December 1983, when civilian rule was restored.

19. The Los Angeles policemen were subsequently retried and convicted by a federal judge.

carries a specific political reference. The title comes from the name of the famous Tibetan Buddhist monastery that was shut down by the Chinese government after the communist takeover of Tibet in 1959. The 250 monks at Drepung who escaped imprisonment and execution moved to India, where they eventually built another monastery. Made after the fall of communism in the Soviet Union and central Europe, *Drepung* honors the memory of the Buddhist monastery while drawing attention to the widespread persecution and destruction perpetrated by the Chinese government in Tibet. In this installation, the artist has created an uncertain structure built on imbalance (such as the chair and the teetering plate glass it supports), and he has covered most of the glass with opaque paint. Specific materials, such as a chair and paint can, should be regarded as volumes of color in an abstract composition rather than as objects. Kopecký's presentation of materials—glass, paint, and wood—considers qualities such as light, shadow, texture, volume, reflection, opacity, fragility, and stability.

War is one of the enduring themes in Western art, and given the generation of the artists who pioneered American studio glass, it is surprising that the subject of the Vietnam War does not appear more often. Two uncommon occurrences are found in the works of Richard Posner and Michael Aschenbrenner.[20] In his panel, Posner uses the metaphor of the window to present himself looking back at his wartime self (Fig. 45). A photographic image of the artist is shown peering through a window at a figure lying in traction on a bed. The scene records Posner's experience in alternative service: a conscientious objector, he sustained a back injury while working as a dishwasher in a civilian hospital. The symbolic imagery of cows, marching soldiers, and an open book is drawn from a dream Posner had while recovering from his injury. The scene re-creates the guilt, isolation,

45 Richard Posner
Another Look at My Beef with the Government
1976
(Plate 14)

46 Michael Aschenbrenner
Damaged Bone Series: No Place Left to Hide
1989
(Plate 36)

20. A related piece in the Museum's collection, which is not illustrated in this book but which should be mentioned, is a cast glass relief by Henry Halem (American, b. 1938). Titled *Ravenna Masked Bandit*, it was made following the National Guard's shooting of students at Kent State University in Kent, Ohio, where Halem taught, in 1972. See Frantz [note 5], p. 100.

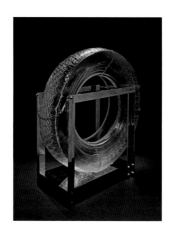

47 Robert Rauschenberg
    Tire
    Designed in 1995–1996
    and made in 2005
    (Plate 53)

48 Clifford Rainey
    Hollow Torso
    1997
    (Plate 57)

Interested equally in popular culture and in social commentary, Robert Rauschenberg was one of an early group of Pop artists who changed the course of modern art. Throughout his long and controversial career, Rauschenberg challenged people's notions of what fine art is and how it is made. His *Tire*, a symbol that has been repeated many times in his work, comments on the preciousness and infallibility of contemporary art (Fig. 47). The rubber tire—a humble, dirty, industrial, and ecologically adverse necessity—is re-created in mold-blown colorless glass and presented as a thing of beauty. Luminous and luxurious, like a diamond in a platinum setting, it casually leans in its silver-plated carrier. As was typical of Rauschenberg, the work is highly ironic, but it also encourages the viewer to consider everyday objects in new ways.

The figure and the self

Although the telling of stories, or narrative, is a primary vehicle for the depiction of the figure in art, figural studies and portraits constitute a significant genre. Glass is an ideal material in which to execute the figure because one of the most powerful analogies for glass is that it holds light in its mass in the same way that the spirit is held in the mass of the physical body. In the Museum's collection, the figure in glass has been addressed by artists such as Hank Murta Adams (American, b. 1956), Erwin Eisch (German, b. 1927), Judy Hill (American, b. 1953), Karen LaMonte (American, b. 1967), Stanislav Libenský and Jaroslava Brychtová, Clifford Rainey (British, b. Northern Ireland, 1948), Jill Reynolds (American, b. 1956), René Roubíček, Gizela Šabóková (Czech, b. 1952), Christopher Wilmarth, and Ann Wolff (German, b. 1937).

Studies of the figure in glass, as in other media, range from lifelike to abstract. Two naturalistic life-size sculptures—*Hollow Torso* by Clifford Rainey (Fig. 48) and *Evening Dress with Shawl* by Karen

and anguish that the artist felt in making his decision to abstain from war. Aschenbrenner served as a medical field technician in Vietnam, and his sculpture addresses the trauma of human casualties. In his *Damaged Bone Series*, which was inspired by his own leg wound, translucent bones are attached by thin wires or carefully bound with rags and supported by wood splints (Fig. 46). The reverence with which the glass bones are treated, as well as their presentation as relics, means to communicate, Aschenbrenner says, feelings of "warmth, gentleness and regret."[21] The glass, in this case, is not functional, as it is in Posner's window onto the past, but it is symbolic of the fragility of the body and the psyche.

21. Michael Aschenbrenner, "Analysis: Personal Imagery," *Glass Art Society Journal* (Corning, New York: Glass Art Society), 1985, p. 70.

LaMonte (Fig. 49)—are inspired by classical art in their monumentality, idealization, and fragmentary state. Both artists use complex molds to create their sculptures, which reveal the human form inside the structure of a supporting brace (Rainey) or an evening gown (LaMonte). Symbolizing the transience of the physical body, Rainey's nude female form is one of a series of torsos that considers the body and time. It is constructed from 13 individually cast sections that are stacked one atop another: although the torso appears to be strong, it is still a vulnerable shell that can be knocked apart. In LaMonte's monumental figure, which is cast in five sections, it is the dress that is emphasized, with only a ghostly impression of the physical body remaining. LaMonte uses clothing as a means to investigate identity, and the dress, always life-size, is a recurring motif. From stiff and frilly Victorian dresses to body-hugging 1930s gowns to voluminous classical drapery, LaMonte's fashion choices look at changing notions of beauty, how women view themselves, and how they have been viewed by others.

When the body is treated in an abstract or symbolic way, a different kind of energy, dynamism, and immediacy is conveyed. Christopher Wilmarth's tribute to the French Symbolist poet Stéphane Mallarmé (1842–1898) is the subject of *Insert myself within your story . . .* (Fig. 50). This work, in which glass is used to suggest spirituality, belongs to a group of sculptures collectively known as the "Breath" series. Mallarmé's poetry, according to Wilmarth (who identified closely with it), contained the "anguish and longing of experience not fully realized."[22] Having previously worked only with "cold" glass, Wilmarth saw the potential of hot, blown glass as a metaphor for the poet Mallarmé's breath and spirit. For the vessel to contain the breath, he chose the form of an egglike head, inspired by the sculpture of Constantin Brancusi (Romanian, 1876–1957). Creating a successful figural form is more challenging in blown glass than it is in

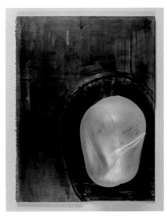

49 Karen LaMonte
Evening Dress with Shawl
2004
(Plate 77)

50 Christopher Wilmarth
Insert myself within your story . . .
1979–1981
(Plate 20)

other techniques, such as casting. The refined, simplified shapes of Brancusi's sculptures parallel the rounded forms of blown glass. The work of Brancusi is echoed again in the ghostly bodies of René Roubíček's figures (Fig. 51).

The study of gesture and mood, rather than the suggestion of human form, is the dominant concern of an abstract cast glass torso by Gizela Šabóková, titled *Come to Me* (Fig. 52). The title, the deep blue color, and the self-confident posture of the sculpture beckon the viewer to come

22. Laura Rosenstock, *Christopher Wilmarth*, New York: Museum of Modern Art, 1989, p. 16. The glass head was made at the California College of Arts and Crafts in Oakland in 1979, when Wilmarth was an artist in residence at the University of California at Berkeley. It was blown by Paul Weber and not by Marvin Lipofsky, as has been reported in various publications.

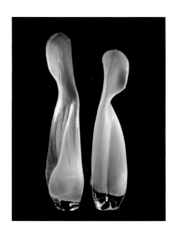

51 René Roubíček
Figures I, II
1980
(Plate 24)

52 Gizela Šabóková
Come to Me
2002–2004
(Plate 75)

53 Erwin Eisch
Eight Heads of Harvey Littleton
1976
(Plate 12)

near. At close range, however, the torso's rough abraded surface, its heavy and unwieldy shape, and its projecting arms visually push away the viewer, keeping all at a distance. The seductive beauty of the material adds to the complexity of the mood being portrayed, creating a sense of ambiguity and capriciousness.

Portraiture is realized in glass in a variety of ways, ranging from depictions of the self to symbolic portraits that communicate through posture, gesture, and emotional nuance. A portrait can be symbolic at the same time that it is naturalistic, and a good portrait will always reflect who the sitter is and not just what he or she may look like.

Studio glass pioneer Erwin Eisch has spent his career blowing glass in molds in his own likeness and in the likenesses of others. In the early years of the Studio Glass movement, he was respected for his approach to the material as poetic and robust rather than sweet, ugly rather than beautiful,

and opaque rather than transparent. In 1962, Eisch met Harvey Littleton, and through their friendship, an important link was established between European and American studio artists working in glass. Eisch's well-known portrait *Eight Heads of Harvey Littleton* shows the many facets of a man Eisch admired and sought to define (Fig. 53). The heads represent, from left to right in the photograph, *Littleton the Spirit; Littleton the Gentleman; Littleton the Fragile; Littleton, Man of Frauenau; Littleton the Teacher; Littleton's Headache; Littleton the Poet;* and *Littleton the Worker. Littleton the Teacher* is inscribed with Littleton's widely known and controversial aphorism, "Technique Is Cheap." Rather than denying the importance of technique, which is how many artists have understood the maxim, Littleton meant to urge artists to focus on the artistic content of their work. Glass is a technically demanding material, and because of this, there is always the threat of artists (and, equally important,

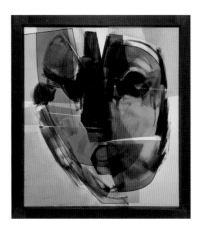

54 Ann Wolff
Double Face
1999
(Plate 65)

55 Hank Murta Adams
Bust with Locator
1995
(Plate 51)

56 Judy Hill
Jump
1993
(Plate 47)

their viewers) becoming arrested at a level that focuses on mastery of skill.[23]

Eisch's portrait illustrates the different aspects and roles of an individual, as does the portrait of a woman by Ann Wolff (Fig. 54). However, Wolff's portrait—which was made by painting on individual glass sheets and then layering the sheets, as in a collage—is more symbolic: while she enters into the realm of the depiction of the self, the subject is really Everywoman. Wolff remarks: "It is natural to take oneself as one's starting point. The situation of women partly determines who I am and leads me to pose particular questions."[24] Throughout her career, Wolff has been interested in the life of women, and her work rarely strays from that topic. The relationships between women as friends, and as mothers and daughters, and the role of women in society deeply concern her. Another kind of symbolic portrait is represented by *Bust with Locator* by Hank Murta Adams, which does not depict an

individual or Everyman, but a state of mind (Fig. 55). Although the somewhat humorous and animated qualities of Adams's portraits make them seem caricaturish, their depictions of mood and feeling are carefully observed.

Self-portraiture is a category that has been explored by relatively few artists in glass. Judy Hill makes female figures that look identical, but they are individualized through posture and gesture (Fig. 56). All of her figures, whether single or grouped, are portraits of herself that represent different states of mind, thoughts, preoccupations, and experiences. Jill Reynolds is an installation artist

23. As Littleton explains it: "[What] I meant by that is that technique is available to everybody, that you can read the technique, if you have any background. Technique in and of itself is nothing. But technique in the hands of a strong, creative person . . . takes on another dimension." Harvey K. Littleton [note 6].

24. Ann Wolff, interview with Helmut Ricke, in Heike Issaias and others, *Ann Wolff*, Stockholm: Raster Förlag, 2002, p. 177.

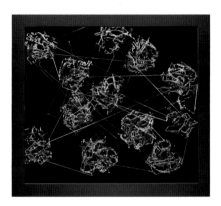

57 Jill Reynolds
Family Matter
2002
(Plate 73)

58 Stanislav Libenský
and Jaroslava Brychtová
Imprint of an Angel II
1999
(Plate 62)

whose work examines relationships between the body, science, nature, and language. *Family Matter* is a portrait of Reynolds and her 11 siblings as interconnected molecules (Fig. 57). Each molecule is made up of sets of letters spelling out a name, and the larger, hollow letters are filled with a bloodlike red liquid. Both molecules and letters, Reynolds explains, can be combined in an infinite variety of ways to create new meaning, whether as physical matter or as written text. The key to this self-portrait is the observation that the self exists within a network of relationships, that each individual constitutes a single molecule in the huge organism that is the world.

The last series of sculptures by Stanislav Libenský and Jaroslava Brychtová, made before Libenský's death in 2002, may be considered as both symbolic portraits and portraits of the self. What they constitute are forms, or portraits, of the soul. While Libenský and Brychtová began their long career together in glass with abstract heads (Fig. 8), most of their efforts over the years have been dedicated to exploring geometric forms and the drama of light captured in the glass mass. *Imprint of an Angel II* (Fig. 58) represents a return to the physical body. It is a soul-portrait that looks at themes of aging, mortality, and the human spirit, which the artists call the "inner light." Made of a blackish gray glass that is the color of the many X-rays that Libenský studied after the discovery of his lung cancer, the sculpture depicts a man's shoulders and chest. The form, described by the artists as a vestment or a shroud, is meant to represent the physical impression of an angel, or the divine part of man.[25]

25. For a discussion of this series of sculptures, see Robert Kehlmann, *The Inner Light: Sculpture by Stanislav Libenský and Jaroslava Brychtová*, Tacoma, Washington: Museum of Glass: International Center for Contemporary Art, 2002.

Nature and landscape

Glass is not usually thought of as a natural or organic material, yet its ability to assume a variety of textures and colors and to hold light makes it the perfect material to explore the natural world. Forms and patterns in landscape, as well as the flora and fauna of the natural world, are all potential themes to be realized in glass. The still life, or *nature morte*, refers to the fecundity and abundance of nature. But it also marks the passing of time in its intimation of death and decay. Representations of still lifes and the world of flowers and animals in glass in the Museum's collection include works by the American artists Beth Lipman (b. 1971), Donald Lipski (b. 1947), Flora Mace (b. 1949) and Joey Kirkpatrick (b. 1952), Sherry Markovitz (b. 1947), Debora Moore (b. 1960), Dennis Oppenheim (b. 1938), Michael Rogers (b. 1955), Therman Statom (b. 1953), and Jack Wax (b. 1954), and the Czech artist Ivan Mareš (b. 1956).

Still Life with Two Plums by Flora Mace and Joey Kirkpatrick consists of an oversize wood bowl filled with an assortment of huge fruit that includes a blushing pear, a glossy Italian plum, a greengage, shiny red and green apples, a textured lemon, a tangelo, and a fuzzy peach (Fig. 59). In order to create realistic colors and textures, the artists built layers of color on their blown glass forms by sifting crushed colored glass powders onto the hot glass during the blowing process. By focusing on something as common as a bowl of fruit, Mace and Kirkpatrick want their giant still lifes to encourage awareness of the cycles and seasons of nature, and to communicate the idea that in the natural world, everything is connected.

A different kind of still life is portrayed in the work of Donald Lipski, whose sculpture and installations examine the properties of organic materials and the operation of ecological systems. Lipski searches out thick-walled industrial and scientific

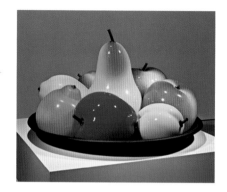

59 Flora C. Mace and Joey Kirkpatrick
Still Life with Two Plums
2001
(Plate 71)

60 Donald Lipski
Water Lilies #52
1990
(Plate 38)

61 Beth Lipman
    Untitled (after A. Martini)
    2001
    (Plate 70)

62 Therman Statom
    Clearly Oranges
    1998
    (Plate 61)

glass containers, such as tanks, spheres, and tubing, that are rated to hold highly toxic acids. Instead of using these vessels for dangerous materials, he encloses delicate and ephemeral substances, such as plants, in order to protect them from an increasingly toxic environment. In *Water Lilies #52*, a bunch of carrots floats inside acid-resistant glass tubing that has been hermetically sealed with a heavy steel clamp (Fig. 60). The preservative solution keeps the carrots in suspended animation, but they will gradually fade and decompose. This still life is not in stasis, but changes over time. Eventually, all that will be left of the carrots is debris at the bottom of the tubing, with only a photograph preserving what the sculpture originally looked like.[26]

In their still lifes, Beth Lipman and Therman Statom are not inspired by objects assembled from nature, but by those preserved in painting. Lipman, who understands the still life as a memento mori, has studied 17th-century Dutch painting, and she interprets selected still-life compositions in hot, sculpted glass (Fig. 61). For this untitled piece, an enamel decal of a still life by the Italian painter A. Martini, found by Lipman, served as a catalyst. Lipman re-created the fruits and vegetables of the still life in glass, and then applied the decal to the sculpture, creating a dialogue between the two- and three-dimensional representations. Statom assembles glass shards, blown glass objects, and found objects that he combines with painting, drawing, and writing (Fig. 62). He encloses his still lifes in sectioned glass boxes, which he calls "divided paintings." In the room-size installations for which Statom is well known, his still-life assemblages evolve into landscape.

---

26. The decomposition is Lipski's intention, and he does not wish for the organic materials in his sculptures to be replaced.

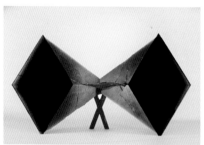

63 Debora Moore
Host IX–Epidendrum
2007
(Plate 81)

64 Ivan Mareš
Blackcoater
1989
(Plate 37)

65 Jack Wax
Fugitive
2003
(Plate 76)

Objects interpreting animals, rocks, flowers, and trees may seem unlikely in glass, but these can be some of the most fluent works in the medium. Debora Moore has spent several years studying orchids, yet her seemingly naturalistic sculptures are interpretations rather than copies that aim to depict the essence of the ephemeral flowers (Fig. 63). Insects and other cold-blooded animals also have potential for glass. Looking out the window of his studio one day, Ivan Mareš was struck by a swarm of black butterflies that looked, he said, as if they were "wearing black evening coats."[27] The form of these butterflies was the basis for *Blackcoater* (Fig. 64). In this abstract, almost batlike shape with an intentionally rough, primitive surface, the thickest parts of the sculpture are a shade of nearly opaque purple that absorbs light. As the glass becomes thinner toward the edges, the color lightens and becomes transparent, like the water at the edge of a pond.

The theme of insects may also be employed for the purpose of analogy, which is suggested in *Fugitive* by Jack Wax (Fig. 65). The shriveled and perforated tubelike structures that make up this sculpture refer to ephemeral things, such as cocoons, husks, and snakeskins, that are both necessary to life and casually discarded when they are no longer useful. These remains allude to the transience of the physical body, and they are symbolic of transformation. Bees, beehives, and the communal industry that they represent are addressed in *Beehive Volcano* by Dennis Oppenheim (Fig. 66). The sculpture, consisting of three mold-blown glass domes, is accompanied by a soundtrack of buzzing bees. In this work,

27. From a statement in object record files at The Corning Museum of Glass.

66 Dennis Oppenheim
Beehive Volcano
Designed in 1979 and made in 1989
(Plate 21)

67 Michael Rogers
13 Crows
2002
(Plate 74)

68 Sherry Markovitz
Big Bear
1997
(Plate 56)

Oppenheim compares the compressed social activity of the hive and, by extension, any situation in which social behavior is controlled and suppressed, with the potentially explosive force of a volcano. The bright primary colors of the hives give the sculpture an innocent air that is belied by the warning it means to convey.

Animals have long been employed as symbolic messengers in art, and glass may be used to underscore their spiritual role. A sculpture by Michael Rogers, titled *13 Crows*, was inspired by the dead crows (acting as scarecrows) that the artist saw hanging in fields throughout Japan (Fig. 67). The number of the birds is unlucky, and their lifeless, inverted bodies are covered in words—in this case, Japanese newspapers—that could convey good news or bad. While ominous signs abound in this piece, the actual birds are toylike and almost humorous, and the meaning is intentionally ambiguous. *Big Bear* by Sherry Markovitz may also be

appreciated as symbolic. The thick encrustation of colorful and eye-catching materials signals that this is a power object rather than a trophy head (Fig. 68). The power object, well known in the art of tribal cultures, is distinguished by the carefully selected accumulation of materials that adorn it. These may be rare or treasured materials or, in the case of *Big Bear*, materials that have meaning for the artist.

Nature may be appreciated as a source of inspiration for artists in additional, and more abstract, ways. Landscape plays a central role because it is through the observation of nature that proportion, composition, volume, color and light, and pattern and line may be discovered. When landscape is understood as an organizing device, and as a model for the creation of structure, then its necessity to artists, and especially to artists working with abstraction, becomes evident. Ideas about landscape and the interpretation of the four elements may

69 Michael Scheiner
Bearing
1998
(Plate 60)

70 Alessandro Diaz de Santillana
Custode di sabbia
1993
(Plate 46)

71 Alessandro Diaz
de Santillana
West Sky
1997
(Plate 55)

be seen in sculptures and panels in the Museum's collection by Nicole Chesney (American, b. 1971), Bernard Dejonghe (French, b. 1942), Alessandro Diaz de Santillana (Italian, b. France, 1959), Eric Hilton (British, b. Scotland, 1937), Franz Xaver Höller (German, b. 1950), Thérèse Lahaie (American, b. 1958), Jessica Loughlin (Australian, b. 1975), Tom Patti (American, b. 1943), Susan Plum (American, b. 1944), Michael Scheiner (American, b. 1956), and Kiki Smith (American, b. Germany, 1954).

The four elements—air, earth, fire, and water—are the physical and metaphysical building blocks of the natural world. Like the four seasons, the four elements provide a handy structure with which ideas about nature may be symbolically expressed. The element of earth, for example, is suggested in works such as *Bearing* by Michael Scheiner (Fig. 69). This abstract, organic sculpture, inspired by the segmented forms found in nature, has the appearance of a giant dirt-colored worm. Made of blown

glass sections joined with epoxy resin, it evokes the cold solidity and immovability of earth.[28] In contrast, Alessandro Diaz de Santillana translates the element of fire and the sensations it evokes of searing, burning, glowing, and smoldering into the brilliant red flamelike form of *Custode di sabbia* (Caretaker of sand; Fig. 70). The word "sand" in the title refers to the heat of the desert and also to the sand that is the main ingredient of glass. In *West Sky*, de Santillana is inspired by another element, air (Fig. 71). Sky and its sense-associations of light, invisibility, wind, and cold are interpreted by de Santillana as a hard, reflective, aerodynamic vertical that looks like a frozen silver zeppelin. The

28. Scheiner's primary interest in glass is process, which, for him, generates ideas. Although he talks about this sculpture as being inspired by segmented forms found in nature, the reading of the sculpture as related to the element of earth is my interpretation.

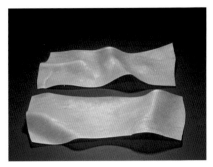

72 Bernard Dejonghe
Cercle
1995
(Plate 52)

73 Franz Xaver Höller
Parchment
1994
(Plate 50)

74 Kiki Smith
Brown Water
1999
(Plate 64)

sculpture is dematerialized, that is, it is made nearly invisible by its mirrored surface filled with air bubbles, which reflects the world around it.

Although it has a close relationship to air and fire, which are the elements involved in its making, glass is perhaps most convincing in its use as a metaphor for water. Water is, visually and symbolically, most akin to glass, and it is not surprising that many artists working in glass examine this relationship. Like glass, water has various grades of transparency, it can acquire a range of colors, and it exists in fluid and rigid states.

Correlations between water and glass are considered in *Cercle* (Circle) by Bernard Dejonghe (Fig. 72). The cold, rigid white blocks of this sculpture are more evocative of snow and ice than of the intense heat of the glass kiln. Dejonghe cast optical-quality lead glass so that it developed a hard, devitrified white crust, which was then chiseled, resulting in a material that has the depth and clarity of rock

crystal with the rough surface of weathered glass or stone. The winter landscape, rather than the element of water, serves as a visual source for *Parchment* by Franz Xaver Höller (Fig. 73). Made of two simple panels, heated over forms inside a kiln, this sculpture brings to mind the soft forms of hills blanketed with snow. In this piece, which externalizes thoughts and emotions using the forms of landscape, there is the illusion of something dynamic beneath the surface, just as the new growth of spring waits under the frozen earth.

Nature and landscape are recurring subjects in the sculpture of Kiki Smith. Glass appears throughout her work, as a spiritual and narrative element, as a bodily fluid, or as a metaphor for sky and water. In *Brown Water*, Smith uses 247 solid teardrop-shaped components, placed in an intentionally patternless and changing arrangement, to evoke glistening beads of water (Fig. 74). Her droplets give physical presence to the random marks made by

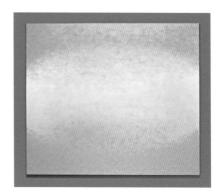

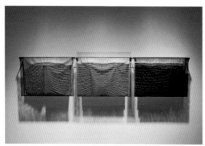

75 Nicole Chesney
Present
2005
(Plate 79)

76 Thérèse Lahaie
Silver Gray Nocturne Triptych
2005
(Plate 80)

77 Eric Hilton
Innerland
1980
(Plate 23)

raindrops as they fall to the ground, and as such, they transform the intangible into physical form.

The complex and shifting relationship between water and air is addressed in the painting *Present* by Nicole Chesney (Fig. 75). In the creation of this image, she was inspired by the writings of the French philosopher Gaston Bachelard (1885–1962) and especially by his vision of the cloudless, empty sky, which refers, he says, to the exterior sky and the "interior skies of dreams." With a luminous and slightly reflective sandblasted mirror as its canvas, the painting is a depiction of fog or clouds, a poetic union of the elements of air and water. There is no perspective and there are no moorings in *Present*; it depicts, rather, the vastness of interior and exterior space. Insight into the actions of light, water, and breath is provided by the kinetic and seemingly fluid wall-mounted work *Silver Gray Nocturne Triptych* by Thérèse Lahaie (Fig. 76). Light is projected through textured glass panels onto a fabric,

while a brush attached to a low-r.p.m. motor pushes the fabric against the back of the glass and then releases it. This activity creates shifting patterns of shadow and reflection that mimic the way that light plays on the surface of water. The shadows expand and contract rhythmically, like breaths, drifting in and out of focus. By giving her pieces movement, Lahaie animates the glass, calling attention to the unique qualities of the material.

Eric Hilton is closely tied to the dramatic and windswept landscapes of northern Scotland, where he lives part of the year, but his most ambitious sculpture, *Innerland*, reflects the landscape of the imagination (Fig. 77). Designed for the highly refractive glass made by Steuben Glass, Hilton's crystal landscape, made up of 25 separate cubes, has dreamlike topographical features that are meticulously engraved, cut, and sandblasted in the glass. When the components are assembled, the optical refraction of the glass makes it appear as if the

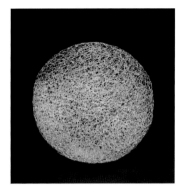

78 Tom Patti
Clear Lumina with Azurlite
1992
(Plate 42)

79 Jessica Loughlin
Vertical Lines 2
2002
(Plate 72)

80 Susan Plum
Woven Heaven, Tangled Earth
1999
(Plate 63)

interior structures have grown inside the sculpture. *Innerland* is meant to express Hilton's ideas about the unity of life and of the "inner being, or inner land, which is shared by all people everywhere."[29]

Cues taken from landscape for the organization of visual studies in abstraction may be observed in the work of Tom Patti and Jessica Loughlin. Patti has devoted much of his career to researching special glasses and glass coatings, and to developing his elaborate fusing methods. His complex and precisely engineered sculptures, such as *Clear Lumina with Azurlite*, appear to be monumental, even architectural, but in reality they are quite small (Fig. 78). The horizontal bands of color in his works mimic the progression of color in landscape as it changes from the darker tones of the earth to the increasingly paler hues of the sky.[30] Loughlin uses the open landscape of Australia as a visual and intellectual model for abstraction. Her forms are minimal, and she replaces color with monochro-

matic tones, such as the gray scale of her kiln-formed sculpture *Vertical Lines 2* (Fig. 79). The hanging elements of this wall piece, which are reduced to flat planes with long, vertical ribs, refer to the shifting space of the horizon, where land and sky meet. The horizon, although visible, can never physically be reached. Unattainable and ever-present, it conveys a sense of endless time.

Ancient cosmologies, archeological and future time, and the celestial landscape are the sources of inspiration for *Woven Heaven, Tangled Earth* by Susan Plum (Fig. 80). This airy, light-filled sphere, constructed from thin rods of borosilicate glass, is an object of curiosity and fascination because

29. From a statement in object record files at The Corning Museum of Glass.
30. The correlation between the progression of color in landscape and the progression of color in Patti's sculptures is my interpretation.

if it were any larger, it could not support its own weight.[31] As a physical thing, it barely exists. Its extreme fragility suggests a sense of otherworldliness, which is what the artist means to convey. Plum is interested in methods of weaving, which she practices in her flameworking technique, and in the archeology of Mexico. She discovered that certain Mesoamerican cultures conceived of the universe as a loom, woven with filaments of light (energy). Around the earth, Plum remarks, "the woven strands of light become entangled, and it is the job of the shaman to untangle this 'discord.' Thus, the act of weaving symbolically rebuilds and re-energizes the world."[32] For Plum, glass is a metaphor for light. It is a way in which form can be given to energy, which, although quantifiable, remains mostly invisible and intangible.

Color, light, reflection, and transparency

The last section of this essay looks at material. What are the unique characteristics of glass, what can it do, and how can it be used? So far, I have addressed the ways in which glass has been employed in the service of narrative, history, and time; in creating the figure; and in constructing forms inspired by the natural world. Yet the artistic process often begins with material. The material aspects of glass are revealed in the way that light, color, and reflection can be controlled, and in the different ways that transparency can be manipulated. In the Museum's collection, such approaches to material are seen in the sculptures of Dale Chihuly, Václav Cigler, Pavel Hlava (Czech, 1924–2003), Jun Kaneko (Japanese, b. 1942), Marian Karel (Czech, b. 1944), Stanislav Libenský and Jaroslava Brychtová, Marvin Lipofsky, Věra Lišková (Czech, 1924–1985), Paul Seide (American, b. 1949), Lino Tagliapietra (Italian, b. 1934), Pavel Trnka (Czech, b. 1948), and Dana Vachtová (Czech, b. 1937).

81   Marvin Lipofsky
IGS VI 1997–1999, #12
1997–1999
(Plate 58)

The exploration of color in space is one of the most engaging aspects of glass as a material for sculpture. Marvin Lipofsky, Dale Chihuly, and Lino Tagliapietra are among the many artists whose work follows this path, and for them, color is all-important. Beginning with a vessellike bubble, Lipofsky breaks apart and sculpts the blown glass shape while the material is hot (Fig. 81).[33] What is

31. Borosilicate glass, also known in the United States as Pyrex, is a low-thermal-expansion glass, which is why it is suitable for cookware. Both "hard" borosilicate and "soft" soda-lime glasses are used in flame-working, in which glass is heated and manipulated over an oxygen-propane-fueled torch.

32. From a statement in object record files at The Corning Museum of Glass.

33. Like Josiah McElheny's installation (Fig. 39), this sculpture has a strong relationship to vessels. The way in which Lipofsky subverts and even destroys the vessel form in the creation of his sculpture led to the placement of this work here.

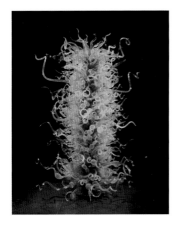

82 Dale Chihuly
Fern Green Tower
2000
(Plate 66)

83 Lino Tagliapietra
Endeavor
2004
(Plate 78)

created is a ragged form that retains the idea of the bubble as symbolic of breath, but that acts as a three-dimensional canvas for the presentation of color. For his chandeliers and towers, of which *Fern Green Tower* (Fig. 82) is an example, Chihuly uses organic shapes and intense hues to create a mass of bright color. He then shoots light through the mass to animate it, creating a moment of pure color energy. When they are lighted, the 500 curling elements of *Fern Green Tower*, which are attached to a steel structure, seem to come alive, as if the construction were some sort of giant underwater plant. Although the piece weighs 1,400 pounds, it imparts a feeling of fluidity and weightlessness.

A sense of weightlessness also characterizes *Endeavor*, Lino Tagliapietra's airy installation of 18 boatlike forms (Fig. 83). Inspired by the sight of the many gondolas that gather at the entrance to the Venetian lagoon on the feast day of the Ascension (Festa della Sensa), Tagliapietra imagined the dis-

tinctive wooden boats, gently bobbing on the water and adorned with colorful standards, as abstract shapes floating in space. For some viewers, Tagliapietra's suspended forms are reminiscent of a flock of birds or a school of fish, or they simply represent powerful strokes of color. However it may be understood, *Endeavor* clearly communicates that glass is a material that visually thrives in light and space.

Neon as a material for art has its own history, which cannot be considered within the confines of this essay, yet any discussion of color and light in glass would be incomplete without mentioning it. Paul Seide is one of a group of pioneering glass artists who began to explore neon in the 1970s. Although neon is seen everywhere in the form of building and product signs, Seide and others, such as Dale Chihuly (with James Carpenter) and Fred Tschida (American, b. 1949), experimented with it for sculptural and installation work. Inspired by the

84   Paul Seide
      Frosted Radio Light
      1986
      (Plate 31)

85   Stanislav Libenský
      and Jaroslava Brychtová
      Red Pyramid
      1993
      (Plate 48)

light objects of such well-known sculptors as Dan Flavin (American, 1933–1996) and Bruce Nauman (American, b. 1941), artists working with glass developed new ideas for neon. In Seide's sculpture *Frosted Radio Light* (Fig. 84), the electrical transformer required for neon is replaced by a radio transmitter. As is typical in his pieces, the colors, which are produced by the enclosed, charged gases, move and change shades when the sculpture is stroked.

When the words *color* and *light* are mentioned in the same sentence as *glass*, the artists that immediately and inevitably come to mind are Stanislav Libenský and Jaroslava Brychtová, who sought to create work that engages light, space, transparency, and volume. They pursued original directions in their sculpture throughout their career together, which spanned more than 45 years. Yet it was not until 1987, when the couple were in their 60s, that they could devote themselves full-time to their art.

In the 1990s, the Czech Republic established its independence, and the artists were finally free to take control of their work. It was a prolific and fruitful decade for them. Although they experimented with many different forms and colors in glass, they were mainly interested in the ways that light could be manipulated in the glass mass.

"Glass is light," says Brychtová. "We introduce the light dynamic into the center of the glass mass. That is the definition of the fourth dimension, which cannot be achieved in any other material."[34] In sculptures such as *Red Pyramid* (Fig. 85), light and color are not used to create space; rather, the drama of light held in mass is the focus of the object. In this

34. Elliott Brown Gallery, *Stanislav Libenský and Jaroslava Brychtová: Paintings, Drawings and Sculpture*, Seattle, Washington: the gallery, 1995, p. 8.

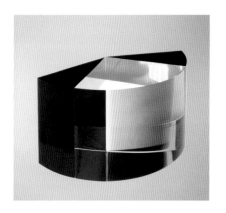

86 Stanislav Libenský
and Jaroslava Brychtová
Contacts III
1984–1987
(Plate 29)

87 Stanislav Libenský
and Jaroslava Brychtová
Big Arcus/Arcus III
1993
Czech Republic, Železný Brod
Mold-melted glass, cut
H. 104.1 cm, W. (base) 86.2 cm,
D. 16.7 cm
93.3.26, gift of the artists

88 Pavel Trnka
Objekt 3-teilig
1984
(Plate 27)

way, the sculpture acts similarly to a stained glass window: through the vehicle of colored glass, space is transformed. In *Contacts III*, two prisms intersect to form a cube (Fig. 86). The combination of two geometric shapes to create a third form is characteristic of the artists' work, and it serves to illustrate their belief that glass is a material in which the fourth dimension can be achieved. Transparency is also a critical aspect of Libenský and Brychtová's work, and they exploit the transparency of the material in order to achieve the effect of light held in color. In *Big Arcus/Arcus III*, this is visible in how the sculpture appears to dematerialize at its edges (Fig. 87). Libenský and Brychtová's understanding of the properties of glass, light, and volume is influenced by the philosophy of Czech Cubism.[35] In spite of their rigorous, intellectual approach, their work—like that of so many artists who have chosen to focus on glass—remains relatively unknown outside the glass world.

Adding reflection to color and light intensifies the glassiness of an object, and this may be seen clearly in the work of Pavel Trnka. Because of the material's ability to magnify and refract light, the colors of Trnka's small sculpture from the "Zyklus Spectrum" series (Fig. 88) appear and disappear as the viewer moves around it. Marian Karel also uses highly reflective glass and light to make illusionistic sculptures that challenge the viewer's perceptions of space and dimension. In contrast to Trnka's work, however, the absence of color is of interest to Karel, as it increases the reflective qualities of the

35. Czech Cubism, which flowered in architecture and the applied arts in the early years of the 20th century, had a strong metaphysical aspect, which the French movement did not share. For more information on Czech Cubism, see *Czech Cubism: Architecture, Furniture, and Decorative Arts, 1910–1925*, ed. Alexander von Vegesack, New York: Princeton Architectural Press, 1992.

89 Marian Karel
    Black Cube
    2000
    (Plate 67)

90 Věra Lišková
    Anthem of Joy in Glass
    1977
    (Plate 15)

91 Marian Karel
    Penetration
    1978
    (Plate 16)

glass. His *Black Cube* (Fig. 89) is so dark and reflective that it is almost invisible; it appears to lack substance, like a shadow. Yet its slightly bulging sides suggest that some sort of energy is contained within it. The sculpture illustrates the Czech notion that dynamic abstraction can be achieved only through the creation of an internal, animating energy.[36] In Karel's drawing for this piece, the hollow space inside the cube is filled with interlocking spheres and squares that act, in theory, as an internal dynamo. This imaginary energy source pushes the walls of the cube outward, creating the bulging

sides and the distortion of the reflective surface. To achieve this effect, the six sides of the sculpture, made of a black architectural glass,[37] were slumped over a curved mold inside a kiln and then assembled.

While glass is an ordinary material that may easily be looked *through*, it is necessary to look *at* it to fully appreciate what it is. Transparency is the most characteristic quality of glass, and it is the most paradoxical. Being transparent, an object may be said to exist, but also not to exist because one can see through it.[38] It is this quality that sets

36. This is illustrated in Josef Kaplický's saying, which was related to me by Marian Karel: "Abstraction in art is like an egg. The geometric shape on the outside is enlivened by the warm and mysterious life inside of it." This principle was taught by Kaplický (Czech, 1889–1962), a painter and sculptor, to his students at the Academy of Applied Arts in Prague, who included Stanislav Libenský and Václav Cigler. In turn, Libenský taught it to his students, who included Marian Karel, and Cigler also taught it.

37. This architectural glass, which is no longer commercially produced, is called Vitrolite in the United States and Chodopak in the Czech Republic.

38. From a Jungian interpretation that is as follows: "The 'state of transparency' is defined as one of the most effective and beautiful conjunctions of opposites: matter 'exists' but it is as if it did not exist, because one can see through it." J. E. Cirlot, *A Dictionary of Symbols*, New York: Philosophical Library, 1962, p. 71.

92 Dana Vachtová
The Elements I
1979
(Plate 19)

93 Pavel Hlava
Red Disks
About 1973
(Plate 8)

glass apart from other materials. In studying the form, content, and execution of a work in glass, one must always consider how an artist has or has not made use of the material's transparency.

Věra Lišková's complex and fragile *Anthem of Joy in Glass*, made of flameworked borosilicate glass, consists of inflated tubes, with pointed ends, that suggest the notes of invisible music (Fig. 90).[39] By using a transparent series of forms, Lišková captured the unique ability of glass to be simultaneously visible and invisible. *Penetration* by Marian Karel, in contrast, employs transparent forms to demonstrate both the fluid and the rigid states of glass (Fig. 91). In her investigations of transparency, Dana Vachtová prefers to juxtapose materials, and her sculptures often impart a sense of dreaminess. The full, fluid mold-blown shapes of *The Elements I* spill over the sharp edges of the rigid metal base, like water flowing over rocks (Fig. 92). Vachtová invites the viewer to visually compare these ma-

terials, noting the flexibility, lightness, and transparency of the glass in contrast to the hardness, solidity, and seeming immovability of the metal base.

Looking at form inside glass—as in the sculpture *Red Disks* by Pavel Hlava (Fig. 93)—is a simple but effective way to accentuate the transparency of glass, as well as its plasticity. In this sculpture, the interior of the reddish orange glass bubble was penetrated with a wood tool during the glassblowing process. Because it contains colloidal gold as a colorant, the glass struck red when it was reheated, which explains why the color of the glass changes from reddish orange on the outside to a deeper red

39. Lišková, who worked as a designer for the Czech glass industry for many years, was the first artist to use flameworking for large-scale sculpture.

94 Marian Karel
    Blue Cone
    1987
    (Plate 34)

95 Stanislav Libenský
    and Jaroslava Brychtová
    The Prism in the Spheric Space
    1978
    (Plate 17)

on the inside. In *Blue Cone* (Fig. 94), Marian Karel demonstrates how transparency is used to bring light into the glass mass to create form. The inside of the square base has a hollow space that reproduces the shape of the cone that sits on top of it. When light shines through the glass, the interior cone appears to be doubled, which is an optical illusion. The form is seen although it does not exist. Similarly, in *The Prism in the Spheric Space* by Stanislav Libenský and Jaroslava Brychtová, the interior rectangular bar assumes a comet-like tail, which is also the result of light refraction (Fig. 95).

The dematerialization of form and the effect of light on color are powerfully demonstrated in *Glass Sticks* by Jun Kaneko (Fig. 96). Kaneko is a sculptor who is chiefly known for his large-scale sculpture in ceramics. He was drawn to work in glass because, he says, "in glass, it's possible to see inside the shape."[40] *Glass Sticks* is one of the first sculptures that he made in glass. It is assembled

from 104 stacked rectangular bars, each of which consists of up to 10 layers of colorless and red glass fused in several firings. Unlike his ceramics, which are opaque, thick, and often brightly glazed, Kaneko's glass is treated as an airy substance, allowing color and light to pass through its mass. He calls attention to the transparency of the form of *Glass Sticks* by using colorless glass and by leaving space between the glass bars. The color of the sculpture appears to be atmospheric; its shades of red vary in intensity, depending on the angle from which the work is viewed.

The last object to be discussed in this essay is simple and wondrous in its emphasis on materiality. *Disk*, by Václav Cigler, is a shimmering block of cast

40. *Bullseye: The Kaneko Project*, Portland, Oregon: Bullseye Glass Co., 2007, p. 19.

96 Jun Kaneko
Glass Sticks
2001
(Plate 69)

97 Václav Cigler
Disk
Designed in 1966 and
made in 1974
(Plate 3)

lead glass that has been shaped inside a mold. The glass is tinted a light brown that looks much darker in the photograph (Fig. 97). The surprise of this piece is that while the glass is entirely transparent, the viewer cannot see through it; instead, the light refraction causes the viewer's image to be inverted and projected back. In this manipulation of the material's natural properties, Cigler presents the idea that transparency in glass can be misleading, a con-

tradition. What appears to be transparent may not be clear at all. Cigler's sculpture illustrates one of the many paradoxes of glass, a material that is fluid and rigid, transparent and opaque, fragile and strong, colored and colorless, and light-reflecting and light-absorbing. Glass is always changing, a material in flux, and it is this seemingly contradictory and inconsistent nature that makes it such a compelling material for art.

Plates

1 Stanislav Libenský (Czech, 1921–2002)
and Jaroslava Brychtová (Czech, b. 1924)
Head I
1957–1958

Czechoslovakia, Železný Brod
Mold-melted glass, ground, polished
H. 35.5 cm, W. 10.7 cm, D. 14.7 cm
62.3.132

2 Václav Cigler (Czech, b. 1929)
Disk
About 1966–1971

Czechoslovakia, Bratislava
Cast optical lead glass, ground, polished
H. 38 cm, Diam. 37.6 cm
72.3.6

3 Václav Cigler (Czech, b. 1929)
Disk
Designed in 1966 and made in 1974

Czechoslovakia, Bratislava
Cast optical lead glass, ground, polished
H. 28.5 cm, W. 32 cm, D. 12.2 cm
82.3.11

4 Marvin Lipofsky (American, b. 1938)
California Loop Series 1969, #29
1969

United States, Berkeley, California, University of California
Blown glass, iridized, hot-worked, sandblasted; rayon flocking, epoxy
H. 15.2 cm, W. 50.8 cm, D. 30.5 cm
2006.4.151

5 Christopher Wilmarth (American, 1943–1987)
Gyes Arcade
1969

United States, New York, New York
Float glass, cut, slumped, acid-etched, assembled
H. 36 cm, W. 238.5 cm, D. 221.5 cm
2000.4.53, purchased in honor of Susanne K. Frantz
with funds provided by the Ben W. Heineman Sr. Family;
the Roger G. and Maureen Ackerman Family; James R.
and Maisie Houghton; the Art Alliance for Contemporary
Glass; The Carbetz Foundation Inc.; The Maxine and Stuart
Frankel Foundation; Daniel Greenberg. Susan Steinhauser,
and The Greenberg Foundation; Polly and John Guth;
and The Jon and Mary Shirley Foundation

6 René Roubíček (Czech, b. 1922)
Untitled
1971

Czechoslovakia, Škrdlovice
Hot-worked glass
H. 55 cm, W. 24.3 cm, D. 21.5 cm
2005.3.18

7 Robert Sowers (American, 1923–1990)
Turkish Delight
1972

United States, Brooklyn, New York
Antique sheet glass, cut; lead came; assembled
H. 82.6 cm, W. 43.7 cm
87.4.18, gift of the artist

8 Pavel Hlava (Czech, 1924–2003)
Red Disks
About 1973

Czechoslovakia, Chlum u Třeboně
Mold-blown and hot-worked glass
H. 37.6 cm, Diam. 37 cm
74.3.73

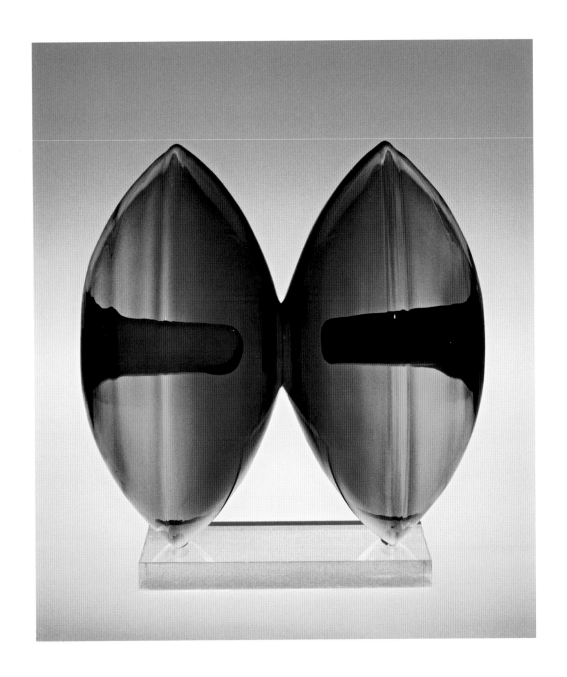

9 Dale Chihuly (American, b. 1941)
and James Carpenter (American, b. 1949)
The Corning Wall
1974

With the assistance of Darrah Cole, Kate Elliott
(American, b. 1950), Phil Hastings, and Barbara
Vaessen (Dutch, b. 1949)
United States, Stanwood, Washington, Pilchuck Glass School,
and Providence, Rhode Island, Rhode Island School of Design
Blown glass, iridized, cut; lead came; assembled
H. 199.4 cm, W. 125.8 cm
74.4.186

10 Paul Marioni (American, b. 1941)
The Conversationalist
1974

United States, Seattle, Washington
Sheet glass, cut, slumped, enameled;
sandblasted wood, photo-silkscreen,
lead came, found eyeglasses; assembled
H. 70.7 cm, W. 71.8 cm
74.4.183

11 Dominick Labino (American, 1910–1987)
Emergence Four-Stage
1975

United States, Grand Rapids, Ohio
Hot-worked glass, internal air trap
H. 22.4 cm, W. 16.2 cm, D. 6.3 cm
76.4.21, purchased with the aid of funds
from the National Endowment for the Arts

12 Erwin Eisch (German, b. 1927)
Eight Heads of Harvey Littleton
1976

Federal Republic of Germany, Frauenau
Mold-blown glass, enameled, assembled
Largest: H. 50.3 cm, W. 20.3 cm
76.3.32

13 Robert Kehlmann (American, b. 1942)
Composition XXXI
1976

United States, Berkeley, California
Sheet glass, cut; lead came; assembled
H. 75.7 cm, W. 74.7 cm
79.4.11

14 Richard Posner (American, b. 1948)
Another Look at My Beef with the Government
1976

United States, Oakland, California, California College
of Arts and Crafts
Sheet glass, cut, sandblasted; lead came, copper foil,
photographic lamination; assembled
H. 69 cm, W. 82 cm
88.4.12

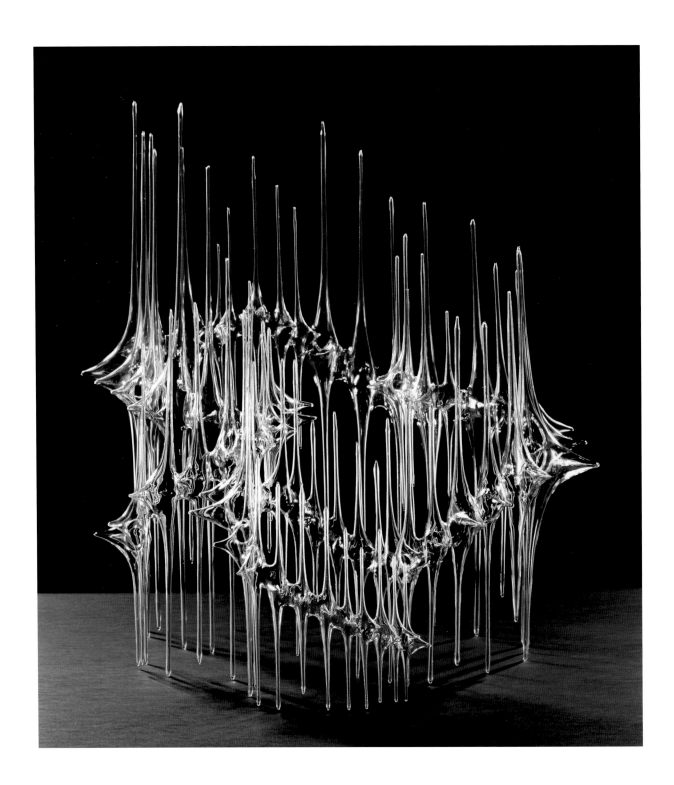

15 Věra Lišková (Czech, 1924–1985)
Anthem of Joy in Glass
1977

Czechoslovakia, Prague
Flameworked borosilicate glass
H. 99.5 cm, W. 95.1 cm, D. 101.6 cm
79.3.14, gift of Art Centrum

16 Marian Karel (Czech, b. 1944)
Penetration
1978

Czechoslovakia, Železný Brod
Cast lead glass, ground, polished
H. 20.3 cm, W. 24.2 cm, D. 24.2 cm
78.3.51

17 Stanislav Libenský (Czech, 1921–2002)
and Jaroslava Brychtová (Czech, b. 1924)
The Prism in the Spheric Space
1978

Czechoslovakia, Železný Brod
Mold-melted glass, ground, polished, assembled
Diam. 30.3 cm
78.3.53

18 Dominick Labino (American, 1910–1987)
Ionic Structure of Glass
1979

United States, Grand Rapids, Ohio
Cast glass, ground, polished, assembled
Diam. 151.8 cm
80.4.30, purchased with the aid of funds
from the National Endowment for the Arts

19 Dana Vachtová (Czech, b. 1937)
The Elements I
1979

Czechoslovakia, Sázava, Kavalier Glassworks
Mold-blown glass; metal base
H. 52 cm, W. 71.5 cm, D. 82 cm
81.3.24

20 Christopher Wilmarth (American, 1943–1987)
Insert myself within your story . . .
from the "Breath" series
1979–1981

With the assistance of Paul Weber (American, b. 1958)
United States, Oakland, California, California College
of Arts and Crafts, and New York, New York
Blown glass, acid-etched; patinated bronze
H. 46.1 cm, W. 35.5 cm
82.4.19, purchased with the aid of funds
from the National Endowment for the Arts

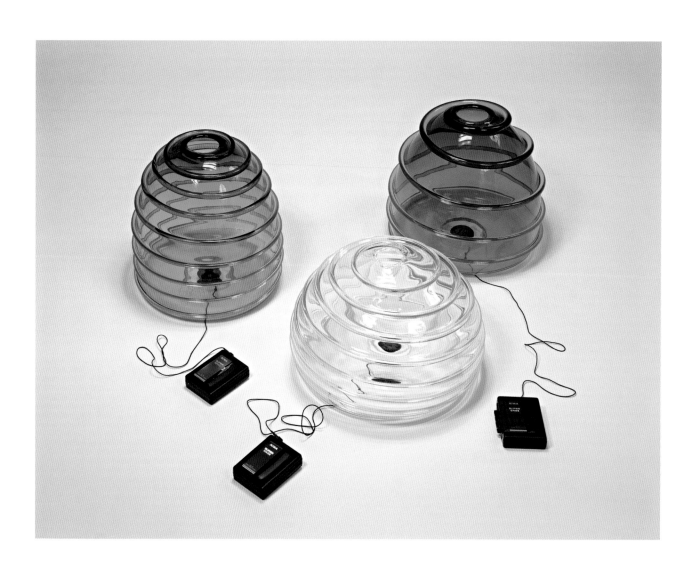

21 Dennis Oppenheim (American, b. 1938)
Beehive Volcano
Designed in 1979 and made in 1989

United States, Stanwood, Washington, Pilchuck Glass School
Blown glass with applied wraps; audiocassette tapes
and players
Largest: H. 35.5 cm, Diam. 38.4 cm
93.4.91, gift in part of the artist

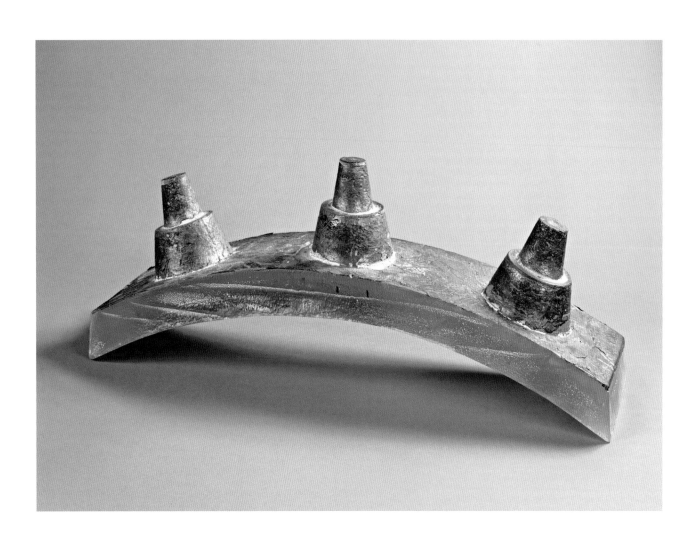

22 Howard Ben Tré (American, b. 1949)
From Jack J
1980

United States, Providence, Rhode Island,
Rhode Island School of Design
Sand-cast glass, sandblasted; copper
H. 19.6 cm, W. 15.1 cm, L. 60.7 cm
80.4.56, purchased with the aid of funds
from the National Endowment for the Arts

23 Eric Hilton (British, b. Scotland, 1937)
Innerland
1980

With the assistance of Ladislav Havlík (Czech, b. 1925),
Lubomír Richter, Peter Schelling, and Roger Selander
(engraving) and Mark Witter (cutting)
United States, Corning, New York, Steuben Glass
Cast lead glass, ground, polished, sandblasted, cut,
engraved, assembled
H. 9.9 cm, W. 49.3 cm, D. 49.3 cm
86.4.180, anonymous gift

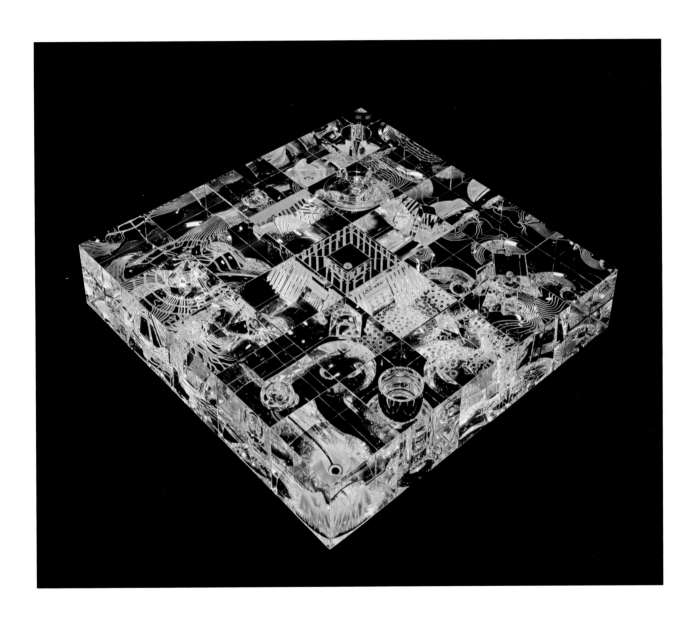

24 René Roubíček (Czech, b. 1922)
Figures I, II
1980

Czechoslovakia, Nový Bor
Mold-blown glass
Larger: H. 95 cm, Diam. 24.6 cm
81.3.25, .26

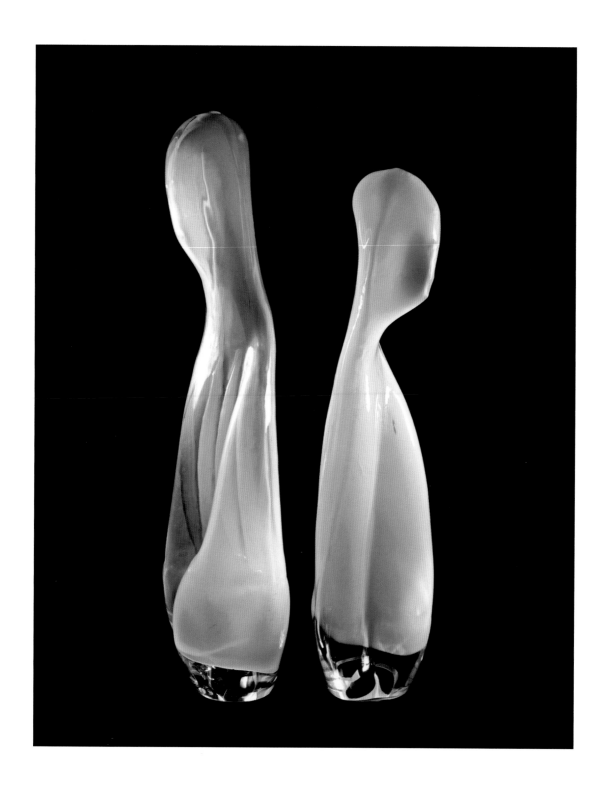

25 Robert Kehlmann (American, b. 1942)
Entombment, Station 14
from "The Stations of the Cross" series
1982

United States, Berkeley, California
Sheet glass, cut, sandblasted, assembled
H. 81.8 cm, W. 61.5 cm
83.4.102

26 William Morris (American, b. 1957)
Standing Stone
1982

United States, Stanwood, Washington,
Pilchuck Glass School
Blown, cased, and mold-blown glass
H. 76.5 cm, W. 31.6 cm, D. 14 cm
82.4.20

27 Pavel Trnka (Czech, b. 1948)
Objekt 3-teilig (Three-part object)
from the "Zyklus Spectrum" (Spectrum cycle) series
1984

With the assistance of Jan Frydrych (Czech, b. 1953)
Czechoslovakia, Prague
Cast glass, ground, polished
H. 10.9 cm, W. 21.8 cm
85.3.72

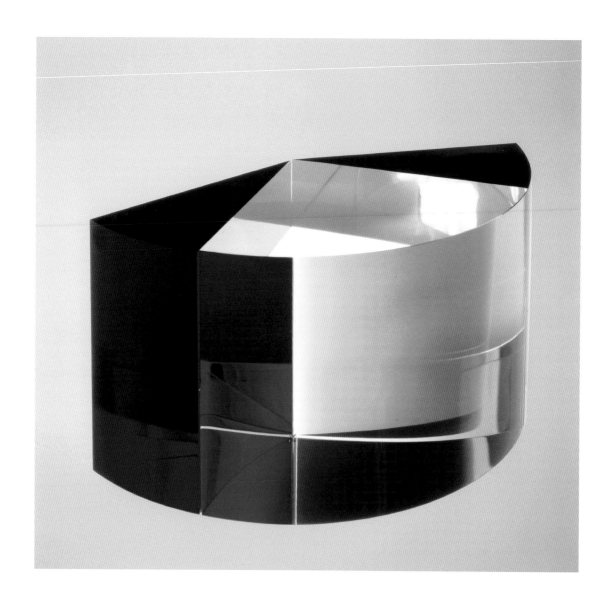

28 Robert Willson (American, 1912–2000)
Ranch Doll
1984

With the assistance of Pino Signoretto
(Italian, b. 1944)
Italy, Murano
Hot-worked glass, applied elements; gold foil
H. 53.3 cm, W. 16.5 cm, D. 12.7 cm
2001.3.34, gift of Margaret Pace Willson

29 Stanislav Libenský (Czech, 1921–2002)
and Jaroslava Brychtová (Czech, b. 1924)
Contacts III
1984–1987

Czechoslovakia, Železný Brod
Mold-melted glass, ground, polished, assembled
H. 121.2 cm, W. 96 cm, D. 26.2 cm
88.3.27, gift in part of Daniel Greenberg
and Susan Steinhauser

30 Judith Schaechter (American, b. 1961)
Nedotykompectomy
1986

United States, Philadelphia, Pennsylvania
Sheet glass, cut, glass crystals, enameled, etched,
stained; lead came; assembled
H. 66.7 cm, W. 33.4 cm
87.4.38

31 Paul Seide (American, b. 1949)
Frosted Radio Light
1986

United States, New York, New York
Blown and hot-worked glass; neon gas,
mercury vapor; radio transmitter
H. 48.4 cm, W. 53.5 cm, D. 30 cm
87.4.41, gift in part of Mike Belkin

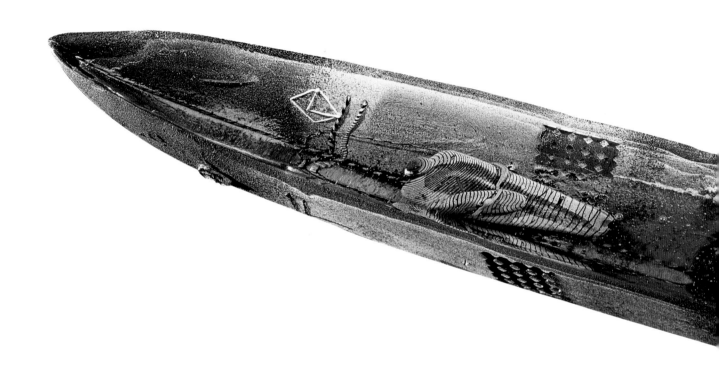

32 Bertil Vallien (Swedish, b. 1938)
Unknown Destination II
1986

With the assistance of William Morris (American, b. 1957)
and Norman Courtney (American, b. 1947)
United States, Stanwood, Washington, Pilchuck Glass School
Sand-cast glass, hot-worked glass inclusions; copper
H. 11 cm, W. 104.5 cm, D. 13.3 cm
87.4.19

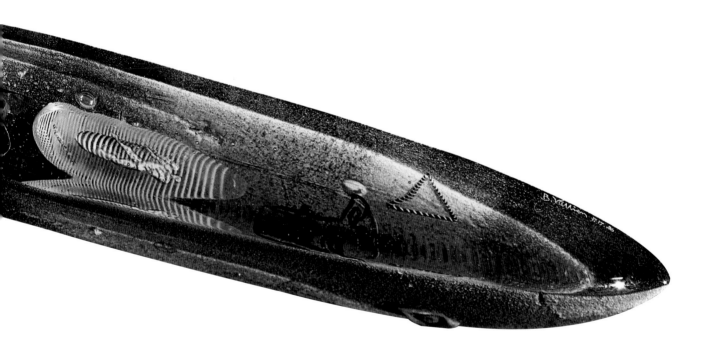

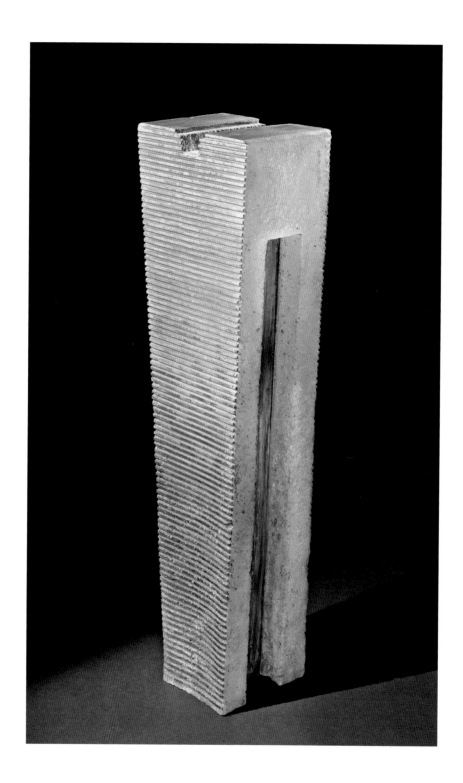

33 Howard Ben Tré (American, b. 1949)
Dedicant 8
1987

United States, Brooklyn, New York, Super Glass,
and Providence, Rhode Island
Sand-cast glass, sandblasted, cut; patinated brass sheet,
gold and copper foils, pigmented wax
H. 121.6 cm, W. 35.9 cm, D. 25.7 cm
87.4.57, the second Rakow Commission

34 Marian Karel (Czech, b. 1944)
Blue Cone
1987

With the assistance of Pavel Satrapa (Czech, b. 1947)
Czechoslovakia, Železný Brod
Cast glass, ground, polished, assembled
H. 23.9 cm, W. 24.5 cm, D. 24.3 cm
91.3.51

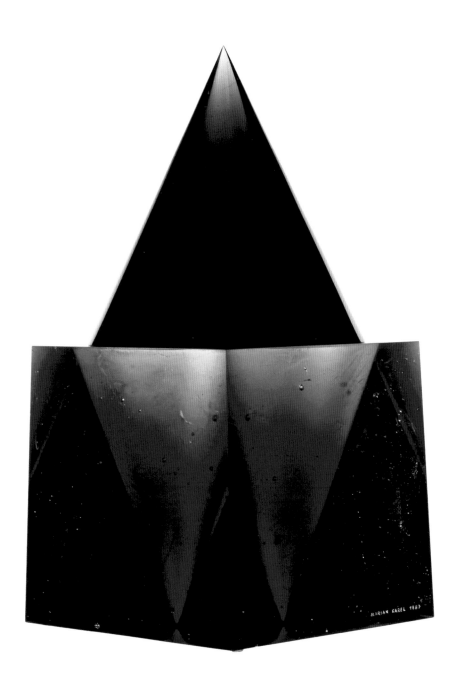

35 Harvey K. Littleton (American, b. 1922)
Gold and Green Implied Movement
1987

United States, Spruce Pine, North Carolina
Hot-worked glass, cut, assembled
H. 82 cm, W. about 48 cm, D. about 35.5 cm
2006.4.112

36 Michael Aschenbrenner (American, b. 1949)
Damaged Bone Series: No Place Left to Hide
1989

United States, New York, New York, New York
Experimental Glass Workshop
Hot-worked glass; wood, wire, cloth; assembled
H. 215.9 cm, W. 165.1 cm
90.4.18

37 Ivan Mareš (Czech, b. 1956)
Blackcoater
1989

Czechoslovakia, Železný Brod
Mold-melted lead glass, ground, polished
H. 57.2 cm, W. 102.8 cm, D. 24.5 cm
92.3.12

38 Donald Lipski (American, b. 1947)
Water Lilies #52
1990

United States, Brooklyn, New York
Machine-blown Pyrex acid-waste-line tubing; metal
couplings; carrots, preservative solution; assembled
H. 39 cm, W. 29.2 cm, D. 10.1 cm
92.4.5, gift of Maureen and Roger Ackerman

39 Judith Schaechter (American, b. 1961)
Caught in a Flood
1990

United States, Philadelphia, Pennsylvania
Sheet glass, cut, engraved; vitreous paint,
patinated copper foil; assembled
H. 61 cm, W. 112.5 cm
91.4.23

40 György Buczkó (Hungarian, b. 1950)
Ti
1991

Hungary, Budapest
Slumped glass; pigments, rope, metal hook
H. 120 cm, W. 38 cm, D. 13.8 cm
95.3.23

41 Vladimír Kopecký (Czech, b. 1931)
Drepung
1992

Czechoslovakia, Prague
Float glass; paint, wood, metal,
found objects; assembled
Dimensions variable
94.3.154

42 Tom Patti (American, b. 1943)
Clear Lumina with Azurlite
1992

United States, Pittsfield, Massachusetts
Heat-formed glass, ground, polished
H. 10.3 cm, W. 15.5 cm, D. 11.3 cm
94.4.1, purchased with funds from the Art Alliance
for Contemporary Glass, the Creative Glass Center
of America, the Ben W. Heineman Sr. Family,
and Carl H. Pforzheimer III

43 Gerhard Ribka (German, b. 1955)
St. Anastasius
1992

United Kingdom, Lincoln
Float glass, cut, enameled, stained, lustered;
lead came; assembled
H. 46.6 cm, W. 60.3 cm
94.2.8

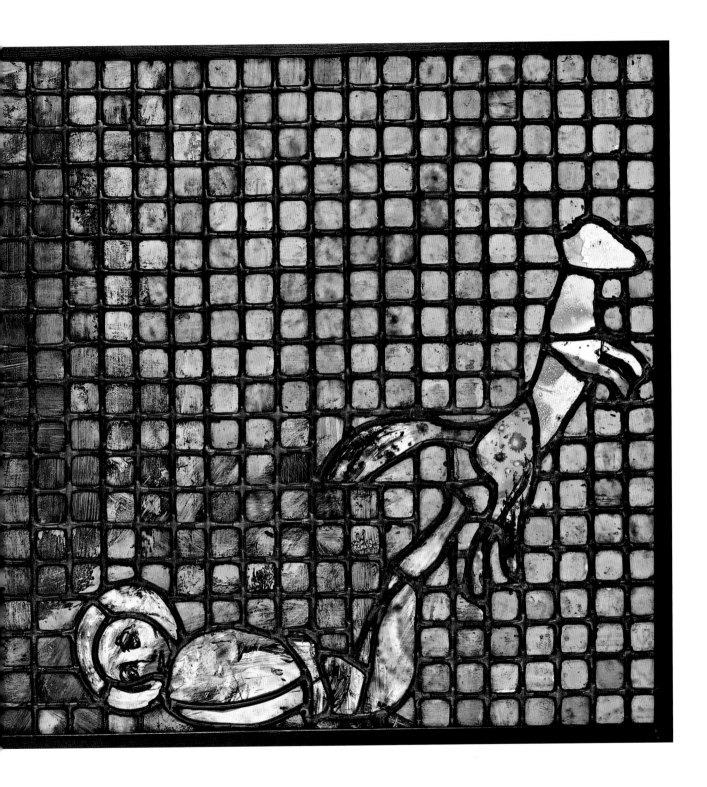

44 Joyce J. Scott (American, b. 1948)
Three Graces Oblivious While Los Angeles Burns
1992

United States, Seattle, Washington, Pilchuck Glass School,
and Baltimore, Maryland
Mold-blown, cased, and flameworked glass; glass beads;
nylon string; assembled
H. 53.7 cm, W. 24.7 cm, D. 22.7 cm
97.4.214

45 Larry Bell (American, b. 1939)
Window Bkd #6
1993

United States, Taos, New Mexico
Float glass; applied vaporized metals (Inconel,
silicon monoxide); wood, black denim
H. 135.2 cm, W. 135.3 cm
94.4.146

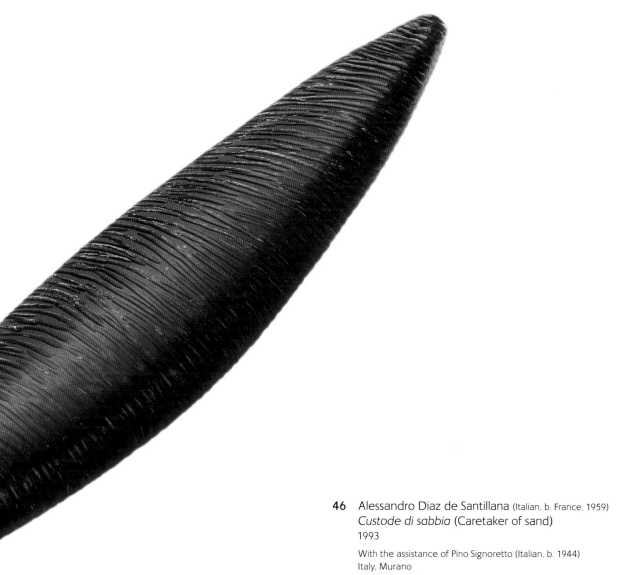

46 Alessandro Diaz de Santillana (Italian, b. France, 1959)
Custode di sabbia (Caretaker of sand)
1993

With the assistance of Pino Signoretto (Italian, b. 1944)
Italy, Murano
Blown glass, cut
H. 25.8 cm, L. 105.2 cm, D. 15.7 cm
95.3.31

47 Judy Hill (American, b. 1953)
Jump
1993

United States, Portland, Oregon
Fused glass; glazed raku-fired ceramic; assembled
H. 51.1 cm, W. 28 cm, D. 13.7 cm
95.4.1

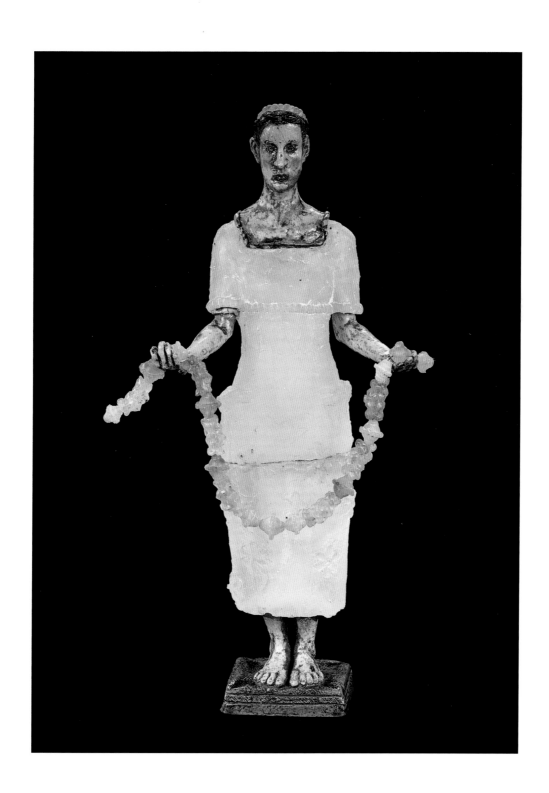

48 Stanislav Libenský (Czech, 1921–2002)
and Jaroslava Brychtová (Czech, b. 1924)
Red Pyramid
1993

Czech Republic, Železný Brod
Mold-melted glass, ground, polished
H. 83.4 cm, W. 119.3 cm, D. 28.2 cm
94.3.101, gift of the artists
Photo: G. Urbanék

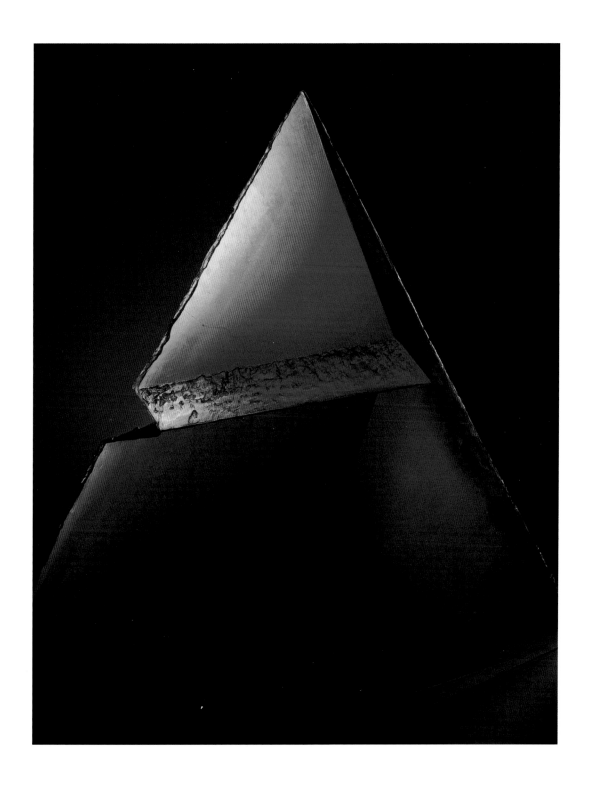

49 Ginny Ruffner (American, b. 1952)
Shirts, Cherries, and Snowflakes, Of Course
1993

United States, Seattle, Washington
Flameworked borosilicate glass, sandblasted;
oil paint, colored pencil
H. 50.4 cm, W. 37.7 cm, D. 35 cm
93.4.89

50 Franz Xaver Höller (German, b. 1950)
Parchment
1994

Germany, Zwiesel
Slumped sheet glass, cut, engraved
Larger: H. 9.3 cm, L. 99.7 cm, D. 50.1 cm
99.3.98

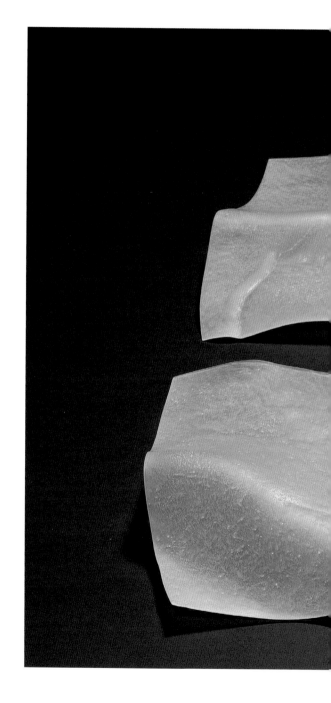

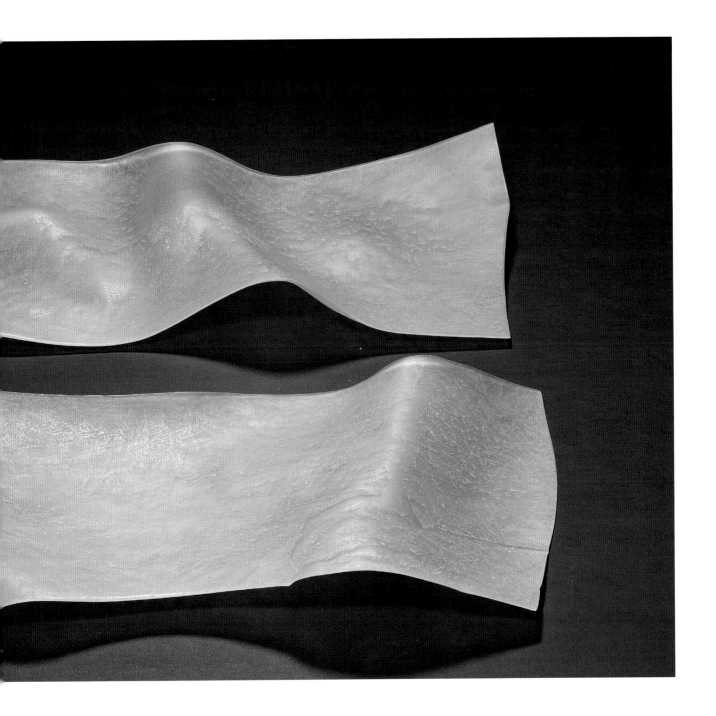

51 Hank Murta Adams (American, b. 1956)
Bust with Locator
1995

United States, Milton, West Virginia, Blenko Glass,
and Troy, New York
Cast glass, sandblasted; copper
H. 73.6 cm, W. 45.7 cm, D. 33 cm
96.4.1

52 Bernard Dejonghe (French, b. 1942)
Cercle (Circle)
1995

France, Briançonnet
Cast optical lead glass, devitrified, ground,
polished, assembled
H. 30 cm, Diam. 60 cm
97.3.72, purchased with funds from the
Ben W. Heineman Sr. Family

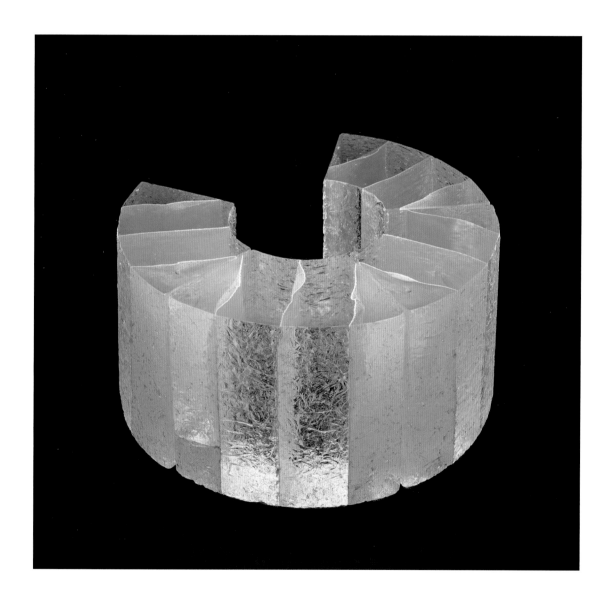

53 Robert Rauschenberg (American, 1925–2008)
Tire
Designed in 1995–1996 and made in 2005

With the assistance of Daniel Spitzer (American, b. 1964)
and Dan Dailey (American, b. 1947)
United States, Brooklyn, New York, UrbanGlass,
and Kensington, New Hampshire
Mold-blown glass; silver-plated steel carrier
H. 78.7 cm, W. 68.5 cm, D. 29.2 cm
2007.4.5, gift in part of Daniel Greenberg,
Susan Steinhauser, and The Greenberg Foundation,
and the F. M. Kirby Foundation

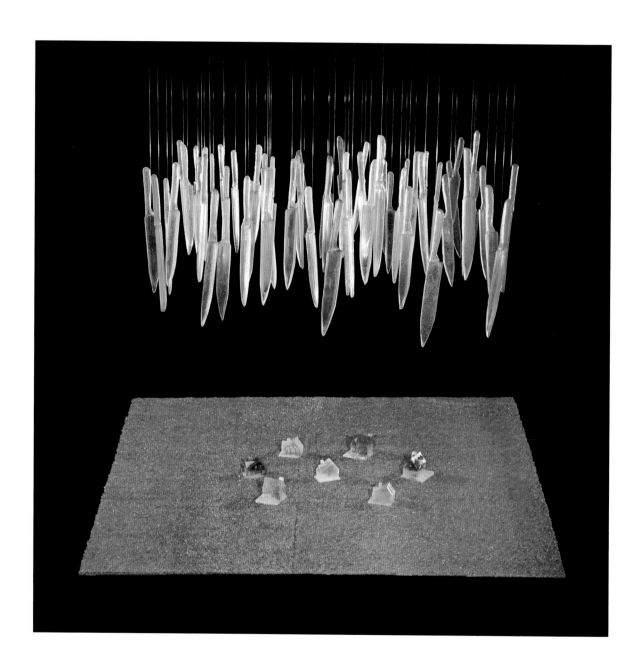

54 Silvia Levenson (Argentinean, b. 1957)
It's Raining Knives
1996–2004

Italy, Vigevano
Cast glass, ground, polished; artificial grass,
nylon line; assembled
H. 120 cm, W. 120 cm
2004.3.29, the 19th Rakow Commission

55 Alessandro Diaz de Santillana (Italian, b. France, 1959)
West Sky
1997

With the assistance of Charles Parriott (American, b. 1952),
Bryan Rubino (American, b. 1958), and Greg Dietrich
(American, b. 1958)
United States, Seattle, Washington, and Stanwood,
Washington, Pilchuck Glass School
Blown glass, silvered; steel structure; assembled
H. 260 cm, W. 26.9 cm
2000.4.5

56 Sherry Markovitz (American, b. 1947)
Big Bear
1997

United States, Seattle, Washington
Glass beads; mixed media; assembled
H. 83 cm, W. 64 cm, D. 86.7 cm
98.4.16, gift of the Ben W. Heineman Sr. Family

57 Clifford Rainey (British, b. Northern Ireland, 1948)
Hollow Torso
1997

United States, Oakland, California
Cast glass, ground, polished, assembled
H. 101.6 cm, W. 62 cm, D. 35.5 cm
2001.4.19, gift of the Ben W. Heineman Sr. Family

58 Marvin Lipofsky (American, b. 1938)
IGS VI 1997–1999, #12
1997–1999

Czech Republic, Nový Bor, and United States,
Berkeley, California
Mold-blown glass, cut, sandblasted, assembled
H. 41.2 cm, W. 65.4 cm, D. 53.4 cm
2006.3.5

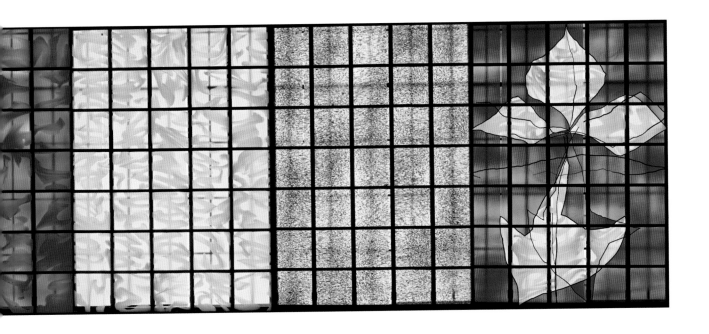

59 Brian Clarke (British, b. 1953)
The Glass Wall
1998

Germany, Munich, Franz Mayer Inc.
Blown sheet glass, cut; aluminum came, steel cable; assembled
H. 6.3 m, L. 22.4 m
99.2.4, purchased with funds from the Arthur Rubloff Residuary Trust

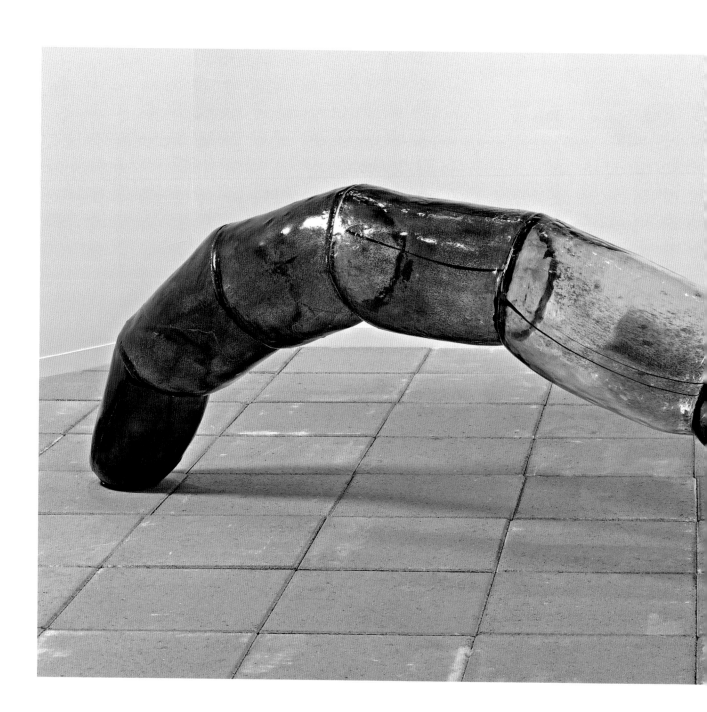

60 Michael Scheiner (American, b. 1956)
Bearing
1998

United States, Central Falls, Rhode Island
Mold-blown glass, cut; pigments;
assembled
H. 73 cm, L. 243.2 cm
98.4.463, the 13th Rakow Commission

61 Therman Statom (American, b. 1953)
Clearly Oranges
1998

United States, Escondido, California
Blown glass, float glass, cut; mixed media; assembled
H. 115.4 cm, W. 115.4 cm, D. 11.8 cm
2003.4.110, gift of the Sidney J. Marx Family
and the Ken Saunders Family

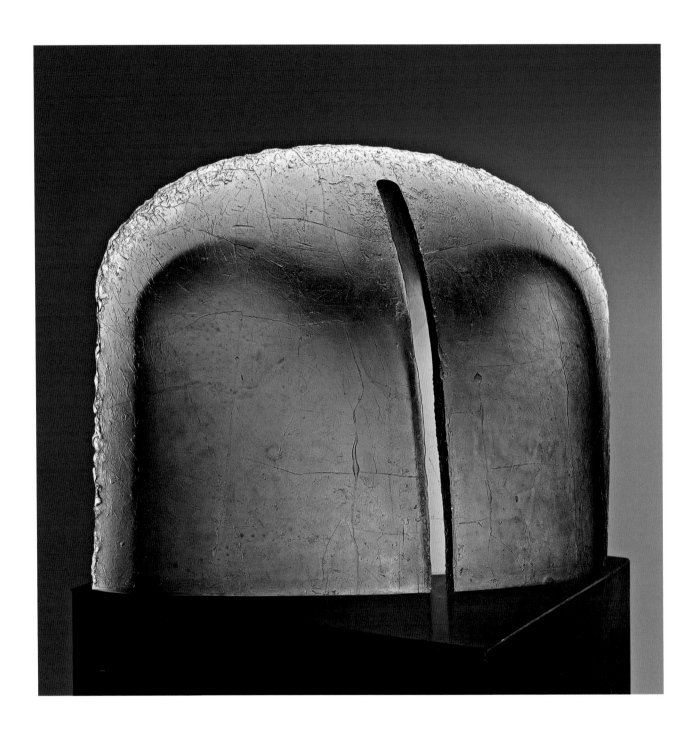

62   Stanislav Libenský (Czech, 1921–2002)
and Jaroslava Brychtová (Czech, b. 1924)
Imprint of an Angel II
1999

Czech Republic, Železný Brod
Mold-melted glass, ground, polished
H. 77.5 cm, W. 108.7 cm, D. 31.5 cm
2004.3.10, purchased with funds from James R. and Maisie Houghton,
The Carbetz Foundation Inc., James B. Flaws and Marcia D. Weber,
the Ben W. Heineman Sr. Family, Joseph A. Miller and Rachel C. Wood,
Peter and Cathy Volanakis, Wendell P. Weeks and Kim Frock, and Alan
and Nancy Cameros

63 Susan Plum (American, b. 1944)
Woven Heaven, Tangled Earth
1999

United States, Brooklyn, New York, UrbanGlass
Flameworked borosilicate glass
Diam. (max.) 91.4 cm
2001.4.70

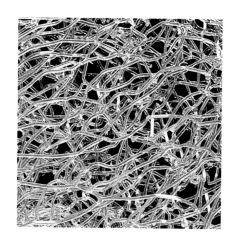

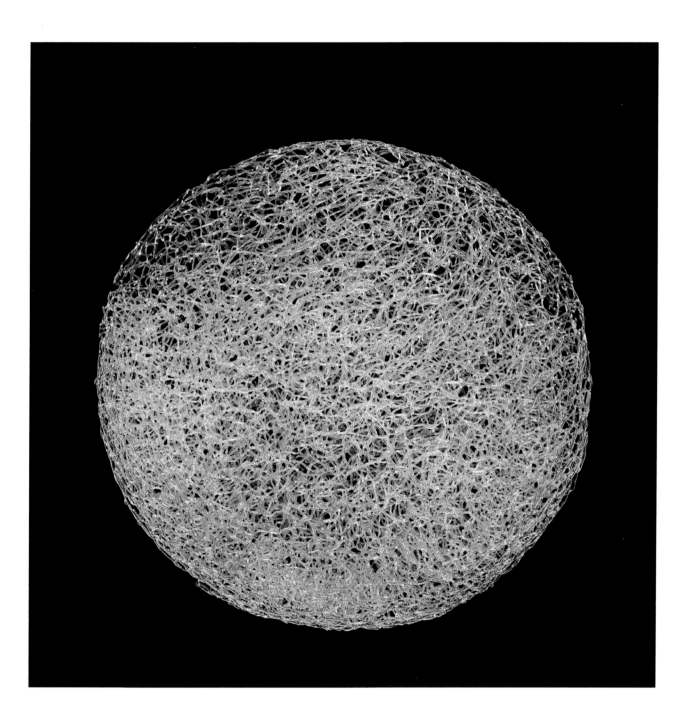

64 Kiki Smith (American, b. Germany, 1954)
Brown Water
1999

With the assistance of Tom Farbanish (American, b. 1963)
United States, Pleasant Gap, Pennsylvania
Hot-worked glass, assembled
Assembled dimensions variable; largest element:
H. 6.4 cm, L. 19.1 cm, D. 5.7 cm
2007.4.6, purchased with funds from the Arthur Rubloff
Residuary Trust

65 Ann Wolff (German, b. 1937)
Double Face
1999

Germany, Berlin
Antique sheet and float glass, cut, enameled;
steel frame; assembled
H. 117.5 cm, W. 107.5 cm, D. 11.1 cm
2004.3.11

66 Dale Chihuly (American, b. 1941)
Fern Green Tower
2000

United States, Seattle, Washington
Blown glass; steel structure; assembled
H. 335.2 cm, Diam. 228.6 cm
2000.4.6, gift of the artist

67 Marian Karel (Czech, b. 1944)
Black Cube
2000

Czech Republic, Prague
Slumped Vitrolite; wood; assembled
H. 103.5 cm, W. 102.6 cm, D. 102.4 cm
2000.3.63, gift of the artist and the Heller Gallery, New York

68 Josiah McElheny (American, b. 1966)
Untitled (White)
2000

United States, Seattle, Washington
Blown glass; display cabinet, lighting
H. 56.5 cm, L. 218.6 cm, D. 40.7 cm
2000.4.9, the 15th Rakow Commission

69 Jun Kaneko (Japanese, b. 1942)
Glass Sticks
2001

United States, Portland, Oregon, Bullseye Glass
Kiln-formed glass, ground, polished, assembled
H. 200 cm, W. 106.6 cm, D. 106.6 cm
2007.4.4, gift of the Ennion Society and funds provided
by Laura Houghton, James R. and Maisie Houghton,
and the Glass Acquisitions and Exhibitions Fund
Photo: Russell Johnson, courtesy Bullseye Gallery, Portland, Oregon

70 Beth Lipman (American, b. 1971)
Untitled (after A. Martini)
2001

United States, Rindge, New Hampshire
Blown, hot-worked, and flameworked glass; enamel
transfer, latex glass paint, stained wood base
H. 50.8 cm, W. 74.9 cm, D. 50.8 cm
2001.4.20

71 Flora C. Mace (American, b. 1949)
and Joey Kirkpatrick (American, b. 1952)
Still Life with Two Plums
2001

United States, Seattle, Washington
Blown glass; glass powders, wood; assembled
H. 69.5 cm, Diam. (bowl) 116.7 cm
2002.4.2, gift in part of the artists

72 Jessica Loughlin (Australian, b. 1975)
Vertical Lines 2
2002

United States, Portland, Oregon, Bullseye Glass
Kiln-formed glass, ground, polished, assembled
H. 159.3 cm, W. 142.4 cm
2003.4.25, gift in part of Daniel Greenberg,
Susan Steinhauser, and The Greenberg Foundation,
and Robert Cole Jr. and E. Marie McKee
Photo: Paul Foster

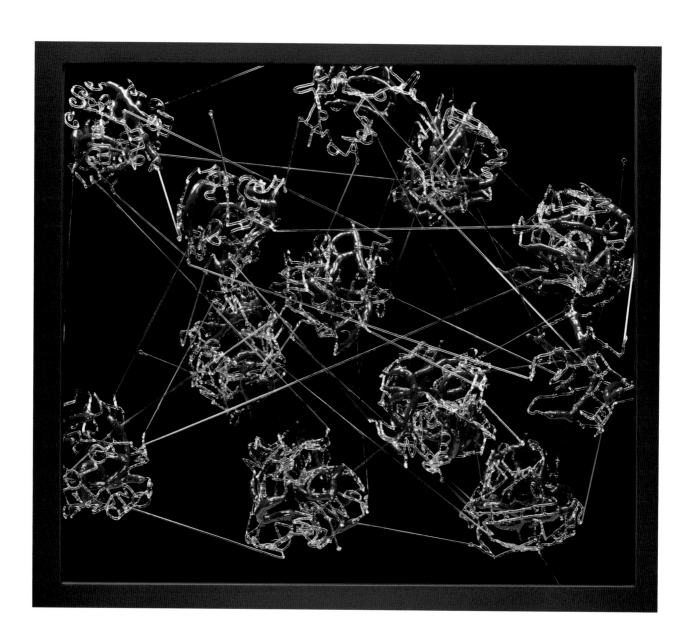

73 Jill Reynolds (American, b. 1956)
Family Matter
2002

United States, Brooklyn, New York
Flameworked borosilicate glass; glycerin,
pigment, cork, wax; assembled
H. 132.1 cm, W. 144.8 cm, D. 68.6 cm
2002.4.64, the 17th Rakow Commission

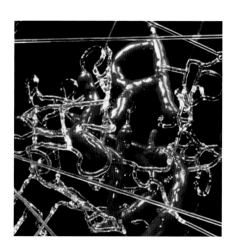

74 Michael Rogers (American, b. 1955)
13 Crows
2002

Japan, Seto, Aichi Prefecture, Aichi University of Education
Cast glass, ground, polished; newspaper, glue; assembled
Assembled dimensions variable; largest crow:
H. 48.4 cm, W. 13.5 cm
2004.6.3

75 Gizela Šabóková (Czech, b. 1952)
Come to Me
2002–2004

Czech Republic, Železný Brod
Mold-melted glass, ground, polished
H. 78.7 cm, W. 50.8 cm, D. 33 cm
2004.3.42

76 Jack Wax (American, b. 1954)
Fugitive
2003

United States, Richmond, Virginia,
Virginia Commonwealth University
Hot-worked glass; pigment; assembled
Dimensions variable
2004.4.15

77 Karen LaMonte (American, b. 1967)
Evening Dress with Shawl
2004

Czech Republic, Železný Brod
Mold-melted glass, ground, polished, assembled
H. 150 cm, W. 121 cm, D. 59.5 cm
2005.3.21, gift in part of the Ennion Society
Photo: G. Urbanék and O. Kocurek

78 Lino Tagliapietra (Italian, b. 1934)
Endeavor
2004

United States, Seattle, Washington
Blown and hot-worked glass, cut, *battuto*-cut; steel cable; assembled
Assembled dimensions variable; largest element: L. 166.3 cm

2005.4.170, purchased in honor of James R. Houghton with funds from Corning Incorporated and gifts from the Ennion Society, The Carbetz Foundation Inc., James B. Flaws and Marcia D. Weber, Maisie Houghton, Polly and John Guth, Mr. and Mrs. Carl H. Pforzheimer III, Wendell P. Weeks and Kim Frock, Alan and Nancy Cameros, the Honorable and Mrs. Amory Houghton Jr., E. Marie McKee and Robert Cole Jr., Robert and Elizabeth Turissini, Peter and Cathy Volanakis, and Lino Tagliapietra and the Heller Gallery, New York

79 Nicole Chesney (American, b. 1971)
Present
2005

United States, Cranston, Rhode Island
Sandblasted mirror; oil paint
H. 172.8 cm, W. 203.2 cm
2005.4.162, the 20th Rakow Commission

80 Thérèse Lahaie (American, b. 1958)
Silver Gray Nocturne Triptych
2005

United States, Emeryville, California
Sheet glass; fabric, brush, acrylic, stainless steel,
motor; assembled
H. 61 cm, W. 237.2 cm, D. 16.5 cm
2005.4.204

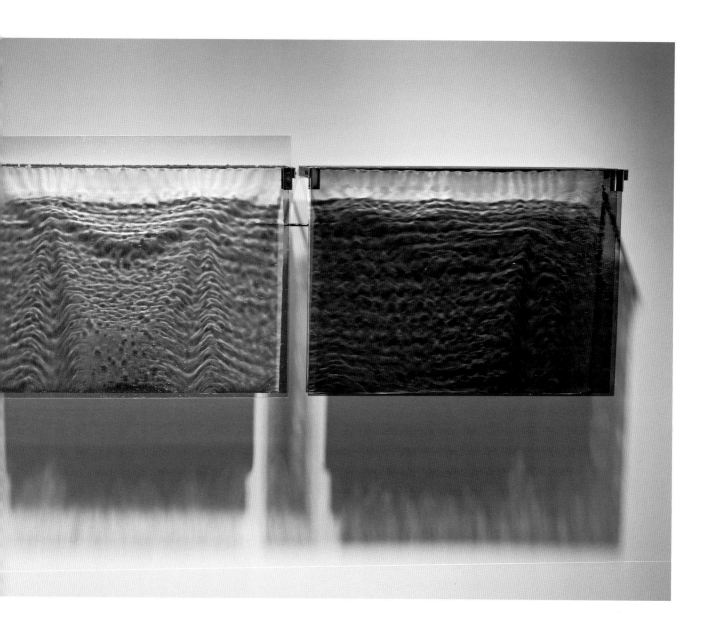

81 Debora Moore (American, b. 1960)
Host IX–Epidendrum
2007

United States, Seattle, Washington
Blown and hot-worked glass, applied glass powders,
acid-etched
H. 96.5 cm, W. 30.5 cm, D. 17.8 cm
2007.4.70, the 22nd Rakow Commission
Photo: Rob Vinnedge

Artists' Biographies

Compiled by Tina Oldknow and Laura Cotton

All of the artists in this publication are professional artists who are, or were, actively exhibiting. Individual exhibition histories may be found in the bibliographic references or in online résumés.

Hank Murta Adams
Born in 1956 in Philadelphia, PA. Lives in Troy, NY.

Adams is creative consultant for the Creative Glass Center of America, Wheaton Arts and Cultural Center, Millville, NJ (since 2001). He was principal designer at Blenko Glass, Milton, WV (1988–1994). He taught at the Center for Creative Studies, Detroit, MI (1997, 1987); Ox-Bow School, Chicago Art Institute, Saugatuck, MI (1996–1997); University of Hawaii, Honolulu, HI (1996); Pilchuck Glass School, Stanwood, WA (1994–1996, 1981); and Tennessee Technological University, Smithville, TN (1995, 1981–1985).
 Adams was a visiting artist at California Polytechnic State University, San Luis Obispo, CA (2002); Vermont Studio School, Johnson, VT (1997); Pennsylvania State University, Reading, PA (1996); Rhode Island School of Design, Providence, RI (1996); Tyler School of Art, Temple University, Philadelphia, PA (1996); Urban-Glass, Brooklyn, NY (1995); Cranbrook Educational Community, Bloomfield Hills, MI (1991); Oberglas, Bärnbach, Austria (1990, 1989); University of Alabama, Tuscaloosa, AL (1988); University of Illinois, Urbana-Champaign, Champaign, IL (1986); Artpark, Lewiston, NY (1985); Toledo Museum of Art School of Design, Toledo, OH (1984); and the University of Hawaii, Honolulu (1982).

Education
 Tennessee Technological University, Cookeville, TN (1981–1984); Rhode Island School of Design, B.F.A. Painting (1978).

Selected honors and awards
 New York State Arts Fellowship (2003); Creative Glass Center of America Fellowship, Millville, NJ (2001); Empire State Crafts Alliance Grant (1993); Shimonoseki City Art Museum Prize, Shimonoseki, Japan (1992); National Endowment for the Arts Fellowships (1990, 1988, 1986).

Selected museum collections
 Arkansas Art Center, Little Rock, AR; Birmingham Museum of Art, Birmingham, AL; Brooks Museum of Art, Memphis, TN; Corning Museum of Glass, Corning, NY; Detroit Institute of Arts, Detroit, MI; Glasmuseum Hentrich, Museum Kunst Palast, Düsseldorf, Germany; Hokkaido Museum of Modern Art, Sapporo, Japan; Honolulu Academy of Art, Honolulu, HI; Mint Museum of Craft + Design, Charlotte, NC; Musée de Design et d'Arts Appliqués Contemporains, Lausanne, Switzerland; Renwick Gallery, Smithsonian American Art Museum, Smithsonian In-

stitution, Washington, DC; Shimonoseki City Art Museum, Shimonoseki, Japan; Speed Art Museum, Louisville, KY; Toledo Museum of Art, Toledo, OH.

Other objects by this artist in the Corning Museum
 Sculptures, *Dumpster Top with Industrial Garbage* and *Garbage Top*, 1983 (2002.4.135, gift of Barry Friedman Ltd.); Sculpture, *Spring Head*, 1984 (84.3.228).

For more information
 Fox 2006, pp. 58 and 60; Frantz, Ricke, and Mizuta 1998, pp. 18–23 and 130; Lynn 2005, p. 174; Michael Oatman, "The Navigator. Hank Murta Adams: Chaos and Control," *Glass* (UrbanGlass Art Quarterly), no. 99, Summer 2005, cover and pp. 52–61; John Perreault, "Hank Murta Adams," *American Craft*, v. 64, no. 6, December 2004/January 2005, pp. 48–51; Warmus 2003, pp. 8–9, 70, and 73–75.

Michael Aschenbrenner
Born in 1949 in Pomona, CA. Lives in Upland, CA.

Aschenbrenner was a visiting artist at the New York Experimental Glass Workshop, New York, NY (1985).

Education
 University of Minnesota, Minneapolis, MN, M.F.A. (1978); California State University, San Bernardino, CA, B.F.A. (1974).

Selected honors and awards
 Pollock/Krasner Foundation Grants (1996, 1989); National Endowment for the Arts Fellowship (1992); Creative Glass Center of America Fellowship, Millville, NJ (1991); New York State Council on the Arts Grant (1985).

Selected museum collections
 Corning Museum of Glass, Corning, NY; Frederick R. Weisman Museum of Art, Pepperdine University, Malibu, CA; Honolulu Academy of the Arts, Honolulu, HI; Metropolitan Museum of Art, New York, NY; Museum of Arts and Design, New York, NY; Vietnam Veterans Arts Museum, Chicago, IL.

Other objects by this artist in the Corning Museum
 Sculpture, *California Sphere*, 1977 (78.4.12); Sculpture, *Bones*, 1980 (80.4.53, purchased with the aid of funds from the National Endowment for the Arts).

For more information
 Fox 2006, pp. 114–115; Janet Kardon and Nancy Princenthal, *Glass Installations*, New York: American Craft Museum, 1993, pp. 30–33; John Perreault, "Michael Aschenbrenner: Glass

Plus," *Glass* (New York Experimental Glass Workshop), no. 40, Spring/Summer 1990, pp. 28–33; Yelle 2000, p. 10.

Larry Bell
Born in 1939 in Chicago, IL. Lives in Taos, NM.

Bell taught at the Taos Institute for the Arts, Taos, NM (1991–1993).

Education
Chouinard Art Institute, Los Angeles, CA (1957–1959).

Selected honors and awards
Governors' Award for Excellence and Achievement in the Arts, State of New Mexico (1990); National Endowment for the Arts Fellowship (1975); Guggenheim Foundation Fellowship (1970); Copley Foundation Grant (1962).

Selected museum collections
Albright-Knox Art Gallery, Buffalo, NY; Art Gallery of New South Wales, Sydney, NSW, Australia; Art Institute of Chicago, Chicago, IL; Centre Georges Pompidou, Paris, France; Corning Museum of Glass, Corning, NY; Dallas Museum of Art, Dallas, TX; Denver Art Museum, Denver, CO; Detroit Institute of Arts, Detroit, MI; Hirshhorn Museum and Sculpture Garden, Smithsonian Institution, Washington, DC; Los Angeles County Museum of Art, Los Angeles, CA; Massachusetts Institute of Technology, Cambridge, MA; Menil Collection, Houston, TX; Milwaukee Museum of Art, Milwaukee, WI; Musée d'Art Contemporain, Lyons, France; Museum Ludwig, Cologne, Germany; Museum of Contemporary Art, Los Angeles, CA; Museum of Fine Arts, Houston, Houston, TX; Museum of Modern Art, New York, NY; Museum of New Mexico, Santa Fe, NM; National Gallery of Australia, Canberra, ACT, Australia; San Antonio Museum of Art, San Antonio, TX; San Francisco Museum of Modern Art, San Francisco, CA; Solomon R. Guggenheim Museum, New York, NY; Stedelijk Museum, Amsterdam, the Netherlands; Tate Gallery, London, U.K.; Wadsworth Atheneum Museum of Art, Hartford, CT; Walker Art Center, Minneapolis, MN; Whitney Museum of American Art, New York, NY.

For more information
www.larrybell.com; Stephanie Barron and others, *Made in California: Art, Image and Identity, 1900–2000*, Berkeley: University of California Press, 2000, pp. 210–211; Gregory Battcock, ed., *Minimal Art: A Critical Anthology*, Berkeley: University of California Press, 1995; Germano Celant, ed., *Venice/Venezia: California Art from The Panza Collection at the Guggenheim Museum*, New York: the museum, 2001, pp. 42–47; Fox 2006, pp. 22–23; Peter Friese, *Minimal Maximal*, Bremen: Neues Museum Weserburg, 2001, pp. 80–85; Lynn 2005, p. 17; Mann 1997, p. 12; Smithsonian Interview.

Howard Ben Tré
Born in 1949 in Brooklyn, NY. Lives in Providence, RI.

Education
Rhode Island School of Design, Providence, RI, M.F.A. (1980);

Portland State University, Portland, OR, B.S.A. Ceramics (1978); Brooklyn College, Brooklyn, NY (1968–1969); Missouri Valley College, Marshall, MO (1967–1968).

Selected honors and awards
Providence Preservation Society Award for Urban Design, Providence, RI (1998); Innovative Use of Glass in Sculpture Award, UrbanGlass, Brooklyn, NY (1997); Pell Award for Excellence in the Arts, Providence, RI (1997); Society of Architects, Art & Architecture Collaboration Award, Boston, MA (1993); National Endowment for the Arts Fellowships (1990, 1984, 1980); Rhode Island State Council on the Arts Fellowships (1990, 1984, 1979); Rakow Commission, Corning Museum of Glass, Corning, NY (1987); Change Inc. Grant (1982).

Selected museum collections
Albright-Knox Art Gallery, Buffalo, NY; Brooklyn Museum, Brooklyn, NY; Centro Cultural/Arte Contemporáneo, Mexico City, DF, Mexico; Chrysler Museum of Art, Norfolk, VA; Corning Museum of Glass, Corning, NY; Detroit Institute of Arts, Detroit, MI; High Museum of Art, Atlanta, GA; Hirshhorn Museum and Sculpture Garden, Smithsonian Institution, Washington, DC; Hokkaido Museum of Modern Art, Sapporo, Japan; Indianapolis Museum of Art, Indianapolis, IN; Los Angeles County Museum of Art, Los Angeles, CA; Metropolitan Museum of Art, New York, NY; Museum of Arts and Design, New York, NY; Museum of Fine Arts, Boston, MA; National Museum of American History, Smithsonian Institution, Washington, DC; National Museum of Modern Art, Tokyo, Japan; Philadelphia Museum of Art, Philadelphia, PA; Phoenix Art Museum, Phoenix, AZ; Renwick Gallery, Smithsonian American Art Museum, Smithsonian Institution, Washington, DC; Rhode Island School of Design Museum, Providence, RI; Royal Ontario Museum, Toronto, ON, Canada; Saint Louis Art Museum, St. Louis, MO; Speed Art Museum, Louisville, KY; Toledo Museum of Art, Toledo, OH.

Other objects by this artist in the Corning Museum (all gifts of the Ben W. Heineman Sr. Family, unless otherwise noted)
Sculpture, *Burial Box, Type II–Rose*, 1978 (79.4.120, purchased with the aid of funds from the National Endowment for the Arts); Sculpture, *Cast Form Type VI*, 1979 (2006.4.17); Sculpture, *From Joe H. 2*, 1980 (2006.4.19); Sculpture, *Dedicant 7*, 1987 (2006.4.18); Sculpture, *Dedicant 11*, 1988 (2007.4.134); Sculpture, *Axis III*, 2001 (2006.4.16).

For more information
www.bentre.com; Buechner 1979, pp. 50 and 251; Arthur C. Danto, *Howard Ben Tré*, New York: Hudson Hills Press, 1999; Fox 2006, pp. 62–64; Eleanor Heartney, *Private Visions, Utopian Ideals: The Art of Howard Ben Tré*, Buffalo, NY: University at Buffalo Art Galleries, UB Anderson Gallery, 2005; Linda L. Johnson, *Howard Ben Tré: Contemporary Sculpture*, Washington, DC: Phillips Collection, 1989; Lynn 2005, pp. 15, 41, 94, and 207; Oldknow 2005, p. 67; Warmus 2003, pp. 42–45; Yelle 2000, pp. 17–19; Smithsonian Interview.

Jaroslava Brychtová
See Stanislav Libenský and Jaroslava Brychtová.

György Buczkó

Born in 1950 in Budapest, Hungary. Lives in Budapest, Hungary.

Buczkó is head of the Glass Department, School of Fine and Applied Arts, Budapest, Hungary (since 1982).

Education
Hungarian Academy of Crafts and Design, Budapest, Hungary (1974).

Selected honors and awards
Hungarian Artists' Association Prize (1997); Special Prize, Small Sculptures Biennial, Pécs, Hungary (1993); Asahi Shimbun Prize, Hokkaido Museum of Modern Art, Sapporo, Japan (1992); Hungarian Art Prize, Budapest, Hungary (1987); Second Prize, Small Sculptures Biennial, Pécs, Hungary (1987).

Selected museum collections
Bakony Museum, Veszprém, Hungary; Corning Museum of Glass, Corning, NY; Glasmuseum Hentrich, Museum Kunst Palast, Düsseldorf, Germany; Hokkaido Museum of Modern Art, Sapporo, Japan; Janus Pannonius Museum, Pécs, Hungary; Kunsthaus am Museum Carola van Harn, Cologne, Germany; Kunstsammlungen der Veste Coburg, Coburg, Germany; Museum of Applied Arts, Budapest, Hungary.

For more information
Frantz, Ricke, and Mizuta 1998, pp. 30–35 and 132.

James Carpenter

Born in 1949 in Washington, DC. Lives in New York, NY.

Carpenter's recent architectural projects include the Israel Museum, Jerusalem, Israel (scheduled completion 2010); 7 World Trade Center, New York, NY (completed 2006); Hearst Corporation Building, New York, NY (completed 2006); Time Warner Center, New York, NY (completed 2004); Deutsche Post Tower, Bonn, Germany (completed 2002); Sandra Day O'Connor Federal Courthouse, Phoenix, AZ (completed 2000); and Millennium Tower, New York, NY (completed 1995). Carpenter was a consultant on new glass materials for Corning Glass Works, Corning, NY (1972–1982).

Education
Rhode Island School of Design, Providence, RI, B.F.A. Sculpture (1972).

Selected honors and awards
American Institute of Architects Merit Award (2006); MacArthur Fellowship, John D. and Catherine T. MacArthur Foundation, Chicago, IL (2004); Benedictus Award (2002); National Environmental Design Award, Smithsonian Institution, Washington, DC (2002); American Institute of Architects Honors Award (1991); New York Foundation for the Arts Fellowship (1990); American Consulting Engineers Council Award (1987); New York Association of Consulting Engineers Award (1987); National Endowment for the Arts Fellowships (1985, 1979).

Selected museum collections
Arts Council of Australia, Sydney, NSW, Australia; Brooklyn Museum, Brooklyn, NY; Corning Museum of Glass, Corning, NY; Kunstgewerbemuseum, Berlin, Germany; Musée du Verre, Liège, Belgium; Museum Bellerive, Zurich, Switzerland; Museum für Kunst und Gewerbe, Hamburg, Germany; Museum of Arts and Design, New York, NY; National Gallery of Australia, Canberra, ACT, Australia; Rhode Island School of Design Museum, Providence, RI; Seattle Art Museum, Seattle, WA; Wadsworth Atheneum Museum of Art, Hartford, CT.

Other objects by this artist in the Corning Museum
Vessel, Untitled, 1974–1979 (98.4.10, gift of the artist); Prismatic Tile Screen, 1992 (2006.4.143, gift of Kathy Duffin).

With Dale Chihuly (American, b. 1941): Sculpture, Untitled (Flood Piece), about 1974 (99.4.248, gift of Dwight P. and Lorri Lanmon).

Design (for Venini, Italy): "Saturno" Bowl, 1972–1974 (80.3.62, anonymous gift).

Design (for Steuben Glass, United States): Bowl, 1979 (97.4.52, gift of Steuben Glass).

For more information
www.jcdainc.com; Fox 2006, pp. 146 and 148; Sandro Marpillero, *James Carpenter: Environmental Refractions*, Princeton, NJ: Princeton Architectural Press, 2006; Moor 1997, pp. 150–153; Oldknow 2005, p. 163; Yelle 2000, pp. 33–34; Smithsonian Interview.

Nicole Chesney

Born in 1971 in Cinnaminson, NJ. Lives in Cranston, RI.

Chesney was a visiting artist at the Massachusetts College of Art, Boston, MA (2004, 2002, 2001), and at The Studio of The Corning Museum of Glass, Corning, NY (2003).

Education
Canberra School of Art, Australian National University (ANU), Canberra, ACT, Australia, M.A. Visual Arts (2000); Massachusetts College of Art, B.F.A. (1997); California College of Arts and Crafts, Oakland, CA (1992–1994).

Selected honors and awards
Rakow Commission, Corning Museum of Glass (2005); New Talent Award, UrbanGlass, Brooklyn, NY (2004); Jutta Cuny-Franz Foundation Award, Museum Kunst Palast, Düsseldorf, Germany (2001); Drawing Prize, Canberra School of Art (ANU) (1999); Graduate Award, Canberra School of Art (ANU) (1999, 1998); David Thomas Foundation Grant, Noosa Heads, QLD, Australia (1998).

Selected museum collections
Corning Museum of Glass, Corning, NY; Glasmuseet Ebeltoft, Ebeltoft, Denmark.

For more information
    Tina Oldknow, "The 2005 Rakow Commission: Nicole Chesney,"
    New Glass Review 27, Corning: Corning Museum of Glass,
    2006, pp. 101–102; Oldknow 2005, p. 132; Helmut Ricke,
    "Jutta Cuny-Franz Memorial Award 2001," *Neues Glas*, no. 3,
    Fall 2001, pp. 73 and 75.

Dale Chihuly

Born in 1941 in Tacoma, WA. Lives in Seattle, WA.

Chihuly was co-founder, artistic director, and a teacher at Pilchuck Glass School, Stanwood, WA (1971–1990); he was also head of the Sculpture and Glass Program and a teacher at the Rhode Island School of Design, Providence, RI (1969–1983). He has taught at Lobmeyr, Baden, Austria (1985); Institute of American Indian Arts, Santa Fe, NM (1974); and the Haystack Mountain School of Crafts, Deer Isle, ME (1968–1971).

Chihuly was a visiting artist at the Rhode Island School of Design (1980–1983), and at Artpark, Lewiston, NY (1975). He is a trustee of The Corning Museum of Glass, Corning, NY (since 1999).

Education
    Rhode Island School of Design, M.F.A. Ceramics (1967–1968);
    University of Wisconsin, Madison, WI, M.S. Sculpture (1967);
    University of Washington, Seattle, WA, B.F.A. Interior Design
    (1965).

Selected honors and awards
    Washington State Medal of Merit, Olympia, WA (2007); Gold
    Medal Award, American Craft Council (2006); Honorary Doc-
    torate, University of Miami, Coral Gables, FL (2006); Honorary
    Doctorate, Kalamazoo College, Kalamazoo, MI (2005); Honor-
    ary Doctorate, Whitman College, Walla Walla, WA (2004);
    Lifetime Achievement Award, Glass Art Society (2003); Gold
    Medal Award, National Arts Club, New York, NY (2002); Hon-
    orary Doctorate, University of Hartford, Hartford, CT (2001);
    Lifetime Achievement in the Arts, Corporate Council for the
    Arts/ArtsFund, Seattle, WA (2001); Distinguished Artist Gold
    Medal Award, University of the Arts, Philadelphia, PA (2000);
    Honorary Doctorate, Brandeis University, Waltham, MA (2000);
    Award for Outstanding Achievement in Glass, UrbanGlass,
    Brooklyn, NY (1996); Honorary Doctorate, Gonzaga University,
    Spokane, WA (1996); Honorary Doctorate, Pratt Institute, New
    York, NY (1995); Distinguished Alumnus Award, University of
    Washington (1993); National Living Treasure, University of
    North Carolina, Wilmington, NC (1992); Honorary Doctorate,
    California College of Arts and Crafts, Oakland, CA (1988); Gov-
    ernors' Writers Award, Seattle, WA (1987); Honorary Doctorate,
    Rhode Island School of Design (1986); Honorary Doctorate,
    University of Puget Sound, Tacoma, WA (1986); Governors' Art
    Award, Providence, RI (1985); Governors' Art Awards, Seattle,
    WA (1985, 1984); Visual Artists Award, American Council for
    the Arts, New York, NY (1984); Achievement in the Arts Award,
    Tacoma, WA (1983); National Endowment for the Arts Fellow-
    ship (1975); Fulbright Foundation Fellowship (1968); Louis
    Comfort Tiffany Foundation Grant, New York, NY (1968);
    Seattle Weavers Guild Award, Seattle, WA (1964).

Selected museum collections
    Albright-Knox Art Gallery, Buffalo, NY; Auckland War Memorial
    Museum, Auckland, New Zealand; Brooklyn Museum, Brooklyn,
    NY; Carnegie Museum of Art, Pittsburgh, PA; Chrysler Museum
    of Art, Norfolk, VA; Cleveland Museum of Art, Cleveland, OH;
    Contemporary Museum, Honolulu, HI; Cooper-Hewitt National
    Design Museum, Smithsonian Institution, New York, NY; Corco-
    ran Gallery of Art, Washington, DC; Corning Museum of Glass,
    Corning, NY; Denver Art Museum, Denver, CO; Design Museum
    Ghent, Ghent, Belgium; Detroit Institute of Arts, Detroit, MI;
    Eretz Israel Museum, Tel Aviv, Israel; Fine Arts Museums of San
    Francisco, San Francisco, CA; Glasmuseet Ebeltoft, Ebeltoft,
    Denmark; Glasmuseum Hentrich, Museum Kunst Palast, Düssel-
    dorf, Germany; High Museum of Art, Atlanta, GA; Indianapolis
    Museum of Art, Indianapolis, IN; Israel Museum, Jerusalem, Is-
    rael; Kemper Museum of Contemporary Art, Kansas City, MO;
    Kunstsammlungen der Veste Coburg, Coburg, Germany; Los
    Angeles County Museum of Art, Los Angeles, CA; Metropol-
    itan Museum of Art, New York, NY; Montreal Museum of Fine
    Arts, Montreal, QC, Canada; Musée d'Art Moderne et d'Art
    Contemporain, Nice, France; Musée de Design et d'Arts Appli-
    qués Contemporains, Lausanne, Switzerland; Musée des Arts
    Décoratifs, Paris, France; Museo del Vetro, Murano, Italy; Mu-
    seum Bellerive, Zurich, Switzerland; Museum Boymans van
    Beuningen, Rotterdam, the Netherlands; Museum of Arts and
    Design, New York, NY; Museum of Contemporary Art, Chicago,
    IL; Museum of Contemporary Art San Diego, La Jolla, CA; Mu-
    seum of Decorative Arts, Prague, Czech Republic; Museum of
    Fine Arts, Boston, MA; Museum of Fine Arts, Houston, Houston,
    TX; National Gallery of Australia, Canberra, ACT, Australia;
    National Museum of Modern Art, Tokyo, Japan; National-
    museum, Stockholm, Sweden; New Orleans Museum of Art,
    New Orleans, LA; Norton Museum of Art, West Palm Beach,
    FL; Philadelphia Museum of Art, Philadelphia, PA; Phoenix Art
    Museum, Phoenix, AZ; Portland Art Museum, Portland, OR;
    Powerhouse Museum, Sydney, NSW, Australia; Queensland Art
    Gallery, South Brisbane, QLD, Australia; Rhode Island School
    of Design Museum, Providence, RI; Royal Ontario Museum,
    Toronto, ON, Canada; Saint Louis Art Museum, St. Louis, MO;
    Seattle Art Museum, Seattle, WA; Singapore Art Museum,
    Singapore; Suntory Museum of Art, Tokyo, Japan; Tacoma Art
    Museum, Tacoma, WA; Toledo Museum of Art, Toledo, OH;
    Victoria and Albert Museum, London, U.K.; Wadsworth Ath-
    eneum Museum of Art, Hartford, CT; Whitney Museum of
    American Art, New York, NY.

Other objects by this artist in the Corning Museum
    Vessel, Untitled, 1971 (71.4.145, gift of the artist); *Tornado
    Vessel*, 1974 (2003.4.66, gift of Kate Elliott in memory of Italo
    Scanga); Vessel, *Indian Blanket Cylinder (Double Saddle
    Blanket)*, 1975 (75.4.56); Vessel, *Navajo Blanket Cylinder (Chief
    Breast Plate)*, 1975 (2007.4.138, gift of the Ben W. Heineman
    Sr. Family); Vessel, *In Honor of Jackson Pollock and Ruth Kligman*,
    1975 (2007.4.139, gift of the Ben W. Heineman Sr. Family);
    Vessel, *Navajo Blanket Cylinder*, 1975 (2007.4.140, gift of the
    Ben W. Heineman Sr. Family); Vessel, *Navajo Blanket Cylinder
    (Chief Pattern Blanket)*, 1975 (2007.4.141, gift of the Ben W.
    Heineman Sr. Family); Vessel, *Navajo Blanket Cylinder (Serape
    Style 1865)*, 1975 (2007.4.142, gift of the Ben W. Heineman Sr.

Family); Vessel, *Navajo Blanket Cylinder (Full Wrap Pueblo Cylinder)*, 1975 (2007.4.143, gift of the Ben W. Heineman Sr. Family); Vessel, *Navajo Basket Cylinder (047-0038)*, 1976 (2007.4.144, gift of the Ben W. Heineman Sr. Family); Vessel, *Navajo Blanket Cylinder (Zig-Zag with Horse Drawing)*, 1976 (2007.4.145, gift of the Ben W. Heineman Sr. Family); Vessel, *Indian Blanket Cylinder (Hudson Bay Style 1890)*, 1976 (2007.4.146, gift of the Ben W. Heineman Sr. Family); Vessel, *Navajo Blanket Cylinder (Star Boyeta)*, 1976 (2007.4.147, gift of the Ben W. Heineman Sr. Family); Vessel, *Navajo Blanket Cylinder with Horses*, 1976 (2008.4.28, gift of Heinz and Elizabeth Wolf in honor of Dale Chihuly); Vessel, *Opal Basket*, 1977 (79.4.123); Sculpture, *Basket Group*, 1979 (80.4.55, purchased with the aid of funds from the National Endowment for the Arts); Sculpture, *Seaforms*, 1981 (81.4.43); Vessel, *Basket*, 1981 (92.4.128, bequest of David Brokars); Sculpture, *Macchia Seaform Group*, 1982 (83.4.45, gift of Michael J. Bove III); Vessel, *Macchia*, 1982 (83.4.144); Sculpture, *Basket Set*, 1984 (95.4.377, gift of Mr. and Mrs. Albert E. St. Denis); Sculpture, *Seaforms*, 1986 (2007.4.150, gift of the Ben W. Heineman Sr. Family); Vessels, *Olive Green Venetian with Sawtooth Flanges* and *Chrome Yellow Venetian with Sawtooth Flanges*, 1988 (89.4.9, gift of the artist); Sculpture, *Gray-Blue and Lavender Persian Set with Red Lip Wraps*, 1988 (2007.4.149, gift of the Ben W. Heineman Sr. Family); Vessel, *Cadmium Yellow-Orange Venetian #398*, 1990 (90.4.129, purchased with funds from Mr. and Mrs. James R. Houghton); Sculpture, *Niijima Floats*, 1993 (94.4.34, gift of the artist); Sculpture, *Erbium Chandelier*, 1993 (2008.4.2, gift of Bullseye Glass Company); Vessel, *Celadon Green Piccolo Venetian with Viridian Lilies*, 1994 (2006.4.24, gift of the Ben W. Heineman Sr. Family); Vessel, *Cylinder with Indian Blanket Drawing*, 1995 (2007.4.148, gift of the Ben W. Heineman Sr. Family); Sculpture, *Putti Lounging on Crab Resting on Orange Madder Vessel*, 1999 (2007.4.151, gift of the Ben W. Heineman Sr. Family).

With James Carpenter (American, b. 1949): Sculpture, Untitled (Flood Piece), about 1974 (99.4.248, gift of Dwight P. and Lorri Lanmon).

For more information
www.chihuly.com; Todd Alden, *Chihuly at the Royal Botanic Gardens, Kew*, Seattle: Portland Press, 2005; Walter Darby Bannard and Henry Geldzahler, *Chihuly: Form from Fire*, Daytona Beach, FL: Museum of Arts and Sciences, and Seattle and London: University of Washington Press, 1993; Sarah Bremser, *Chihuly: Glass in Architecture*, Kaohsiung, Taiwan: Kaohsiung Museum of Fine Arts, 1994; Buechner 1979, pp. 60–62 and 253; Timothy Anglin Burgard, *The Art of Dale Chihuly*, San Francisco: Chronicle Books, 2008; Dale Chihuly and others, *Chihuly: Color, Glass, and Form*, Tokyo: Kodansha International, 1986; Jack Cowart and Karen Chambers, *Chihuly: A Decade of Glass*, Bellevue, WA: Bellevue Art Museum, 1984; Sylvia Earle and others, *Chihuly Seaforms*, Seattle: Portland Press, 1995; Henry Geldzahler and Robert Hobbs, *Dale Chihuly: Objets de verre*, Paris: Musée des Arts Décoratifs, 1986; Ron Glowen, *Venetians: Dale Chihuly*, Altadena, CA: Twin Palms Publishers, 1989; Donald B. Kuspit, *Chihuly*, Seattle: Portland Press in association with Harry N. Abrams, New York, 1997; Donald Kuspit

and Kathryn Kanjo, *Chihuly: The George R. Stroemple Collection*, Portland, OR: Portland Art Museum, 1997; Lynn 2005, pp. 113, 172–173, and 190–191; Linda Norden, *Chihuly Baskets*, Seattle: Portland Press, 1994; Nordness 1970, pp. 160–161; Tina Oldknow, *Chihuly Persians*, Seattle: Portland Press, 1996; Tina Oldknow, *Pilchuck: A Glass School*, Seattle: the school in association with the University of Washington Press, Seattle and London, 1996; Oldknow 2005, p. 21; Jennifer Hawkins Opie and others, *Chihuly at the V&A*, Seattle: Portland Press in association with V&A Publications, London, 2001; Barbara Rose and others, *Chihuly Gardens & Glass*, Seattle: Portland Press, 2002; Barbara Rose and others, *Chihuly Projects*, Seattle: Portland Press in association with Harry N. Abrams, New York, 2000; Patterson Sims, *Dale Chihuly: Installations, 1964–1992*, Seattle: Seattle Art Museum, 1992; Davira S. Taragin, *Dale Chihuly 2002*, Hamilton, NJ: Grounds for Sculpture, 2003; William Warmus, *Chihuly in the Light of Jerusalem 2000*, Seattle: Portland Press, 1999.

Václav Cigler
Born in 1929 in Vsetín, Czechoslovakia. Lives in Prague, Czech Republic.

Cigler was head of the Glass Architecture Studio, Academy of Fine Arts, Bratislava, Czechoslovakia (1966–1979).

Education
Academy of Applied Arts, Prague, Czechoslovakia (1951–1957); Specialized School for Glassmaking, Nový Bor, Czechoslovakia (1948–1951).

Selected honors and awards
Coburg Glass Prize, Kunstsammlungen der Veste Coburg, Coburg, Germany (1985); Glaskunst '81, Orangerie, Kassel, Germany (1981); Silver Medal, International Exhibition, Jablonec nad Nisou, Czechoslovakia (1966).

Selected museum collections
Badisches Landesmuseum, Karlsruhe, Germany; Corning Museum of Glass, Corning, NY; Glasmuseum Hentrich, Museum Kunst Palast, Düsseldorf, Germany; Hokkaido Museum of Modern Art, Sapporo, Japan; Kunstgewerbemuseum, Berlin, Germany; Kunstsammlungen der Veste Coburg, Coburg, Germany; Moravian Gallery, Brno, Czech Republic; Musée de Design et d'Arts Appliqués Contemporains, Lausanne, Switzerland; Musée des Arts Décoratifs, Paris, France; Museum Bellerive, Zurich, Switzerland; Museum Boymans van Beuningen, Rotterdam, the Netherlands; Museum für Kunsthandwerk, Frankfurt am Main, Germany; Museum of Arts and Design, New York, NY; Museum of Decorative Arts, Prague, Czech Republic; National Gallery, Prague, Czech Republic; North Bohemian Museum, Liberec, Czech Republic; Stedelijk Museum, Amsterdam, the Netherlands.

Other objects by this artist in the Corning Museum
Vase with Two Female Figures, 1958 (62.3.131); Sculpture, *Object-Mat VI*, 1981 (2001.3.58, gift of Charles and Gail Puckette).

For more information
  Milena Lamarová and Václav Cigler, *Václav Cigler: Projeckty, sklo, kresby = Václav Cigler: Projects, Glass, Drawings*, Prague: Cigler, 1993; Opie 2004, pp. 26–27; Petrová 2001; Petrová 2004, pp. 30–31; Ricke 1990, pp. 200–203 and 252–254; Ricke 2005, pp. 146–154 and 372–373; Schack von Wittenau 2005, pp. 200–201; Sekera and Šetlík 1998.

Brian Clarke
Born in 1953 in Oldham, U.K. Lives in London, U.K.

Clarke's recent architectural projects include the Pyramid of Peace, Astana Kazakhstan (2006); Ascot Racecourse, Ascot, U.K. (2003); Pfizer Inc., New York, NY (2001); Al-Faisaliah Complex, Riyadh, Saudi Arabia (2000); Olympus Optical Europa Building, Hamburg, Germany (2000); Casa Austria, Salzburg, Austria (1999); RWE Energie AG, Essen, Germany (1997); Centre Norte Shopping, Rio de Janeiro, Brazil (1996); Swiss Bank Corporation, Stamford, CT (1996); and Stansted Airport, Stansted, U.K. (1991).

Education
  North Devon College of Art and Design, Barnstaple, Devon, U.K. (1970); Burnley School of Art, Burnley, U.K. (1968); Oldham School of Arts and Crafts, Oldham, U.K. (1965).

Selected honors and awards
  Comité d'Honneur, Fondation Vincent van Gogh, Arles, France; Fellow, Royal Society of Art, London, U.K.; Honorary Fellow, Royal Institute of British Architects, London, U.K.; Leeds Award for Architecture, Leeds, U.K. (1991); Winston Churchill Memorial Traveling Fellowship (1974–1975).

Selected museum collections
  Corning Museum of Glass, Corning, NY.

Other object by this artist in the Corning Museum
  Architectural Panel, *The Glass Dune/Hamburg*, 1992 (95.3.32).

For more information
  www.brianclarke.co.uk; *Brian Clarke: Architectural Artist*, London: Academy Editions, 1994; *Brian Clarke: Lamina*, London: Gagosian Gallery, 2005; *Brian Clarke: Transillumination*, New York: Tony Shafrazi Gallery, 2002; Clarke 1979; Lynn 2005, p. 59; Moor 1997, pp. 106–111; Oldknow 2005, p. 165.

Bernard Dejonghe
Born in 1942 in Chantilly, France. Lives in Briançonnet, France.

Education
  Ecole des Métiers d'Art, Paris, France (1960–1964).

Selected honors and awards
  Bettencourt Prize, Paris, France (2001); Culture Prize, Bourges, France (1996); National Grand Prize, Ministry of Culture, Paris, France (1995); Asahi Shimbun Prize, Hokkaido Museum of Modern Art, Sapporo, Japan (1994).

Selected museum collections
  Corning Museum of Glass, Corning, NY; Fonds National d'Art Contemporain, Paris, France; Fonds Régional d'Art Contemporain, Marseilles, France; Hokkaido Museum of Modern Art, Sapporo, Japan; Musée Ariana, Geneva, Switzerland; Musée d'Art Contemporain, Dunkirk, France; Musée d'Art Moderne, Nice, France; Musée Réattu, Arles, France.

Other objects by this artist in the Corning Museum
  Sculpture, *Little Glass Maul*, 1995 (97.3.82, gift of the artist).

For more information
  Frantz, Ricke, and Mizuta 1998, pp. 40–43 and 134; Jacqueline Lerat, *Bernard Dejonghe: Siliciums–nuages clairs*, Bourges, France: Ville de Bourges, Agence Culturelle, 1999; Opie 2004, pp. 36–37; Schack von Wittenau 2005, pp. 82–83; Weschenfelder 2006, pp. 292 and 337.

Alessandro Diaz de Santillana
Born in 1959 in Paris, France. Lives in Venice, Italy.

De Santillana taught at the University of California, San Diego, CA (1997).

Education
  University of Venice, Venice, Italy (1977–1981).

Selected museum collections
  Corning Museum of Glass, Corning, NY; Musée des Beaux Arts, Rouen, France.

Other object by this artist in the Corning Museum
  Sculpture, *Balistide Verde*, 1992 (93.3.39).

For more information
  Frantz, Ricke, and Mizuta 1998, pp. 44–47 and 135; Lynn 2005, p. 65; Oldknow 2005, pp. 76–77.

Erwin Eisch
Born in 1927 in Frauenau, Germany. Lives in Frauenau, Germany.

Eisch organized the summer school Bild-Werk Frauenau, Frauenau, Germany (1988). He taught at Pilchuck Glass School, Stanwood, WA (1984, 1983, 1981); Alfred University, Alfred, NY (1976); Foley College of Art, Stourbridge, U.K. (1973); Haystack Mountain School of Crafts, Deer Isle, ME (1972); California State University, San Jose, CA (1968); and the University of Wisconsin, Madison, WI (1968, 1964).

Education
  Academy of Fine Arts, Munich, Germany (1956–1959, 1949–1952); apprenticeship to Valentin Eisch, Frauenau, Germany (1946–1949); School for Glassmaking, Zwiesel, Germany (1946–1948).

Selected honors and awards
  Lifetime Achievement Award, UrbanGlass, Brooklyn, NY (2002); Gold Award, American Interfaith Institute, Philadelphia,

PA (1992); Kulturpreis Ostbayern, Germany (1987); First Prize, Coburg Glass Prize, Kunstsammlungen der Veste Coburg, Coburg, Germany (1985); Honorary Lifetime Member, Glass Art Society (1982); Coburg Glass Prize, Kunstsammlungen der Veste Coburg (1977).

Selected museum collections
Badisches Landesmuseum, Karlsruhe, Germany; Corning Museum of Glass, Corning, NY; Glasmuseum Hentrich, Museum Kunst Palast, Düsseldorf, Germany; Hessisches Landesmuseum, Darmstadt, Germany; Kunstsammlungen der Veste Coburg, Coburg, Germany; Metropolitan Museum of Art, New York, NY; Musée des Arts Décoratifs, Paris, France; Museum Bellerive, Zurich, Switzerland; Museum für Kunst und Gewerbe, Hamburg, Germany; National Museum of Modern Art, Kyoto, Japan; Renwick Gallery, Smithsonian American Art Museum, Smithsonian Institution, Washington, DC; Toledo Museum of Art, Toledo, OH; Yokohama Museum of Art, Yokohama, Japan.

Other objects by this artist in the Corning Museum
Bottle, *Flight into Egypt/St. George and the Dragon*, 1964 (64.3.29, gift of the artist); Cup, 1964 (64.3.31, gift of the artist); Sculpture, Untitled, 1966–1969 (98.3.13, gift of the artist); Sculptures, Untitled, 1967 (98.3.9, .12, gifts of the artist); Vessel, 1968 (89.4.74, gift of the Robert C. Florian Estate); Vessel, 1968 (98.3.10, gift of the artist); Sculpture, *Hand*, 1968 (98.3.11, gift of the artist); Sculpture, *Telefon*, 1971 (76.3.3); Vessels, *Variations to a Wine Glass*, 1978 (80.3.24, .25, gifts of Erwin and Gretl Eisch); Sculpture, *To the Big Corning Day/May 29th 1980*, 1980 (80.3.18, gift of the artist); Vessel, *Bottle Spirits: Hobby Horse*, 1980 (80.3.60); Vase, *Lethe*, 1980 (80.3.61, gift/exchange of Harvey K. and Bess Littleton); Bottle, Vessel, and Bowl, *Poesie in Glas*, 1981 (81.3.39–.41); Vase, 1981 (81.3.42); Bowl, 1981 (2008.3.6, gift of Heinz and Elizabeth Wolf); Sculpture, *Buddha's Inner Smile*, 1982 (82.3.47); Sculpture, *Finger's Studies (Finger's Thought)*, 1982 (82.3.84, gift of the artist); Bottle, *Four Seasons*, 1982 (2008.3.7, gift of Heinz and Elizabeth Wolf); Vase, *Poesie*, 1984 (84.3.44); Sculpture, *Self-Portrait from the Outside*, 1997 (2000.3.59).

For more information
www.eisch.de; Yvonne Brunhammer and others, *Erwin Eisch: Sensualité du verre*, Charleroi, Belgium: Musée du Verre, 1997; Buechner 1979, pp. 78–79 and 255; Frantz, Ricke, and Mizuta 1998, pp. 48–53 and 136; Igor A. Jenzen, ed., *Da Bin I: Selbstporträts in Glas von Erwin Eisch*, Dresden: Staatliche Kunstsammlungen Dresden, 2002; Lynggaard 1998, pp. 35–40; Lynn 2005, pp. 40 and 187; Oldknow 2005, p. 78; Opie 2004, pp. 40–41; Ricke 1990, pp. 60–63 and 254–257; Schack von Wittenau 2005, pp. 36–39; Yelle 2000, pp. 63–64.

Judy Hill
Born in 1953 in Galveston, TX. Lives in Portland, OR.

Hill taught at California State University, Fresno, CA (2002); BildWerk Frauenau, Frauenau, Germany (2000); Penland School of Crafts, Penland, NC (1997); Pratt Fine Arts Center, Seattle, WA (1991); and Pilchuck Glass School, Stanwood, WA (1988).

She was a visiting artist at the Oregon School of Arts and Crafts, Portland, OR (1989–1990).

Education
Louisiana State University, Baton Rouge, LA, M.F.A. (1987); Falmouth School of Art, Falmouth, U.K., B.F.A. (1976).

Selected honors and awards
Bonnie Bronson Award (1998); Western States Arts Federation/National Endowment for the Arts Fellowship (1995); Sculpture Fellowship, Oregon Arts Commission, Portland, OR (1994); Great American Gallery Scholarship (1988); Pilchuck Glass School Scholarships (1987, 1986).

Selected museum collections
Corning Museum of Glass, Corning, NY; Philbrook Museum of Art, Tulsa, OK; Portland Art Museum, Portland, OR; Speed Art Museum, Louisville, KY; Tacoma Art Museum, Tacoma, WA.

For more information
Frantz 2003, pp. 12–15 and 49; Frantz, Ricke, and Mizuta 1998, pp. 66–71 and 139; Graham 1999, cover and pp. 6–7 and 18; Mann 1997, p. 13.

Eric Hilton
Born in 1937 in Bournemouth, U.K. Lives in Odessa, NY.

Hilton is a designer for Steuben Glass, Corning, NY (since 1974). He taught at the State University of New York, College of Ceramics, Alfred, NY (1970); University of Victoria, Victoria, BC, Canada (1968); Birmingham College of Art, Birmingham, U.K. (1967); Stourbridge College of Art, Stourbridge, U.K. (1963); and the Edinburgh College of Art, Edinburgh, U.K. (1961).

Education
Edinburgh College of Art, M.F.A. (1961) and B.F.A. (1959).

Selected honors and awards
National Endowment for the Arts Fellowship (1981) and Research Grant (1980).

Selected museum collections
Corning Museum of Glass, Corning, NY; Hokkaido Museum of Modern Art, Sapporo, Japan; Lowe Art Museum, University of Miami, Coral Gables, FL; Musée de Design et d'Arts Appliqués Contemporains, Lausanne, Switzerland; Musée des Arts Décoratifs, Paris, France; Otari Memorial Art Museum, Nishinomiya, Japan; Renwick Gallery, Smithsonian American Art Museum, Smithsonian Institution, Washington, DC.

Other objects by this artist in the Corning Museum
Sculpture, Untitled, 1973 (73.4.73); Sculpture, *Life Sanctuary 2001*, 2001 (2007.4.161, gift of the Ben W. Heineman Sr. Family).

Design (for Steuben Glass, United States): *Tall Sun Dance Bowl*, 1985 (99.4.70, gift of Steuben Glass); *The Golden Bowl*, 2000 (2001.4.14, gift of Steuben Glass).

For more information
Buechner 1979, pp. 98 and 257; Mary Jean Madigan, *Steuben Glass: An American Tradition in Crystal*, New York: Harry N. Abrams, 2003; Chloe Zerwick, *Aldridge, Dowler, Hilton. The Steuben Project: Sculptures in Crystal*, New York: Steuben Glass, 1988, plates 18–25.

Pavel Hlava
Born in 1924 in Semily, Czechoslovakia. Died in 2003 in Prague, Czech Republic.

Hlava, who was chief designer at Crystalex for almost 20 years, was also a designer for the Center for Home and Fashion Culture, Prague, Czechoslovakia (1959–1985). He taught at the Royal College of Art, London, U.K. (1967).

Education
Academy of Applied Arts, Prague, Czechoslovakia (1942–1948); Specialized School for Glassmaking, Železný Brod, Czechoslovakia (1939–1942).

Selected honors and awards
Academic Art Prize, Prague, Czech Republic (1993); Design Centrum Prize, Brno, Czechoslovakia (1991, 1989); Gold Medal, Kanazawa International Glass, Kanazawa, Japan (1988); Coburg Glass Prize, Kunstsammlungen der Veste Coburg, Coburg, Germany (1985, 1977); Grand Prize, Jablonec nad Nisou, Czechoslovakia (1979, 1976, 1973); Bavarian State Prize and Gold Medal, Internationale Handwerksmesse, Munich, Germany (1971); Gold Medal, Leipzig-Messe, Leipzig, Germany (1966).

Selected museum collections
Art Gallery of New South Wales, Sydney, NSW, Australia; Carnegie Museum of Art, Pittsburgh, PA; Corning Museum of Glass, Corning, NY; Glasmuseet Ebeltoft, Ebeltoft, Denmark; Glasmuseum Hentrich, Museum Kunst Palast, Düsseldorf, Germany; High Museum of Art, Atlanta, GA; Kunstsammlungen der Veste Coburg, Coburg, Germany; Moravian Gallery, Brno, Czech Republic; Musée de Design et d'Arts Appliqués Contemporains, Lausanne, Switzerland; Museum Bellerive, Zurich, Switzerland; Museum Boymans van Beuningen, Rotterdam, the Netherlands; Museum für Kunst und Gewerbe, Hamburg, Germany; Museum of Decorative Arts, Barcelona, Spain; Museum of Decorative Arts, Prague, Czech Republic; National Gallery, Prague, Czech Republic; North Bohemian Museum, Liberec, Czech Republic; Victoria and Albert Museum, London, U.K.; Yokohama Museum of Art, Yokohama, Japan.

Other objects by this artist in the Corning Museum
"Single-Bloom" Vase, 1958 (62.3.125); Vase with Three Ballerinas, 1958 (62.3.127); Vase with Lens-Shaped Cuts, 1958 (62.3.128); Pierced Vase, 1960 (2005.3.19); Sculptural Vessel, 1965 (74.3.75); Vase with Abstract Decoration, 1965 (99.3.11, gift of Mr. and Mrs. Dwight P. Lanmon); Tall Square Vase, 1965–1975 (99.3.12, gift of Mr. and Mrs. Dwight P. Lanmon); Sculptural Vessel, 1970 (74.3.74); Sculpture, *Two Hemispheres*, 1974 (75.3.18); *Crystal Glass Sculpture*, 1978 (78.3.50); Jardiniere, 1979 (79.3.62); Vase, 1979 (79.3.63); Sculpture, *Space 1980*,

1980 (82.3.1, gift of Art Centrum and Pavel Hlava); Sculpture, *Intrusion Series*, 1984 (2006.3.32, gift of the Ben W. Heineman Sr. Family); Sculpture, *Rainbow I*, 1986 (2006.3.11, gift of the Ben W. Heineman Sr. Family); Sculpture, *Contradiction*, 1987 (2007.3.77, gift of the Ben W. Heineman Sr. Family); Sculpture, *Fish*, 1988 (89.3.3); Sculpture, *Fata Morgana*, 1991 (2006.3.31, gift of the Ben W. Heineman Sr. Family); Sculpture, *Crystal Flower*, 1997 (2006.3.10, gift of the Ben W. Heineman Sr. Family).

For more information
Buechner 1979, pp. 99 and 257; Antonín Langhamer, *Pavel Hlava: Život a Práce*, Nový Bor: Crystalex, 1986; Oldknow 2005, p. 175; Sylva Petrová, *Pavel Hlava*, Děčín: Grafiatisk, 1995; Ricke 1990, pp. 144–147 and 264–266; Ricke 2005, pp. 174–180 and 376–377; Schack von Wittenau 2005, pp. 204–205.

Franz Xaver Höller
Born in 1950 in Leopoldsdorf, Germany. Lives in Zwiesel, Germany.

Höller teaches at the National School for Glassmaking, Zwiesel, Germany (since 1981). He taught at the Canberra School of Art, Australian National University, Canberra, ACT, Australia (1993), and at the Toledo Museum of Art School of Design, Toledo, OH (1981).

Education
Academy of Fine Arts, Munich, Germany (1973–1978); National School for Glassmaking, Zwiesel, Germany (1970–1973); apprenticeship in glass cutting, Passau, Germany (1964–1967).

Selected honors and awards
Bavarian State Prize, Internationale Handwerksmesse, Munich, Germany (1995, 1975); Coburg Glass Prize, Kunstsammlungen der Veste Coburg, Coburg, Germany (1985); Bayerwald Glass Prize, Frauenau, Germany (1984); Glaskunst '81, Orangerie, Kassel, Germany (1981).

Selected museum collections
Badisches Landesmuseum, Karlsruhe, Germany; Corning Museum of Glass, Corning, NY; Glasmuseum Hentrich, Museum Kunst Palast, Düsseldorf, Germany; Kunstsammlungen der Veste Coburg, Coburg, Germany; Musée de Design et d'Arts Appliqués Contemporains, Lausanne, Switzerland; Museum Bellerive, Zurich, Switzerland; Museum für Kunst und Gewerbe, Hamburg, Germany; Museum für Kunsthandwerk, Frankfurt am Main, Germany; Württembergisches Landesmuseum, Stuttgart, Germany.

Other objects by this artist in the Corning Museum
Vessel, *The Communication*, 1981 (83.3.11); Sculpture, *Balloon I*, 1994 (99.3.97); Vessel, Untitled, 1996 (97.3.36); Sculpture, *Pair*, 1997 (2003.3.14, gift of Barry Friedman Ltd.).

For more information
Buechner 1979, pp. 100 and 257; Frantz, Ricke, and Mizuta 1998, pp. 72–79 and 140; Helmut Ricke, *Franz-Xaver Höller: Glasobjekte und Zeichnungen, 1977–1990*, Zwiesel: Höller, 1990; Ricke 1990, pp. 174–179 and 266–267; Schack von Wit-

tenau 2005, pp. 42–43; Weschenfelder 2006, pp. 129, 267, and 345.

Jun Kaneko
Born in 1942 in Nagoya, Japan. Lives in Omaha, NE.

Kaneko taught at the Cranbrook Academy of Art, Bloomfield Hills, MI (1979–1986); Rhode Island School of Design, Providence, RI (1973–1975); Scripps College, Claremont, CA (1974); and the University of New Hampshire, Durham, NH (1972–1973).

Education
Claremont Graduate School, Claremont, CA (1970); University of California, Berkeley, CA (1966); California Institute of Art, Los Angeles, CA (1964); Chouinard Art Institute, Los Angeles, CA (1964).

Selected honors and awards
Honorary Doctorate, Royal College of Art, London, U.K. (2005); Fellow, American Craft Council (1995); Honorary Member, National Council on Education for the Ceramic Arts (1994); Nebraska Arts Council Fellowship (1994); National Endowment for the Arts Fellowship (1979); Archie Bray Foundation Fellowship, Helena, MT (1967).

Selected museum collections
Aichi-Prefecture Museum of Ceramics, Japan; Arabia Museum, Helsinki, Finland; Arkansas Art Center, Little Rock, AR; Corning Museum of Glass, Corning, NY; Cranbrook Academy of Art Museum, Bloomfield Hills, MI; Detroit Institute of Arts, Detroit, MI; Fine Arts Museums of San Francisco, San Francisco, CA; Gifu-Ken Museum, Gifu, Japan; Honolulu Academy of Art, Honolulu, HI; Japan Foundation, Tokyo, Japan; Joslyn Art Museum, Omaha, NE; Los Angeles County Museum of Art, Los Angeles, CA; Museum Het Kruithis, s'Hertogenbosch, the Netherlands; Museum of Arts and Design, New York, NY; Museum of Contemporary Art, Honolulu, HI; Nagoya City Museum, Nagoya, Japan; Nelson-Atkins Museum of Art, Kansas City, MO; Oakland Museum of California, Oakland, CA; Olympic Museum of Ceramic Sculpture, Athens, Greece; Philadelphia Museum of Art, Philadelphia, PA; Queensland Art Gallery, South Brisbane, QLD, Australia; Renwick Gallery, Smithsonian American Art Museum, Smithsonian Institution, Washington, DC; Shigaraki Ceramic Museum, Shigaraki, Japan; Toyota City Museum, Toyota, Japan; Yamaguchi Museum, Yamaguchi, Japan.

For more information
Bullseye: The Kaneko Project, Portland, OR: Bullseye Glass Co., 2007; Douglass Freed and Glen R. Brown, *Jun Kaneko*, Sedalia, MO: Daum Museum of Contemporary Art, 2002; Susan Peterson, *Jun Kaneko*, London: Laurence King, 2001; Smithsonian Interview.

Marian Karel
Born in 1944 in Pardubice, Czechoslovakia. Lives in Prague, Czech Republic.

Karel is head of the Fine Art Department at the Academy of Arts, Architecture, and Design, Prague, Czech Republic (since 1999). He was head of the academy's Glass in Architecture Program (1995–1999), and he taught at the Toyama Institute of Glass Art, Toyama, Japan (1999); University of Auckland, Auckland, New Zealand (1998); Niijima Glass Center, Niijima, Japan (1992); and Pilchuck Glass School, Stanwood, WA (1989, 1983).

Education
Academy of Applied Arts, Prague, Czechoslovakia (1965–1972); Secondary School of Applied Arts, Jablonec nad Nisou, Czechoslovakia (1959–1963).

Selected museum collections
Auckland War Memorial Museum, Auckland, New Zealand; Badisches Landesmuseum, Karlsruhe, Germany; Corning Museum of Glass, Corning, NY; Czech Museum of Fine Arts, Prague, Czech Republic; East Bohemian Museum, Pardubice, Czech Republic; Glasmuseum Hentrich, Museum Kunst Palast, Düsseldorf, Germany; Hokkaido Museum of Modern Art, Sapporo, Japan; Kunstsammlungen der Veste Coburg, Coburg, Germany; Moravian Gallery, Brno, Czech Republic; Musée de Design et d'Arts Appliqués Contemporains, Lausanne, Switzerland; Musée des Arts Décoratifs, Paris, France; Museum Bellerive, Zurich, Switzerland; Museum für Kunst und Gewerbe, Hamburg, Germany; Museum of Decorative Arts, Budapest, Hungary; Museum of Decorative Arts, Prague, Czech Republic; National Gallery, Prague, Czech Republic; National Museum of Modern Art, Tokyo, Japan; North Bohemian Museum, Liberec, Czech Republic; Pushkin Museum of Arts, Moscow, Russia; Württembergisches Landesmuseum, Stuttgart, Germany; Yokohama Museum of Art, Yokohama, Japan.

Other objects by this artist in the Corning Museum
Sculpture, *Pyramid III*, 1989 (94.3.156, gift of Michael and Douglas Heller); Sculpture, *The Pyramid*, 1989 (2007.3.84, gift of the Ben W. Heineman Sr. Family).

For more information
www.mariankarel.cz; Buechner 1979, pp. 116–117 and 259; Lynn 2005, p. 64; Oldknow 2005, p. 88; Petrová 2001; Ricke 1990, pp. 204–207 and 273–274; Schack von Wittenau 2005, pp. 206–207; Sekera and Šetlík 1998; Yelle 2000, pp. 111–112.

Robert Kehlmann
Born in 1942 in Brooklyn, NY. Lives in Berkeley, CA.

Kehlmann taught at the California College of Arts and Crafts, Oakland, CA (1991, 1978–1980); Miasa Bunker Center, Nagano, Japan (1985); Honolulu Academy of Arts, Honolulu, HI (1983); and Pilchuck Glass School, Stanwood, WA (1980, 1978). He was a visiting artist at Pilchuck Glass School (1985).

Education
University of California, Berkeley, CA, M.A. English Literature (1966); Antioch College, Yellow Springs, OH, B.A. (1963).

Selected honors and awards
Honorary Lifetime Member, Glass Art Society (1994); National Endowment for the Arts Fellowships (1978, 1977).

Selected museum collections
Corning Museum of Glass, Corning, NY; Glasmuseet Ebeltoft, Ebeltoft, Denmark; Glasmuseum, Immenhausen, Germany; Hessisches Landesmuseum, Darmstadt, Germany; Hokkaido Museum of Modern Art, Sapporo, Japan; Musée de Design et d'Arts Appliqués Contemporains, Lausanne, Switzerland; Museo del Vidrio, Monterrey, Mexico; Museum of Arts and Design, New York, NY; Renwick Gallery, Smithsonian American Art Museum, Smithsonian Institution, Washington, DC; Toledo Museum of Art, Toledo, OH.

Other objects by this artist in the Corning Museum
Panel, *Composition XXIX*, 1976 (79.4.130); Mosaic Panel, *Piano*, 1994 (96.4.57, gift of the artist).

For more information
www.robertkehlmann.com; Buechner 1979, pp. 121 and 260; Susanne K. Frantz and William Warmus, *Robert Kehlmann. Painting with Glass: A Retrospective*, Moraga, CA: Hearst Art Gallery, Saint Mary's College of California, 1996; Matthew Kangas, "Robert Kehlmann: Aspects of Meaning," in Kangas 2006, pp. 241–245; Kehlmann 1992; Oldknow 2005, pp. 138–139; Yelle 2000, pp. 113–114.

Joey Kirkpatrick
See Flora C. Mace and Joey Kirkpatrick.

Vladimír Kopecký
Born in 1931 in Svojanov, Czechoslovakia. Lives in Prague, Czech Republic.

Kopecký is director of the glass studio at the Academy of Art, Architecture, and Design, Prague, Czech Republic (since 1990).

Education
Academy of Applied Arts, Prague, Czechoslovakia (1949–1956); Specialized School for Glassmaking, Nový Bor, Czechoslovakia (1948–1949); Specialized School for Glassmaking, Kamenický Šenov, Czechoslovakia (1946–1948).

Selected honors and awards
Bridgestone Museum of Art Prize, Tokyo Metropolitan Art Museum, Tokyo, Japan (1984); Gold Medal, Expo '58, Brussels, Belgium (1958).

Selected museum collections
Corning Museum of Glass, Corning, NY; Dudley Museum and Art Gallery, Dudley, U.K.; Glasmuseum Hentrich, Museum Kunst Palast, Düsseldorf, Germany; Kunstsammlungen der Veste Coburg, Coburg, Germany; Moravian Gallery, Brno, Czech Republic; Musée de Design et d'Arts Appliqués Contemporains, Lausanne, Switzerland; Musée-Atelier du Verre, Sars-Poteries, France; Museum of Decorative Arts, Prague,

Czech Republic; National Gallery, Prague, Czech Republic; National Museum of Modern Art, Kyoto, Japan; North Bohemian Museum, Liberec, Czech Republic; Victoria and Albert Museum, London, U.K.; Yokohama Museum of Art, Yokohama, Japan.

Other objects by this artist in the Corning Museum
Vase with Abstract Decoration, 1957 (83.3.235); Vase with Abstract Decoration, 1958 (83.3.234); Vase with Abstract Decoration, 1959 (83.3.233); Plate with Abstract Decoration, 1960 (2006.3.67); Vase with Abstract Decoration, 1965 (99.3.41, gift of The Steinberg Foundation).

For more information
Susanne K. Frantz and others, *Vladimír Kopecký*, Prague: Galerie Hlavního Města Prahy, 1999; Oldknow 2005, pp. 178–179; Petrová 2001; Petrová 2004, p. 38; Ricke 1990, pp. 222–225 and 275–276; Ricke 2005, pp. 206–217 and 383–384; Schack von Wittenau 2005, pp. 208–209; Sekera and Šetlík 1998.

Dominick Labino
Born in 1910 in Fairmount City, PA. Died in 1987 in Grand Rapids, OH.

Labino organized the first studio glassblowing workshops in the United States, with Harvey K. Littleton, at The Toledo Museum of Art, Toledo, OH (1962).
He was a research consultant (1965–1974), president and research director (1959–1965), and vice president and director of research and development (1946–1958) at the Johns-Manville Fiber Glass Corporation, Toledo, OH. Labino also worked as project engineer and combustion engineer at Owens-Illinois Glass, Alton, IL (1941–1946), and as assistant plant engineer and batch supervisor at Owens-Illinois Glass, Clarion, PA (1934–1940). He taught at Ohio University, Athens, OH (1966); Bowling Green State University, Bowling Green, OH (1966, 1965, 1964); and the University of Wisconsin, Madison, WI (1964).

Education
Carnegie Institute of Technology, Pittsburgh, PA, Electrical Engineering (1932).

Selected honors and awards
Rakow Award for Excellence in Glass, Corning Museum of Glass, Corning, NY (1985); Toledo Glass and Ceramic Award, Toledo, OH (1972); Governors' Award for the Arts, State of Ohio (1971); Honorary Doctorate, Bowling Green State University (1970); Second Prize, Toledo Federation of Art Societies (1965, 1964).

Selected museum collections
Art Institute of Chicago, Chicago, IL; Chrysler Museum of Art, Norfolk, VA; Cleveland Museum of Art, Cleveland, OH; Corning Museum of Glass, Corning, NY; Glasmuseum, Leerdam, the Netherlands; Glasmuseum Hentrich, Museum Kunst Palast, Düsseldorf, Germany; Metropolitan Museum of Art, New York, NY; Museum für Kunst und Gewerbe, Hamburg, Germany; Museum of Arts and Design, New York, NY; Renwick Gallery,

Smithsonian American Art Museum, Smithsonian Institution, Washington, DC; Toledo Museum of Art, Toledo, OH; Victoria and Albert Museum, London, U.K.

Other objects by this artist in the Corning Museum
String of 20 Beads, 1958 (71.4.144, gift of Dorothy Blair); Vase, 1965 (66.4.50, gift of the artist); Egyptian Core Vessels, 1965 (66.4.105, .109, .110, gifts of the artist); Egyptian Pitcher, 1965 (66.4.108, gift of the artist); Footed Bowl, 1966 (67.4.16, gift of the artist); Sculpture, *Torso*, 1966 (70.4.16); Vase, 1966 (86.4.71, gift of Mrs. Jerome Strauss); Paperweight, 1967 (67.4.15, gift of the artist); Sculpture, *Overflight*, 1967 (70.4.17); *Schmelzglas* Vase, 1967 (70.4.19); Footed Tumbler, 1967 (79.4.474, bequest of Jerome Strauss); Jack-in-the-Pulpit Vase, 1967 (2004.4.392, gift of Gerald M. and Holly C. Eggert); Paperweight, 1968 (68.4.69, gift of the artist); Vase, 1968 (70.4.18); Bottle-Necked Vase, 1968 (70.4.20); Paperweight Vases, 1968 (70.4.21, .22); Footed Bowl, 1968 (70.4.23); Bowl, 1968 (83.4.22, gift of Rudy Eswarin); Gold Ruby Vase, 1969 (70.4.24); Paperweight Vase, 1969 (70.4.25); Dichroic Bowl, 1969 (70.4.26); Paperweight, 1969 (70.4.27, gift of the artist); Wineglass, 1969 (79.4.440, bequest of Jerome Strauss); Vase, 1969 (99.4.87, gift of Mr. and Mrs. Clinton B. Burnett); Paperweight, probably 1969 (99.4.88, gift of Mr. and Mrs. Clinton B. Burnett); *Air Sculpture*, 1970 (70.4.15); *Air Sculpture*, 1970 (99.4.90, gift of Mr. and Mrs. Clinton B. Burnett); Vase, 1971 (99.4.89, gift of Mr. and Mrs. Clinton B. Burnett); Bowl, 1973 (80.4.2, gift of Dorothy Blair); Goblet, 1973 (95.4.267, gift of The Ruth Bryan Strauss Memorial Foundation); Vase, 1976 (2003.4.1, gift of Barry Friedman Ltd.); Paperweight, 1978 (99.4.249, gift of Dwight P. and Lorri Lanmon); *Emergence Series*, 1980 (2007.4.165, gift of the Ben W. Heineman Sr. Family).

For more information
Buechner 1979, pp. 130 and 261; Joan Falconer Byrd, *Dominick Labino: Glass Retrospective*, Cullowhee, NC: Western Carolina University, 1982; *Dominick Labino: A Decade of Glass Craftsmanship, 1964–1974*, Toledo: Toledo Museum of Art, 1974; Frantz 1989; Lynn 2004; Nordness 1970, p. 156; Otto Wittmann, *Dominick Labino: A Half Century with Glass*, Toledo: Owens-Illinois Arts Center, 1983.

Thérèse Lahaie
Born in 1958 in Joliet, IL. Lives in Emeryville, CA.

Lahaie taught at the California College of the Arts, Oakland, CA (2007). She was a visiting artist at California State University, Sacramento, CA (2007), and at the Alberta College of Art, Calgary, AB, Canada (1999).

Education
Massachusetts College of Art, Boston, MA, B.F.A. Glass Sculpture (1986); Emmanuel College, Boston, MA, B.F.A. Fine Art (1980).

Selected honors and awards
Djerassi Resident Artist Program Fellowship, Woodside, CA (2008, 2006); Second Prize, International Kinetic Sculpture

Competition, Palm Beach, FL (2004); Kala Institute Merit Award (2002) and Fellowship (2001), Berkeley, CA; Visiting Artist Award, Alberta College of Art (1999); Silver Award, "Kristallnacht Project," American Interfaith Institute, Philadelphia, PA (1992).

Selected museum collections
Corning Museum of Glass, Corning, NY.

For more information
www.thereselahaie.com; Chandra Cerrito, *Lucid*, Oakland: Contemporary Quarterly Project Space, 2006; Stuhr and others 1997, pp. 56 and 105; Watson and others 2007, cover and pp. [2–5].

Karen LaMonte
Born in 1967 in New York, NY. Lives in Prague, Czech Republic, and New York, NY.

LaMonte was the director of education at UrbanGlass, Brooklyn, NY (1995–1997), and coordinator of the glass program at the Parsons School of Design, New York, NY (1993–1997). She served on the staff of Pilchuck Glass School, Stanwood, WA (1992–1996). LaMonte taught at Pilchuck Glass School (2003); American Academy Summer Workshop, Engelsholm Hojskole, Engelsholm, Denmark (1996); and UrbanGlass (1991–1996). She was a visiting artist at North Lands Creative Glass, Lybster, Caithness, U.K. (1999).

Education
Academy of Art, Architecture, and Design, Prague, Czech Republic (1999–2000); New School for Social Research, New York, NY (1991); Parsons School of Design, New York, NY (1991); Rhode Island School of Design, Providence, RI, B.F.A. Glass (1990); Brown University, Providence, Rhode Island (1987–1990); Pilchuck Glass School (1989); Penland School of Crafts, Penland, NC (1988).

Selected honors and awards
Jutta Cuny-Franz Foundation Award, Museum Kunst Palast, Düsseldorf, Germany (2007); Japan–United States Friendship Commission, National Endowment for the Arts Fellowship (2006); Virginia A. Groot Foundation Award (2005); Award for New Talent in Glass, UrbanGlass (2002); Creative Glass Center of America Fellowship (2002, 1991); Louis Comfort Tiffany Foundation Grant, New York, NY (2001); Fulbright Foundation Fellowship (1999); Empire State Crafts Alliance Award (1992).

Selected museum collections
Chrysler Museum of Art, Norfolk, VA; Corning Museum of Glass, Corning, NY; Fine Arts Museums of San Francisco, San Francisco, CA; National Gallery of Australia, Canberra, ACT, Australia; Racine Art Museum, Racine, WI; Tucson Museum of Art, Tucson, AZ.

Other objects by this artist in the Corning Museum
Sculpture, *Specimen IV: Sloth*, 1997 (97.4.20, gift of Heller Gallery and an anonymous donor); Sculpture, *Blue Dress*, 1998 (2001.3.227, gift of Mike and Annie Belkin).

For more information
www.karenlamonte.com; Arthur Danto and Juli Cho Bailer, *Karen LaMonte: Absence Adorned*, Tacoma, WA: Museum of Glass: International Center for Contemporary Art in association with University of Washington Press, 2005; *Karen LaMonte: Vanitas*, Prague: Czech Museum of Fine Arts, 2005; Oldknow 2005, p. 92; John Perreault, "Karen LaMonte: Reflections on Glass," *American Craft*, v. 65, no. 3, June/July 2005, cover and pp. 42–45; Stuhr and others 1997, pp. 58 and 106; Watson and others 2007, pp. 28–29; Yelle 2000, pp. 130–131.

Silvia Levenson

Born in 1957 in Buenos Aires, Argentina. Lives in Lesa, Lago Maggiore, Italy.

Levenson taught at North Lands Creative Glass, Lybster, Caithness, U.K. (2007); Vetro & Ricerca Glass School, Bolzano, Italy (2000, 1997–1998); Leon Rigaulleau Glass School, Buenos Aires, Argentina (1997, 1995); and Escuela de Arte Palermo, Buenos Aires, Argentina (1997). She was a visiting artist at the Bullseye Glass Company, Portland, OR (1998, 1995), and at Musée-Atelier du Verre, Sars-Poteries, France (1996).

Education
Musée-Atelier du Verre (1994, 1991); Creative Glass, Zurich, Switzerland (1987); Escuela Grafica Martin Garcia, Buenos Aires, Argentina (1973–1977).

Selected honors and awards
Rakow Commission, Corning Museum of Glass, Corning, NY (2004).

Selected museum collections
Casa de la Americas, Havana, Cuba; Corning Museum of Glass, Corning, NY; Ernsting Stiftung Alter Hof Herding, Coesfeld, Germany; Glasmuseet Ebeltoft, Ebeltoft, Denmark; Musée-Atelier du Verre, Sars-Poteries, France; Museo del Vetro, Altare, Italy; Museo Leon Rigaulleau, Buenos Aires, Argentina; Museum of Fine Arts, Houston, Houston, TX.

For more information
www.silvialevenson.com; Orietta Berlanda, *Silvia Levenson: Bambina spinosa*, Rovereto, Italy: Nicolodi, 2001; Fox 2006, pp. 106–108; Chiara Guidi, *Fashion Glass: Silvia Levenson*, Milan: Galleria Maria Cilena Arte Contemporanea, 1999; Musée-Atelier du Verre, *Le Cannibalisme des sentiments: Silvia Levenson*, Sars-Poteries: the museum, 1996; Tina Oldknow, *Silvia Levenson: I See You're a Bit Nervous*, Portland, OR: Bullseye Glass Co., 2005; Oldknow 2005, pp. 182–183; *Silvia Levenson*, Milan: Silvana Editoriale, 2001; Weschenfelder 2006, pp. 299 and 352.

Stanislav Libenský and Jaroslava Brychtová

Libenský: Born in 1921 in Sezemice, Czechoslovakia. Died in 2002 in Železný Brod, Czech Republic.

Brychtová: Born in 1924 in Železný Brod, Czechoslovakia. Lives in Železný Brod, Czech Republic.

Libenský served as head of the Glass Department, Academy of Applied Arts, Prague, Czechoslovakia (1963–1987); director of the Specialized School for Glassmaking, Železný Brod, Czechoslovakia (1953–1962); a designer at the Nový Bor State Glassworks (1945–1953); and head of glass painting, etching, and stained glass at the Specialized School for Glassmaking, Nový Bor, Czechoslovakia (1945–1953). He also taught at the Center for Creative Studies, Detroit, MI; Kent State University, Kent, OH; Pilchuck Glass School, Stanwood, WA; Royal College of Art, London, U.K.; University of California, Berkeley, CA; and the University of Massachusetts, Boston, MA (1982–2000).

Education
Academy of Applied Arts, Prague (1949–1950); School of Decorative Arts, Prague (1939–1944); Specialized School for Glassmaking, Železný Brod (1938–1939); Specialized School for Glassmaking, Nový Bor (1937–1938).

Brychtová was a designer for the Glass in Architecture Development Department, Železný Brod State Glassworks (1950–1984). She taught at the Center for Creative Studies, Pilchuck Glass School, Royal College of Art, and the University of Massachusetts (1982–2000).

Education
Academy of Fine Arts, Prague (1947–1950); Academy of Applied Arts, Prague (1945–1947).

Selected honors and awards (Libenský)
Honorary Doctorate, Royal College of Art, London, U.K. (1994); Chevalier, Ordre des Arts et des Lettres, Ministry of Culture and Communication, Paris, France (1989); Herder-Prize, Universität Wien, Vienna, Austria (1975). Other awards (with Jaroslava Brychtová): Lifetime Achievement Award, Urban-Glass, Brooklyn, NY (1997); Visionaries! Award, Museum of Arts and Design, New York, NY (1997); Lifetime Achievement Award, Glass Art Society (1996); Bavarian State Prize and Gold Medal, Internationale Handwerksmesse, Munich, Germany (1995, 1967); Rakow Award for Excellence in Glass, Corning Museum of Glass, Corning, NY (1984); Coburg Glass Prize, Kunstsammlungen der Veste Coburg, Coburg, Germany (1977); Gold Medal, Internationales Kunsthandwerk, Stuttgart, Germany (1969); Award of the Capital City of Prague, Czechoslovakia (1968); Gold Medal, VIII Bienal de São Paulo, São Paulo, Brazil (1965); Grand Prize, Expo '58, Brussels, Belgium (1958).

Selected museum collections
Art Gallery of Western Australia, Perth, WA, Australia; Brooklyn Museum, Brooklyn, NY; Chrysler Museum of Art, Norfolk, VA; Corning Museum of Glass, Corning, NY; East Bohemian Museum, Pardubice, Czech Republic; Glasmuseum Hentrich, Museum Kunst Palast, Düsseldorf, Germany; Hokkaido Museum of Modern Art, Sapporo, Japan; Indianapolis Museum of Art, Indianapolis, IN; Kunstsammlungen der Veste Coburg, Coburg, Germany; Los Angeles County Museum of Art, Los Angeles, CA; Manchester City Art Gallery, Manchester, U.K.; Metropolitan Museum of Art, New York, NY; Mint Museum of Art, Charlotte, NC; Moravian Gallery, Brno, Czech Republic;

Musée de Design et d'Arts Appliqués Contemporains, Lausanne, Switzerland; Musée des Arts Décoratifs, Paris, France; Musée des Beaux-Arts, Lyons, France; Museo Provincial de Bellas Artes, Valencia, Spain; Museum Bellerive, Zurich, Switzerland; Museum für Kunst und Gewerbe, Hamburg, Germany; Museum of Arts and Design, New York, NY; Museum of Decorative Arts, Prague, Czech Republic; Museum voor Sierkunst, Ghent, Belgium; National Gallery, Prague, Czech Republic; National Museum of Modern Art, Tokyo, Japan; North Bohemian Museum, Liberec, Czech Republic; Toledo Museum of Art, Toledo, OH; Ulster Museum, Belfast, Northern Ireland; Victoria and Albert Museum, London, U.K.; Yokohama Museum of Art, Yokohama, Japan.

Other objects by these artists in the Corning Museum
Architectural Sculpture, *Zoomorphic Stone*, 1957–1958 (94.3.100, gift of the artists); Sculpture, *The Kiss*, about 1958–1960 (62.3.24, gift of the artists); Sculpture, *The Kiss*, designed about 1958–1960 and remade in 1985 (88.3.21, gift of Mr. and Mrs. Donald O. Wiiken); Architectural Sculpture, *Paříž*, designed in 1962, dated 1965 (2001.3.61, gift of Mike and Annie Belkin); Sculpture, *Cube*, 1970 (75.3.17); Sculpture, *Five Parts*, 1973 (2007.3.85, gift of the Ben W. Heineman Sr. Family); Sculpture, *Heart/Red Flower*, designed in 1973 and made in 1976 (81.3.38, gift of the artists); Sculpture, *The Cylinder in the Spheric Space*, 1977 (78.3.52); Architectural Sculpture, *Meteor/Flower/Bird*, completed 1980 (80.3.13); Sculpture, *Family Eye*, 1982 (2001.4.22, gift in part of Peter and Margarete Harnisch); Sculpture, *Head IV*, 1986 (2006.3.13, gift of the Ben W. Heineman Sr. Family); Sculpture Maquettes, *Diagonal*, 1989 (94.3.162, .165, anonymous gifts); Sculpture Maquettes, *Spatia Virides I (Illusive Cube with Prism)* and *II*, 1991–1992 (93.3.18, .19, gifts of the artists); Sculpture, *Spaces I*, 1991–1992 (2007.3.86, gift of the Ben W. Heineman Sr. Family); Sculpture, *Big Arcus/Arcus III*, 1993 (93.3.26, gift of the artists).

By Stanislav Libenský
Vases, *Pelicans* and *Sea Forms*, 1946 (92.3.68, .69, gifts of Prof. and Mrs. Stanislav Libenský); Vase, *Butterfly*, 1948 (83.3.236); Vase, 1955 (99.3.45, gift of The Steinberg Foundation); Bowl, 1957 (99.3.44, gift of The Steinberg Foundation); Bottle, 1964 (2003.3.71, gift of the Ben W. Heineman Sr. Family); Pitcher and Two Cups, 1965 (99.3.46, gift of The Steinberg Foundation); Jardiniere, designed in 1973 and made in 1974 (76.3.2).

For more information
Buechner 1979, pp. 132, 252, and 261; Fox 2006, pp. 67–70; Susanne K. Frantz, *Stanislav Libenský and Jaroslava Brychtová: A 40-Year Collaboration in Glass*, Corning: Corning Museum of Glass, and Munich: Prestel Verlag, 1994; Frantz 1999, pp. 18–21; Robert Kehlmann, *The Inner Light: Sculpture by Stanislav Libenský and Jaroslava Brychtová*, Tacoma, WA: Museum of Glass: International Center for Contemporary Art, 2002; Milena Klasová, *Stanislav Libenský, Jaroslava Brychtová*, Prague: Gallery, 2002; Lynn 2005, pp. 61, 91, 123, 127, and 141; Mann 1997, p. 29; Oldknow 2005, pp. 94–95; Tomáš Vlček, *Stanislav Libenský/Jaroslava Brychtová: Retrospektiva*, Prague: National Gallery, 2002; Yelle 2000, pp. 137–141.

Beth Lipman
Born in 1971 in Philadelphia, PA. Lives in Sheboygan Falls, WI.

Lipman is arts/industry coordinator at the John Michael Kohler Arts Center, Sheboygan, WI (since 2005). She was studio director of education and artist services at the Creative Glass Center of America, Wheaton Village, Millville, NJ (2004–2005); head of the Glass Department at the Worcester Center for Crafts, Worcester, MA (2002–2004); and education director at UrbanGlass, Brooklyn, NY (1996–2000).
Lipman has taught at the Pittsburgh Glass Center, Pittsburgh, PA (2007); Penland School of Crafts, Penland, NC (2006, 2004, 2003); Corning Museum of Glass, Corning, NY (2005, 2003, 2001); UrbanGlass (1996–2001); Parsons School of Design, New York, NY (1999, 1998); and New York University, New York, NY (1999, 1998, 1997). She was an artist in residence at the Museum of Glass, Tacoma, WA (2006); The Studio of The Corning Museum of Glass (2006); and the John Michael Kohler Arts Center (2003).

Education
Temple University, Philadelphia, PA, B.F.A. Glass and Fibers (1994); Massachusetts College of Art, Boston, MA (1989–1990).

Selected honors and awards
Young Talent Award, UrbanGlass (2006); Louis Comfort Tiffany Foundation Grant (2005); Travel Grant, American/Swedish Exchange, American-Scandinavian Foundation (2003); Fellowship, Creative Glass Center of America, Wheaton Village (2001); National Endowment for the Arts Grant (2001); Professional Advancement Grant, New Hampshire State Council on the Arts (2001); Ruth Chenven Foundation Grant (2001); Peter S. Reed Foundation Grant (2000).

Selected museum collections
Brooklyn Museum, Brooklyn, NY; Corning Museum of Glass, Corning, NY; John Michael Kohler Arts Center, Sheboygan, WI; Museum of American Glass, Wheaton Arts and Cultural Center, Millville, NJ; Museum of Glass, Tacoma, WA; Renwick Gallery, Smithsonian American Art Museum, Smithsonian Institution, Washington, DC; Speed Art Museum, Louisville, KY.

For more information
www.bethlipman.com; *Beth Lipman: Still Lifes in Glass*, Sheboygan, WI: John Michael Kohler Arts Center, 2005; John Perreault, "Riffs in Glass," *Glass* (UrbanGlass Art Quarterly), no. 79, Summer 2000, pp. 42–47; Watson and others 2007, pp. 20–21; Yelle 2000, p. 144.

Marvin Lipofsky
Born in 1938 in Barrington, IL. Lives in Berkeley, CA.

Lipofsky taught at Pilchuck Glass School, Stanwood, WA (1988, 1984, 1974); California College of Arts and Crafts, Oakland, CA (1967–1987); Columbus College of Art and Design, Columbus, OH (1979); Southwest Craft Center, San Antonio, TX (1977); Haystack Mountain School of Crafts, Deer Isle, ME (1973, 1967); University of California, Berkeley, California (1964–1972); Bezalel Academy of Arts and Design, Jerusalem, Israel (1971); San Francisco Art Institute, San Francisco, CA (1968); and the University of Wisconsin, Madison, WI (1964).

He was a visiting artist at the Bezalel Academy of Arts and Design (2005); Fundación Centro Nacional del Vidrio, La Granja, Spain (2000); Pilchuck Glass School (1995, 1981, 1977); International Center for Glass, Meisenthal, France (1992); Union of Bulgarian Artists, Sofia, Bulgaria (1991); Konstfack, Stockholm, Sweden (1989); California State University, Chico, CA (1988); Haystack Mountain School of Crafts (1987); Miasa Bunker Center, Nagano, Japan (1987); Washington University, St. Louis, MO (1985); University of California, Los Angeles, CA (1973); and the Gerrit Rietveld Academie, Amsterdam, the Netherlands (1970).

Education
University of Wisconsin, M.S. and M.F.A. Sculpture (1964); University of Illinois, Urbana-Champaign, Champaign, IL, B.F.A. Industrial Design (1962).

Selected honors and awards
Lifetime Achievement Award, Art Alliance for Contemporary Glass, Chicago, IL (2005); Master of the Medium Award, Renwick Gallery, Smithsonian American Art Museum, Smithsonian Institution, Washington, DC (2003); Fellow, American Craft Council, New York, NY (1991); Hokkaido Prefecture Fellowship, Hokkaido, Japan (1987); Honorary Lifetime Member, Glass Art Society (1986); California Living Treasure, Sacramento, CA (1985); National Endowment for the Arts Fellowship (1976, 1974); Toledo Glass National Award, Toledo Museum of Art, Toledo, OH (1968); American Craftsmen's Council National Merit Award, New York, NY (1966); Media '65 & '66 Award, Walnut Creek, CA (1966, 1965); Milwaukee Arts Festival Award, Milwaukee, WI (1964).

Selected museum collections
Auckland City Art Gallery, Auckland, New Zealand; Badisches Landesmuseum, Karlsruhe, Germany; Carnegie Museum of Art, Pittsburgh, PA; Cincinnati Art Museum, Cincinnati, OH; Cooper-Hewitt National Design Museum, Smithsonian Institution, New York, NY; Corning Museum of Glass, Corning, NY; Detroit Institute of Arts, Detroit, MI; Eretz Israel Museum, Tel Aviv, Israel; Fonds National d'Art Contemporain, Paris, France; Glasmuseet Ebeltoft, Ebeltoft, Denmark; Glasmuseum, Leerdam, the Netherlands; High Museum of Art, Atlanta, GA; Hokkaido Museum of Modern Art, Sapporo, Japan; Indianapolis Museum of Art, Indianapolis, IN; Kunstgewerbemuseum, Berlin, Germany; Kunstsammlungen der Veste Coburg, Coburg, Germany; Los Angeles County Museum of Art, Los Angeles, CA; Lowe Art Museum, University of Miami, Coral Gables, FL; Metropolitan Museum of Art, New York, NY; Mint Museum of Craft + Design, Charlotte, NC; Montreal Museum of Fine Arts, Montreal, QC, Canada; Musée de Design et d'Arts Appliqués Contemporains, Lausanne, Switzerland; Musée-Atelier du Verre, Sars-Poteries, France; Museo del Vidrio, La Granja, Spain; Museo del Vidrio, Monterrey, Mexico; Museum Bellerive, Zurich, Switzerland; Museum Boymans van Beuningen, Rotterdam, the Netherlands; Museum für Kunst und Gewerbe, Hamburg, Germany; Museum für Kunsthandwerk, Frankfurt am Main, Germany; Museum of Applied Arts, Belgrade, Serbia; Museum of Arts and Design,

New York, NY; Museum of Contemporary Art, Skopje, Macedonia; Museum of Decorative Arts, Prague, Czech Republic; Museum of Decorative Arts, Sofia, Bulgaria; Museum of Fine Arts, Boston, MA; National Gallery of Australia, Canberra, ACT, Australia; National Museum, L'viv, Ukraine; National Museum, Wrocław, Poland; Oakland Museum of California, Oakland, CA; Philadelphia Museum of Art, Philadelphia, PA; Racine Art Museum, Racine, WI; Renwick Gallery, Smithsonian American Art Museum, Smithsonian Institution, Washington, DC; Saint Louis Art Museum, St. Louis, MO; San Francisco Museum of Modern Art, San Francisco, CA; Seattle Art Museum, Seattle, WA; Smålands Museum, Växjö, Sweden; Stedelijk Museum, Amsterdam, the Netherlands; Tacoma Art Museum, Tacoma, WA; Toledo Museum of Art, Toledo, OH; Württembergisches Landesmuseum, Stuttgart, Germany; Zsolnay Museum, Pécs, Hungary.

Other objects by this artist in the Corning Museum
Sculpture, *California Loop Series*, 1968–1973 (74.4.211); Sculpture, *Stripe (Venini Series)*, 1972 (74.3.120); Sculptures (4), *Sketches*, 1974 (91.4.63, gift of Jean and Martin Mensch); Sculpture, *Holding Series 1976–1979 (Fratelli Toso Series Shard)*, 1977 (2006.4.39, gift of the Ben W. Heineman Sr. Family); Sculpture, *Fratelli Toso Series*, 1977–1978 (79.4.15); Sculpture, *Pilchuck Series 1984–1985 #7 (Summer Rain)*, 1985 (2006.4.40, gift of the Ben W. Heineman Sr. Family).

For more information
www.marvinlipofsky.com; Austin and others 1993; Suzanne Baizerman, ed., *Marvin Lipofsky: A Glass Odyssey*, Oakland: Oakland Museum of California in association with the University of Washington Press, 2003; Buechner 1979, pp. 134 and 261; Matthew Kangas, "Marvin Lipofsky: Concealing the Void," in Kangas 2006, pp. 246–249; Lynn 2005, pp. 86 and 160–163; Mann 1997, p. 13; Nordness 1970, pp. 152–153; Oldknow 2005, p. 96; Warmus 2003, pp. 41 and 52–53; Yelle 2000, pp. 145–146; Smithsonian Interview.

Donald Lipski
Born in 1947 in Chicago, IL. Lives in Sag Harbor, NY.

Education
Cranbrook Academy of Art, Bloomfield Hills, MI, M.F.A. (1973); University of Wisconsin, Madison, WI, B.F.A. (1970).

Selected honors and awards
The Rome Prize, American Academy, Rome, Italy (2000); Academy Award, American Academy of Arts and Letters, New York, NY (1993); National Endowment for the Arts Fellowship (1990); Guggenheim Foundation Fellowship (1988); New York Foundation on the Arts Fellowship (1986); Visual Arts Award, National Endowment for the Arts (1984, 1978).

Selected museum collections
Brooklyn Museum, Brooklyn, NY; Corcoran Gallery of Art, Washington, DC; Corning Museum of Glass, Corning, NY; Denver Art Museum, Denver, CO; Detroit Institute of Arts, Detroit, MI; Fabric Workshop and Museum, Philadelphia, PA; Indianapolis

Museum of Art, Indianapolis, IN; Jewish Museum, New York, NY; Laumeier Sculpture Park, St. Louis, MO; Menil Collection, Houston, TX; Metropolitan Museum of Art, New York, NY; Miami Art Museum, Miami, FL; Minneapolis Museum of Fine Art, Minneapolis, MN; Museum of Contemporary Art, Chicago, IL; Museum of Contemporary Art, La Jolla, CA; Museum of Fine Arts, Boston, MA; Museum of Fine Arts, Houston, Houston, TX; New Orleans Museum of Art, New Orleans, LA; Phoenix Museum of Art, Phoenix, AZ; Walker Art Center, Minneapolis, MN; Whitney Museum of American Art, New York, NY.

For more information
www.donaldlipski.net; Peter Bellamy, *The Artist Project*, New York: IN Publishing, 1991; Brooklyn Museum 1985, pp. 7–9; Frantz 1999, pp. 22–25; Andrea Inselmann, *Threshold: Invoking the Domestic in Contemporary Art*, Sheboygan, WI: John Michael Kohler Arts Center, 1999; Lynn 2005, pp. 63 and 112; Mann 1997, p. 29; Ruffner and others 1991, pp. 36–37 and 65; David Levy Strauss, *Donald Lipski*, Vienna: Bawag Foundation, 1999; Terrie Sultan, *Donald Lipski: A Brief History of Twine*, Madison, WI: Madison Art Center, 2000; John Yau, *Donald Lipski: Who's Afraid of Red, White & Blue?* Philadelphia: Fabric Workshop, 1991; Yelle 2000, pp. 147–148.

Věra Lišková
Born in 1924 in Prague, Czechoslovakia. Died in 1985 in Prague, Czechoslovakia.

Lišková was a designer at the Artistic Center for the Glass and Fine Ceramics Industry, Prague, Czechoslovakia (1952–1985), and at the Moser Glassworks, Karlovy Vary, Czechoslovakia (1950–1985).

Education
Academy of Applied Arts, Prague, Czechoslovakia (1945–1949); School of Decorative Arts, Prague (1941–1943); State School for Graphic Arts, Prague (1939–1941).

Selected honors and awards
Coburg Glass Prize, Kunstsammlungen der Veste Coburg, Germany (1977); Bavarian State Prize and Gold Medal, Internationale Handwerksmesse, Munich, Germany (1973); Ministry of Culture Award, Prague, Czechoslovakia (1960); Ministry of Industry Award, Prague, Czechoslovakia (1947).

Selected museum collections
Corning Museum of Glass, Corning, NY; East Bohemian Museum, Pardubice, Czech Republic; Essen Museum, Essen, Germany; Glasmuseum Hentrich, Museum Kunst Palast, Düsseldorf, Germany; Kunstsammlungen der Veste Coburg, Coburg, Germany; Museum für Angewandtekunst, Vienna, Austria; Museum für Kunst und Gewerbe, Hamburg, Germany; Museum of Decorative Arts, Prague, Czech Republic; Museum of Modern Art, New York, NY; North Bohemian Museum, Liberec, Czech Republic.

Other objects by this artist in the Corning Museum
Chandelier, about 1968 (2002.3.8, gift of Eleanore and Charles Stendig); Vase, about 1969–1970 (71.3.10); Vase, 1970 (71.3.7);

Sculpture, *Hedgehog with Fruit*, 1970 (71.3.9); Vase, about 1970 (71.3.8); Sculpture, *Hedgehog*, about 1970 (81.3.71, gift of the artist); Sculpture, *Soul–Small Object I*, 1970–1979 (99.3.67, gift of The Steinberg Foundation); Decanter, 1970–1979 (99.3.68, gift of The Steinberg Foundation); *Ikebana Vase*, 1970–1979 (99.3.69, gift of The Steinberg Foundation); Sculpture, *Hedgehog*, 1972–1980 (81.3.11, gift of the artist); Sculpture, *Birth of a Star*, 1978 (78.3.54); Sculpture, *Red Flower*, about 1980 (84.3.1, gift of the Corning Glass Center); Sculptures, *Owl* and *Hedgehog*, about 1980–1981 (91.3.89, .90, gifts of Mr. and Mrs. Dwight P. Lanmon).

Design (for Moser Glassworks, Czechoslovakia): Tumbler with Bird of Paradise, 1949 (64.3.89, gift of the artist); Sculpture, *Frog*, 1957 (62.3.136).

Design (for Harrachov Glassworks, Czechoslovakia): Vase, 1953 (83.3.237); Tumblers (2), Bowl, and Dish, 1957 (58.3.123).

Design (for J. & L. Lobmeyr, Czechoslovakia): Beakers, 1958 (58.3.58).

For more information
Buechner 1979, pp. 135–136 and 261; Fox 2006, p. 16; Petrová 2001; Ricke 2005, pp. 258–261 and 388–389; Schack von Wittenau 2005, pp. 214–215; František Stehlík, *Věra Lišková: Práce z let, 1972–1974*, Liberec: Northern Bohemian Museum, 1974.

Harvey K. Littleton
Born in 1922 in Corning, NY. Lives in Spruce Pine, NC.

Littleton organized the first studio glassblowing workshops in the United States, with Dominick Labino, at The Toledo Museum of Art, Toledo, OH (1962).
He was chairman of the Department of Art, University of Wisconsin, Madison, WI (1969–1971, 1964–1967), where he taught (1951–1977; professor emeritus, 1977). He also taught at the University of California, Los Angeles, CA (1975); School of Design, Toledo Museum of Art (1949–1951); and the Ann Arbor Potters' Guild, Ann Arbor, MI (1947–1949). He was a visiting artist at the Gerrit Rietveld Academie, Amsterdam, the Netherlands (1973).
Littleton is a Fellow of The Corning Museum of Glass, Corning, NY (since 1982).

Education
Cranbrook Academy of Art, Bloomfield Hills, MI, M.F.A. Ceramics (1951); University of Michigan, Ann Arbor, MI, B.F.A. Design (1947); Brighton School of Art, Brighton, U.K. (1945).

Selected honors and awards
Honorary Doctorate, North Carolina State University, Raleigh, NC (2004); Wisconsin Visual Art Lifetime Achievement Award, Milwaukee, WI (2004); Fellow, Wisconsin Academy of Arts, Sciences, and Letters, Madison, WI (2001); Honorary Doctorate, University of Wisconsin (2000); Lifetime Achievement Award, UrbanGlass, Brooklyn, NY (1998); James Renwick Alliance Award, Renwick Gallery, Smithsonian American Art Museum,

Smithsonian Institution, Washington, DC (1997); Citation for Distinguished Service, National Association of Schools of Art and Design, Reston, VA (1996); Honorary Doctorate, Rhode Island School of Design, Providence, RI (1996); Visionaries! Award, Museum of Arts and Design, New York, NY (1994); Distinguished Alumnus Award, University of Michigan (1993); Lifetime Achievement Award, Glass Art Society (1993); Western North Carolina Creative Arts Hall of Fame (1989); Governor's Award for the Arts, State of North Carolina (1987); Rakow Award for Excellence in Glass, Corning Museum of Glass (1985); Gold Medal, American Craft Council, New York, NY (1983); Honorary Doctorate, University of the Arts, Philadelphia, PA (1982); National Endowment for the Arts Fellowship (1982); Research Grants, University of Wisconsin (1975, 1971, 1967, 1962, 1957, 1954); Corning Glass Works Grant, Corning, NY (1974); Louis Comfort Tiffany Foundation Grant, New York, NY (1970).

Selected museum collections
Addison Gallery of American Art, Andover, MA; Brooks Museum of Art, Memphis, TN; Chrysler Museum of Art, Norfolk, VA; Cleveland Museum of Art, Cleveland, OH; Cooper-Hewitt National Design Museum, Smithsonian Institution, New York, NY; Corning Museum of Glass, Corning, NY; Detroit Institute of Arts, Detroit, MI; Fine Arts Museums of San Francisco, San Francisco, CA; Glasmuseet Ebeltoft, Ebeltoft, Denmark; High Museum of Art, Atlanta, GA; Hokkaido Museum of Modern Art, Sapporo, Japan; Kunstsammlungen der Veste Coburg, Coburg, Germany; Los Angeles County Museum of Art, Los Angeles, CA; Metropolitan Museum of Art, New York, NY; Mint Museum of Craft + Design, Charlotte, NC; Mobile Museum of Art, Mobile, AL; Musée du Verre, Liège, Belgium; Museum Bellerive, Zurich, Switzerland; Museum Boymans van Beuningen, Rotterdam, the Netherlands; Museum für Angewandtekunst, Vienna, Austria; Museum für Kunst und Gewerbe, Hamburg, Germany; Museum für Kunsthandwerk, Frankfurt am Main, Germany; Museum of Arts and Design, New York, NY; Museum of Decorative Arts, Prague, Czech Republic; Museum of Fine Arts, Houston, Houston, TX; Museum of Modern Art, New York, NY; National Museum of Modern Art, Kyoto, Japan; New Orleans Museum of Art, New Orleans, LA; Saint Louis Art Museum, St. Louis, MO; Speed Art Museum, Louisville, KY.

Other objects by this artist in the Corning Museum
Sculpture, *Torso*, 1942 (78.4.38, gift of Dr. and Mrs. Fred A. Bickford); Vase, 1963 (2001.4.256, gift of J. Bruce Whyte and Gerald L. Boone); Vase, 1965 (66.4.47); Sculpture, *Eye*, 1969 (2007.4.166, gift of the Ben W. Heineman Sr. Family); Sculpture, *Upward Undulation*, 1974 (79.4.145, purchased with the aid of funds from the National Endowment for the Arts); Sculpture, *Four Square*, 1975 (75.4.54); Sculpture, *Inverted Tube/Cut Line*, 1977 (82.4.76, gift of Harvey K. and Bess Littleton); Sculpture, *Interrupted Loop Series*, 1978 (2007.4.167, gift of the Ben W. Heineman Sr. Family); Sculpture, *Pile Up*, 1979 (80.4.8); Sculpture, Untitled, 1979 (2008.4.31, gift of Heinz and Elizabeth Wolf); Sculpture, *Red/Amber Sliced Descending Form*, 1984 (2007.4.168, gift of the Ben W. Heineman Sr. Family); Sculpture, *Ruby Conical Intersection with Amber Sphere*, 1984 (2007.4.169, gift of the Ben W. Heineman Sr. Family).

For more information
www.littletoncollection.com; Buechner 1979, pp. 137 and 262; Joan Falconer Byrd, *Harvey K. Littleton: A Retrospective Exhibition*, Atlanta: High Museum of Art, 1984; Mary F. Douglas, *Harvey K. Littleton: Reflections, 1946–1994*, Charlotte, NC: Mint Museum of Craft + Design, 1999; Fox 2006, p. 31; Frantz 1989, pp. 45–46; Lynggaard 1998, pp. 13–26; Lynn 2004, pp. 51–54; Lynn 2005, pp. 38, 87, 93, and 116; Mann 1997, p. 13; Nordness 1970, pp. 144–145; Oldknow 2005, p. 97; Warmus 2003, pp. 41 and 54–55; Yelle 2000, pp. 149–151; Smithsonian Interview.

Jessica Loughlin
Born in 1975 in Melbourne, VIC, Australia. Lives in Adelaide, SA, Australia.

Loughlin taught at the University of South Australia, Adelaide, SA, Australia (2006), and at North Lands Creative Glass, Caithness, U.K. (2003). She was a visiting artist at the Bullseye Glass Company, Portland, OR (2002, 1998), and at UrbanGlass, Brooklyn, NY (2000).

Education
Canberra School of Art, Australian National University, Canberra, ACT, Australia, B.A. (1997); Pilchuck Glass School, Stanwood, Washington (1997).

Selected honors and awards
Tom Malone Prize, Art Gallery of Western Australia, Perth, WA, Australia (2004); Outstanding New Artist in Glass Award, UrbanGlass (2001); RFC Award, Resource Finance Corporation, Sydney, NSW, Australia (1997).

Selected museum collections
Art Gallery of Western Australia, Perth, WA, Australia; Corning Museum of Glass, Corning, NY; Glasmuseet Ebeltoft, Ebeltoft, Denmark; Mobile Museum of Art, Mobile, AL; Museu do Vidrio, Marinha Grande, Portugal; National Gallery of Australia, Canberra, ACT, Australia; National Glass Collection, Wagga Wagga, NSW, Australia.

Other object by this artist in the Corning Museum
Vessel, *Horizon Line Series #14*, 1997 (2008.6.1, gift of Irene and Bob Sinclair).

For more information
Grace Cochrane, *International Young Artists in Glass: Australia*, Portland, OR: Bullseye Glass Co., 1998, pp. 18–23; Grace Cochrane and Susanne K. Frantz, *Jessica Loughlin at Bullseye Glass*, Portland, OR: Bullseye Glass Co., 2002; Fox 2006, p. 26; Bruce Guenther, *Jessica Loughlin: Shifting Views*, Portland, OR: Bullseye Glass Co., 2005; Brett Littman, "Landscapes: Jessica Loughlin," *Glass* (UrbanGlass Art Quarterly), no. 83, Summer 2001, pp. 34–39; Oldknow 2005, pp. 36–37.

Flora C. Mace and Joey Kirkpatrick
Mace: Born in 1949 in Exeter, NH. Lives in Seattle, WA.

Kirkpatrick: Born in 1952 in Des Moines, IA. Lives in Seattle, WA.

Mace taught at the Toyama Institute of Glass Art, Toyama, Japan (1996); Haystack Mountain School of Crafts, Deer Isle, ME (1994, 1985); University of Hawaii, Honolulu, HI (1993); Pilchuck Glass School, Stanwood, WA (1986–1990, 1981–1983); Lobmeyr School, Vienna, Austria (1985); University of Illinois, Urbana-Champaign, Champaign, IL (1981–1982); and the University of California, Los Angeles, CA (1981).

Education
    University of Illinois, Urbana-Champaign, M.F.A. Sculpture/ Glass (1976); University of Utah, Salt Lake City, UT (1975); Plymouth State College, Plymouth, NH, B.F.A. (1972).

Kirkpatrick taught at the University of Hawaii (1993); Pilchuck Glass School (1986–1990, 1981–1983); Haystack Mountain School of Crafts (1985); Lobmeyr School (1985); University of Illinois, Urbana-Champaign (1981–1982); and the University of California, Los Angeles (1981).

Education
    Pilchuck Glass School (1979); Iowa State University, Ames, IA (1978–1979); University of Iowa, Iowa City, IA, B.F.A. Drawing (1975).

Mace and Kirkpatrick are Fellows of the American Craft Council (2005). They were visiting artists at the Museum of Glass, Tacoma, WA (2002); Pilchuck Glass School (2001, 1987, 1980); and the Rhode Island School of Design, Providence, RI (1980). Mace was the Goodwill Ambassador to Norway on the International Farm Exchange Program (1973–1974).

Selected museum collections
    Broadfield House Glass Museum, Kingswinford, U.K.; Cleveland Museum of Art, Cleveland, OH; Corning Museum of Glass, Corning, NY; Dayton Art Institute, Dayton, OH; Detroit Institute of Arts, Detroit, MI; Fine Arts Museums of San Francisco, San Francisco, CA; Glasmuseet Ebeltoft, Ebeltoft, Denmark; Hokkaido Museum of Modern Art, Sapporo, Japan; Metropolitan Museum of Art, New York, NY; Mobile Museum of Art, Mobile, AL; Montgomery Museum of Fine Art, Montgomery, AL; Musée de Design et d'Arts Appliqués Contemporains, Lausanne, Switzerland; Renwick Gallery, Smithsonian American Art Museum, Smithsonian Institution, Washington, DC; Seattle Art Museum, Seattle, WA; Speed Art Museum, Louisville, KY; Tacoma Art Museum, Tacoma, WA; Toledo Museum of Art, Toledo, OH.

Other objects by these artists in the Corning Museum
    Vessel, *Kally*, 1980 (84.4.20); Untitled Cylinder (with Doll), 1980 (2006.4.41, gift of the Ben W. Heineman Sr. Family); Sculpture, *Water Catcher*, 1984 (85.4.3).

By Flora C. Mace
    Vessel, *Seated Figure III*, 1976 (76.4.27, purchased with the aid of funds from the National Endowment for the Arts); *Cylinder with Figure*, 1977 (2007.4.171, gift of the Ben W. Heineman Sr. Family).

For more information
    www.kirkpatrick-mace.com; Dorigato and Klein 1996, p. 122; Fox 2006, pp. 55–56; Lynn 2005, p. 210; Mann 1997, p. 13; Oldknow 2005, p. 99; Warmus 2003, pp. 72 and 80–81; Watson 2002, pp. 16–17; Yelle 2000, pp. 120–122; Smithsonian Interview.

Ivan Mareš
Born in 1956 in Děčín, Czechoslovakia. Lives in Prague and Děčín, Czech Republic.

Education
    Academy of Applied Arts, Prague, Czechoslovakia (1977–1983); Specialized School for Glassmaking, Kamenický Šenov, Czechoslovakia (1971–1975).

Selected honors and awards
    Honorary Prize, World Glass Now, Hokkaido Museum of Modern Art, Sapporo, Japan (1991).

Selected museum collections
    Corning Museum of Glass, Corning, NY; Glasmuseum Hentrich, Museum Kunst Palast, Düsseldorf, Germany; Hokkaido Museum of Modern Art, Sapporo, Japan; Koganezaki Glass Museum, Shizuoka, Japan; Moravian Gallery, Brno, Czech Republic; Museum of Decorative Arts, Prague, Czech Republic.

For more information
    Fox 2006, pp. 76–77; Frantz, Ricke, and Mizuta 1998, pp. 84–87 and 142; Lynn 2005, p. 122; Petrová 2001; Petrová 2004; Ricke 1990, pp. 160–161 and 290.

Paul Marioni
Born in 1941 in Cincinnati, OH. Lives in Seattle, WA.

Marioni taught at Pilchuck Glass School, Stanwood, WA (2001, 1996, 1974–1988); Penland School of Crafts, Penland, NC (2000, 1996, 1994, 1988–1990, 1978); California College of Arts and Crafts, Oakland, CA (1974–1977); San Francisco State University, San Francisco, CA (1974–1977); and the San Francisco Art Institute, San Francisco, CA (1973–1974).

Education
    University of Cincinnati, Cincinnati, OH, B.A. Philosophy, English Literature (1964–1967); San Francisco State University (1963–1964).

Selected honors and awards
    Recognition Award, National Terrazzo Association, Purcellville, VA (1997); First Prize, Pacific Northwest Annual, Bellevue Art Museum, Bellevue, WA (1993); Silver Award, "Kristallnacht Project," The American Interfaith Institute, Philadelphia, PA (1992); National Endowment for the Arts Fellowship (1989, 1982, 1976).

Selected museum collections
    Corning Museum of Glass, Corning, NY; Hessisches Landes-

museum, Darmstadt, Germany; Museum of Arts and Design, New York, NY; Oakland Museum of California, Oakland, CA; Renwick Gallery, Smithsonian American Art Museum, Smithsonian Institution, Washington, DC.

Other objects by this artist in the Corning Museum
Vessel, *The Visitor (Green)*, 1984 (86.4.55).

With Ann Troutner (American, b. 1958): Sculptures, *Miniature Skulls* (5), 1987 (87.4.65, gift of the artists).

For more information
Austin and others 1993; Buechner 1979, pp. 145 and 262; Matthew Kangas, "Paul Marioni: The Visitor," in Kangas 2006, pp. 236–240; Albert Lewis, "The Gifts of the Gods: A Conversation with Paul Marioni," *Glass* (Portland, OR), v. 6, no. 2, October 1978, pp. 24–40; Oldknow 2005, pp. 186–187; Stuhr and others 1997, pp. 62 and 107; Weiss 1998, pp. 8 and 20; Yelle 2000, pp. 160–162; Smithsonian Interview.

Sherry Markovitz
Born in 1947 in Chicago, IL. Lives in Seattle, WA.

Education
University of Washington, Seattle, WA, M.F.A. Printmaking (1972–1975); University of Wisconsin, Madison, WI, B.A. (1965–1969).

Selected honors and awards
Seattle Arts Commission Grant, Seattle, WA (1990); Washington State Arts Commission Grant, Olympia, WA (1979).

Selected museum collections
Corning Museum of Glass, Corning, NY; John Michael Kohler Arts Center, Sheboygan, WI; Mint Museum of Craft + Design, Charlotte, NC; Museum of Arts and Design, New York, NY; Seattle Art Museum, Seattle, WA.

For more information
Chris Bruce, *Sherry Markovitz: Shimmer Paintings and Sculptures*, Pullman, WA: Museum of Art, Washington State University, 2008; Anne Focke, *U.S. Projects*, New York: Artist's Space, 1986; Vicki Halper, *Documents Northwest: Sherry Markovitz*, Seattle: Seattle Art Museum, 1987; Matthew Kangas, *Breaking Barriers: Recent American Craft*, New York: American Craft Museum, 1995, pp. 15 and 38–39; Mark Leach, *ARTcurrents 10: Sherry Markovitz*, Charlotte, NC: Mint Museum of Craft + Design, 1992.

Josiah McElheny
Born in 1966 in Boston, MA. Lives in New York, NY.

McElheny was senior critic in the Sculpture Department at the School of Art, Yale University, New Haven, CT (2004–2005). He taught at the Haystack Mountain School of Crafts, Deer Isle, ME (1996); Pilchuck Glass School, Stanwood, WA (1995); and the Rhode Island School of Design, Providence, RI (1995). He was a

visiting artist at the University of Nevada, Las Vegas, NV (2000), and the Isabella Stewart Gardner Museum, Boston, MA (1998), and a visiting critic at Yale University, New Haven, CT (2001–2003).

Education
Apprentice to master glassblowers Lino Tagliapietra, Seattle, WA, and Murano, Italy (1992–1997), and Jan-Erik Ritzman and Sven-Ake Carlsson, Transjö, Sweden (1989–1991); Rhode Island School of Design, B.F.A., 1988.

Selected honors and awards
MacArthur Fellowship, John D. and Catherine T. MacArthur Foundation, Chicago, IL (2006); Rakow Commission, Corning Museum of Glass, Corning, NY (2000); American-Scandinavian Foundation Fellowship, New York, NY (1998); Bagley Wright Fund Award, Seattle, WA (1998); Artist Grant, Art Matters Inc., New York, NY (1996); Louis Comfort Tiffany Foundation Award, New York, NY (1995); Betty Bowen Special Recognition Award, Seattle Art Museum, Seattle, WA (1993).

Selected museum collections
Albright-Knox Art Gallery, Buffalo, NY; Centro Galego de Arte Contemporánea, Santiago de Compostela, Spain; Corning Museum of Glass, Corning, NY; Dallas Art Museum, Dallas, TX; Detroit Institute of Arts, Detroit, MI; Henry Art Gallery, University of Washington, Seattle, WA; Institute of Contemporary Art, Boston, MA; Los Angeles County Museum of Art, Los Angeles, CA; Milwaukee Art Museum, Milwaukee, WI; Moderna Museet, Stockholm, Sweden; Museum of Contemporary Art, San Diego, CA; Museum of Modern Art, New York, NY; Philbrook Museum of Art, Tulsa, OK; Phoenix Art Museum, Phoenix, AZ; Seattle Art Museum, Seattle, WA; Tate Modern, London, U.K.; Whitney Museum of American Art, New York, NY.

Other object by this artist in the Corning Museum
Sculpture, untitled commission for Dale Anderson, 1992 (2006.4.174, gift of Lucy G. Feller).

For more information
Jan Avgikos, "Josiah McElheny: The Art of Authentic Forgery," *Glass* (New York Experimental Glass Workshop), no. 54, Winter 1993, pp. 22–29; *Art21 Season Three: Art in the 21st Century*, Alexandria, VA: Art21 Inc., distributed by PBS Home Video, 2005; Miguel Fernández-Cid and others, *Josiah McElheny*, Santiago de Compostela, Spain: Centro Galego de Arte Contemporánea, 2002; Fox 2006, pp. 127 and 130–131; Dave Hickey and others, *Josiah McElheny*, Boston: Isabella Stewart Gardner Museum, 1998; Lynn 2005, p. 62; Richard Martin and others, *An Historical Anecdote about Fashion*, Seattle: Henry Art Gallery, 1999; Josiah McElheny, "Invisible Hand," *Artforum*, v. 42, no. 10, Summer 2004, pp. 209–210; Josiah McElheny, "Proposal for Total Reflective Abstraction," *Cabinet*, no. 14, August 2004, pp. 98–100; Helen Molesworth, ed., *Notes for a Sculpture and a Film*, Columbus: Wexner Center for the Arts, Ohio State University, 2006; Apollonia Morrill, ed., *Josiah McElheny: The Metal Party*, New York: Public Art Fund, and San Francisco: Yerba Buena Center for the Arts, 2002; Louise Neri, "Josiah McElheny: Model for Total Reflective Abstraction

(after Buckminster Fuller and Isamu Noguchi)," in *Antipodes: Inside the White Cube*, London: White Cube, 2003, pp. 34–47.

Debora Moore
Born in 1960 in St. Louis, MO. Lives in Seattle, WA.

Moore is the owner of Fiori Studio, Seattle, WA (since 1994). She has taught at Pilchuck Glass School, Stanwood, WA (2001); Hilltop Artist-in-Residence Program, Tacoma, WA (1995–1997); and the Pratt Fine Arts Center, Seattle, WA (1992–1993). She worked as a glassblower for The Glass Eye, Seattle, WA (1992–1994), and for Chihuly Studio, Seattle, WA (1992). She was an artist in residence at the Museum of Glass, Tacoma, WA (2005), and at Scuola Abate Zanetti, Venice, Italy (2005).

Education
　　Pilchuck Glass School (1995, 1992, 1990); Pratt Fine Arts Center (1989).

Selected honors and awards
　　Rakow Commission, Corning Museum of Glass, Corning, NY (2007); Scholarship, Pilchuck Glass School (1995, 1992, 1990).

Selected museum collections
　　Cooper-Hewitt National Design Museum, Smithsonian Institution, New York, NY; Corning Museum of Glass, Corning, NY; Muskegon Museum of Art, Muskegon, MI.

For more information
　　www.deboramoore.com; Juli Cho Bailer, *Fresh! Contemporary Takes on Nature and Allegory*, Tacoma, WA: Museum of Glass: International Center for Contemporary Art, 2006, pp. 9, 46–47, and 63; Tina Oldknow, "The 2007 Rakow Commission: Debora Moore," *New Glass Review 29*, Corning: Corning Museum of Glass, 2008, pp. 98–99.

William Morris
Born in 1957 in Carmel, CA. Lives in Stanwood, WA.

Morris taught at Pilchuck Glass School, Stanwood, WA (1979–2007); California College of Arts and Crafts, Oakland, CA (1992); University of Hawaii, Manoa, HI (1991); Penland School of Crafts, Penland, NC (1988); Appalachian Center for Crafts, Smithville, TN (1987, 1982); Rochester Institute of Technology, Rochester, NY (1986); Carnegie-Mellon University, Pittsburgh, PA (1985); Haystack Mountain School of Crafts, Deer Isle, ME (1985, 1983, 1981); New York Experimental Glass Workshop, New York, NY (1985, 1983, 1981); Rhode Island School of Design, Providence, RI (1984); Illinois State University, Normal, IL (1982); Lobmeyr School, Vienna, Austria (1979); Royal College of Art, London, U.K. (1979); and the Alberta College of Art, Calgary, AB, Canada (1978).

Education
　　Central Washington University, Ellensburg, WA (1978–1979); California State University, Chico, CA (1976–1977).

Selected honors and awards
　　James Renwick Alliance Award, Renwick Gallery, Smithsonian American Art Museum, Smithsonian Institution, Washington, DC (2005); Visionaries! Award, Museum of Arts and Design, New York, NY (2001); Distinguished Alumnus Award, California State University (1997); Outstanding Achievement in Glass Award, UrbanGlass, Brooklyn, NY (1997); National Endowment for the Arts Fellowship (1994).

Selected museum collections
　　Auckland War Memorial Museum, Auckland, New Zealand; Carnegie Museum of Art, Pittsburgh, PA; Chrysler Museum of Art, Norfolk, VA; Cincinnati Art Museum, Cincinnati, OH; Corning Museum of Glass, Corning, NY; Daichi Museum, Nagoya, Japan; Detroit Institute of Arts, Detroit, MI; Hokkaido Museum of Modern Art, Sapporo, Japan; Joslyn Art Museum, Omaha, NE; Los Angeles County Museum of Art, Los Angeles, CA; Metropolitan Museum of Art, New York, NY; Milwaukee Art Museum, Milwaukee, WI; Mobile Museum of Art, Mobile, AL; Musée des Arts Décoratifs, Paris, France; Museum für Kunst und Gewerbe, Hamburg, Germany; Museum of Arts and Design, New York, NY; Museum of Fine Arts, Houston, Houston, TX; Norton Museum of Art, West Palm Beach, FL; Portland Art Museum, Portland, OR; Renwick Gallery, Smithsonian American Art Museum, Smithsonian Institution, Washington, DC; Seattle Art Museum, Seattle, WA; Shimonoseki City Art Museum, Shimonoseki, Japan; Speed Art Museum, Louisville, KY; Toledo Museum of Art, Toledo, OH; Victoria and Albert Museum, London, U.K.; Virginia Museum of Fine Arts, Richmond, VA.

Other objects by this artist in the Corning Museum
　　Shard Vessel, 1980 (2006.4.173); *Stone Vessel*, 1984 (84.4.31); *Petroglyphic Urn*, 1990 (2007.4.180, gift of the Ben W. Heineman Sr. Family); Vessel, *Scoop*, 1999 (2007.4.39, gift of Charles Bronfman).

For more information
　　www.wmorris.com; Isabel Allende and James Yood, *William Morris. Mazorca: Objects of Common Ceremony*, Seattle: Marquand Books, 2004; Gary Blonston, *William Morris: Artifacts/ Glass*, New York: Abbeville Press, 1996; Blake Edgar and others, *William Morris: Man Adorned*, Seattle: Marquand Books, 2001; Fox 2006, pp. 82–85 and 87; Frantz 1999, pp. 25–29; Henry Geldzahler and Patterson Sims, *William Morris: Glass, Artifact, and Art*, Seattle: distributed by University of Washington Press, 1989; Ilse-Neuman 1997, pp. 34–53; Matthew Kangas, "William Morris: Paleoglass," in Kangas 2006, pp. 206–211; Lynn 2005, pp. 42, 79, 108–109, 114, 125, and 155; William Warmus, *William Morris: Native Species*, Portland, OR: Belzar Springs Press, 2006; Warmus 2003, pp. 68, 69, 71–72, and 86; *William Morris: Cinerary Urn Installation*, Seattle: Marquand Books, 2002; *William Morris: Myth, Object, and the Animal*, Norfolk, VA: Chrysler Museum of Art, 1999; Yelle 2000, pp. 173–176; James Yood and Tina Oldknow, *William Morris: Animal/Artifact*, New York: Abbeville Press, 2000.

Dennis Oppenheim
Born in 1938 in Electric City, WA. Lives in New York, NY.

Education
    Stanford University, Stanford, CA, M.F.A. (1966); California
    College of Arts and Crafts, Oakland, CA, B.F.A. (1965).

Selected honors and awards
    Lifetime Achievement Award, Vancouver Sculpture Biennale,
    Vancouver, BC, Canada (2007); National Endowment for the
    Arts Fellowship (1981, 1974); Guggenheim Foundation Fellow-
    ship (1971).

Selected museum collections
    Albright-Knox Art Gallery, Buffalo, NY; Art Gallery of New
    South Wales, Sydney, NSW, Australia; Art Gallery of Ontario,
    Toronto, ON, Canada; Art Institute of Chicago, Chicago, IL;
    Brooklyn Museum, Brooklyn, NY; Centre d'Art Plastique Con-
    temporain, Bordeaux, France; Chiba City Museum, Chiba City,
    Japan; Corcoran Gallery of Art, Washington, DC; Corning
    Museum of Glass, Corning, NY, Denver Art Museum, Denver,
    CO; Detroit Institute of Arts, Detroit, MI; Fonds National d'Art
    Contemporain, Paris, France; Fort Lauderdale Museum of Art,
    Fort Lauderdale, FL; Gemeentemuseum, The Hague, the
    Netherlands; Helsinki City Art Museum, Helsinki, Finland; High
    Museum of Art, Atlanta, GA; Indianapolis Museum of Art, In-
    dianapolis, IN; Israel Museum, Jerusalem, Israel; Jewish Museum
    of Art, New York, NY; Kunsthaus Zurich, Zurich, Switzerland;
    Los Angeles County Museum of Art, Los Angeles, CA; Louisiana
    Museum of Modern Art, Humlebaek, Denmark; Ludwig Mu-
    seum, Cologne, Germany; Metropolitan Museum of Art, New
    York, NY; Milwaukee Art Museum, Milwaukee, WI; Mint Muse-
    um of Art, Charlotte, NC; Musée d'Art et d'Histoire, Geneva,
    Switzerland; Musée d'Art Moderne et d'Art Contemporain,
    Nice, France; Musée National d'Art Moderne, Centre Georges
    Pompidou, Paris, France; Musées Royaux d'Art et d'Histoire,
    Brussels, Belgium; Museo de Arte Reina Sofia, Madrid, Spain;
    Museum Boymans van Beuningen, Rotterdam, the Nether-
    lands; Museum of Contemporary Art, Chicago, IL; Museum
    of Contemporary Art, Los Angeles, CA; Museum of Fine Arts,
    Houston, Houston, TX; Museum of Modern Art, New York,
    NY; National Gallery of Art, Washington, DC; National Gallery
    of Australia, Canberra, ACT, Australia; Nationalgalerie, Berlin,
    Germany; Norton Museum of Art, West Palm Beach, FL; Penn-
    sylvania Academy of Fine Arts, Philadelphia, PA; Philadelphia
    Museum of Art, Philadelphia, PA; Phoenix Art Museum, Phoenix,
    AZ; San Diego Museum of Contemporary Art, La Jolla, CA;
    San Francisco Museum of Modern Art, San Francisco, CA;
    Seattle Art Museum, Seattle, WA; Staatsgalerie Stuttgart,
    Stuttgart, Germany; Stadtisches Kunstmuseum Bonn, Bonn,
    Germany; Stedelijk Museum, Amsterdam, the Netherlands;
    Tate Gallery, London, U.K.; Wadsworth Atheneum Museum
    of Art, Hartford, CT; Whitney Museum of American Art, New
    York, NY.

For more information
    www.dennis-oppenheim.com; Suzaan Boettger, *Earthworks:
    Art and the Landscape of the Sixties*, Berkeley: University of
    California Press, 2002; Germano Celant, *Oppenheim: Explo-
    rations*, Milan: Charta, 2001; *Dennis Oppenheim: Land Art,
    1968-78*, Storgade, Denmark: Vestsjaellands Kunstmuseum,
    1996; *Dennis Oppenheim: Recent Sculpture and Large Scale*

Project Proposals, Mannheim: Mannheimer Kunstverein, 1996;
James Dickinson, ed., *Technologies of Landscape*, Amherst, MA:
University of Massachusetts Press, 1999; Lorand Hegyi, *Domi-
cile: Privé/public*, Paris: Somogy Editions d'Art, 2005; Alanna
Heiss and Thomas McEvilley, *Dennis Oppenheim: Selected
Works, 1967-1991*, Lille, France: Musée d'Art Moderne de la
Communauté Urbaine de Lille, 1991; Thomas McEvilley, *Sculp-
ture in the Age of Doubt*, New York: Allworth Press, 1999;
Demetrio Paparoni, *Dennis Oppenheim: Project Drawings*,
Turin: In Arco Books, 2005; Ruffner and others 1991, pp. 40–
41 and 66; Seth Siegelaub and others, *The Context of Art/The
Art of Context*, Trieste: Navado Press, 2004; Marion Boulton
Stroud, *New Materials as New Media*, Cambridge, MA: MIT
Press, 2002, pp. 210–213; Yelle 2000, pp. 187–188; Smithso-
nian Interview.

Tom Patti
Born in 1943 in Pittsfield, MA. Lives in Plainfield, MA.

Patti worked as a design consultant for Solutia, St. Louis, MO (1999–
2000); GE Bayer Silicones, Leverkusen, Germany (1998–2000);
PPG Industries, Pittsburgh, PA (1996–2000); Owens Corning, Toledo,
OH (1992–2000); and the Appalachian Project, American Feder-
ation of the Arts, New York, NY (1968). He taught at Berkshire
Community College, Pittsfield, MA (1971), and at the Pratt Institute,
New York, NY (1968). He served on the board of directors of the
Norman Rockwell Museum, Stockbridge, MA (1993–2000), and
the Creative Glass Center of America, Wheaton Arts Center, Mill-
ville, NJ (1984–1992).
    Patti's recent architectural commissions include Morton Square,
New York, NY (completed 2004); Roosevelt Intermodal Station,
Queens, NY (completed 2004); Museum of Fine Arts, Boston, MA
(2000); Mint Museum of Craft + Design, Charlotte, NC (1999);
University of North Carolina Law School, Chapel Hill, NC (1999);
and Owens Corning World Headquarters, Toledo, OH (completed
1996).

Education
    New School for Social Research, New York, NY (1969); Pratt
    Institute, M.F.A. Industrial Design (1967-1969) and B.F.A. Indus-
    trial Design (1963-1967).

Selected honors and awards
    Fellow, American Craft Council, New York, NY (2001); Out-
    standing Achievement in Glass Award, UrbanGlass, Brooklyn,
    NY (1999); Massachusetts Living Treasure (1987) and Fellow-
    ship (1981), Massachusetts Foundation on the Arts, Boston, MA;
    National Endowment for the Arts Fellowship (1979); Owens
    Corning Education Fellowship (1967-1969); Society of Plastic
    Engineers Research Grant (1966).

Selected museum collections
    Art Institute of Chicago, Chicago, IL; Berkshire Museum, Pitts-
    field, MA; Carnegie Museum of Art, Pittsburgh, PA; Chrysler
    Museum of Art, Norfolk, VA; Corning Museum of Glass, Cor-
    ning, NY; Glasmuseum Hentrich, Museum Kunst Palast, Düs-
    seldorf, Germany; Indianapolis Museum of Art, Indianapolis,
    IN; Kestner Museum, Hanover, Germany; Kunstsammlungen

der Veste Coburg, Coburg, Germany; Metropolitan Museum of Art, New York, NY; Mint Museum of Craft + Design, Charlotte, NC; Montreal Museum of Fine Arts, Montreal, QC, Canada; Musée de Design et d'Arts Appliqués Contemporains, Lausanne, Switzerland; Musée des Arts Décoratifs, Paris, France; Museum of Arts and Design, New York, NY; Museum of Fine Arts, Boston, MA; Museum of Fine Arts, Houston, Houston, TX; Museum of Modern Art, New York, NY; National Gallery of Victoria, Melbourne, VIC, Australia; Philadelphia Museum of Art, Philadelphia, PA; Renwick Gallery, Smithsonian American Art Museum, Smithsonian Institution, Washington, DC; Saint Louis Art Museum, St. Louis, MO; Toledo Museum of Art, Toledo, OH; Victoria and Albert Museum, London, U.K.

Other objects by this artist in the Corning Museum
Vessel, *Opal Green*, 1976 (76.4.30); Vessel, *Banded Bronze*, 1976 (79.4.134, purchased with the aid of funds from the National Endowment for the Arts); Sculpture, *Bronze and Clear Planar Lamination*, 1976 (85.4.101, gift of Norman Whitney); Untitled Bowl, 1977 (2007.4.182, gift of the Ben W. Heineman Sr. Family); Sculpture, *Inverted Series*, 1977 (2007.4.183, gift of the Ben W. Heineman Sr. Family); Vessel, *Solar Riser Series #LH*, 1978 (79.4.3); Sculpture, *Solar Gray Compound*, 1980 (80.4.61); Sculpture, *Compacted Horizontal Solarized Blue*, 1987 (2007.4.184, gift of the Ben W. Heineman Sr. Family); Sculpture, *Split Fire Riser*, 1988 (2007.4.185, gift of the Ben W. Heineman Sr. Family); Sculpture, *Parallel Echo with Line*, 1989 (2007.4.186, gift of the Ben W. Heineman Sr. Family); Sculpture, *Asahi Lumina with Bronze and Mirrorized Disk*, 1991–1993 (2007.4.187, gift of the Ben W. Heineman Sr. Family); Sculpture, *Red Lumina Spectral Starphire with Green*, 1994–1996 (2007.4.188, gift of the Ben W. Heineman Sr. Family); Sculpture, *Red Lumina with Amber*, 1996 (2007.4.189, gift of the Ben W. Heineman Sr. Family).

For more information
www.tompatti.com; Buechner 1979, cover and pp. 174 and 266; Dorigato and Klein 1996, pp. 144 and 215; Fox 2006, pp. 22 and 24–26; Kehlmann 1992, p. 131; Lynn 2005, pp. 74, 121, and 146; Mann 1997, p. 29; Oldknow 2005, p. 105; Warmus 2003, pp. 38–40, 42, and 56–59; William Warmus and Donald Kuspit, *Tom Patti: Illuminating the Invisible*, Tacoma, WA: Museum of Glass: International Center for Contemporary Art, 2004; Yelle 2000, pp. 194–197.

Susan Plum
Born in 1944 in Houston, TX. Lives in San Miguel de Allende, Guanajuato, Mexico.

Plum taught at Espace Verre, Montreal, QC, Canada (2002); The Studio of The Corning Museum of Glass, Corning, NY (2001, 1997); Penland School of Crafts, Penland, NC (2000, 1997, 1995, 1993); California College of Arts and Crafts, Oakland, CA (1996); California State University, San Jose, CA (1996); Pilchuck Glass School, Stanwood, WA (1995, 1991, 1990); and the Pratt Fine Arts Center, Seattle, WA (1985–1990). She was a visiting artist at UrbanGlass, Brooklyn, NY (1999).

Education
Pilchuck Glass School (1987, 1986); East West University, Tamil Nadu, India (1984–1985); University of Houston, Houston, TX (1979–1980); University of the Americas, Mexico City, D.F., Mexico (1963–1964); University of Arizona, Tucson, AZ (1962–1963).

Selected museum collections
Corning Museum of Glass, Corning, NY; Hunter Museum of American Art, Chattanooga, TN; Mobile Museum of Art, Mobile, AL; Museum of Arts and Design, New York, NY; Renwick Gallery, Smithsonian American Art Museum, Smithsonian Institution, Washington, DC.

Other objects by this artist in the Corning Museum
Vessel, *Copa de Ceremonia I*, 1989 (89.4.5); Vessel, *Copa de Ceremonia II*, 1989 (89.4.12, gift of Regalo Vetro).

For more information
www.susanplum.net; Dalai Lama Foundation, *The Missing Peace: Artists Consider the Dalai Lama*, Redwood City, CA: the foundation, 2006; Graham 1999, pp. 7–8 and 17; Ruffner and others 1991, pp. 44–45 and 67; Stuhr and others 1997, pp. 72 and 108.

Richard Posner
Born in 1948 in Los Angeles, CA. Lives in Berlin, Germany.

Posner taught at North Lands Creative Glass, Lybster, Caithness, U.K. (2004); University of California, Los Angeles, CA (1991–1992); Konstfackskolan, Stockholm, Sweden (1990, 1979); Minneapolis College of Art and Design, Minneapolis, MN (1988–1990); and the California College of Arts and Crafts, Oakland, CA (1978). Posner was a visiting artist at the Bauhaus, Dessau, Germany (2000); Hochschule der Kunst, Berlin, Germany (2000); Hochschule der Kunst, Halle, Germany (2000); Royal College of Art, London, U.K. (2000); California State University, San Bernardino, CA (1998); Djerassi Foundation, Woodside, CA (1997); Blue Mountain Center, Blue Mountain Lake, NY (1996, 1989); Santa Monica Museum of Art, Santa Monica, CA (1995); Bild-Werk Frauenau, Frauenau, Germany (1993); Littleton Studios, Spruce Pine, NC (1993); Yaddo Artists Colony, Saratoga Springs, NY (1989); Banff Centre for Fine Arts, Banff, AB, Canada (1988); MacDowell Colony, Peterborough, NH (1988); Virginia Center for the Creative Arts, Amherst, VA (1988); Ragdale Foundation, Lake Forest, IL (1987); Pilchuck Glass School, Stanwood, WA (1985); Arrowmont School of Arts and Crafts, Gatlinburg, TN (1983); Haystack Mountain School of Crafts, Deer Isle, ME (1983); and the Penland School of Crafts, Penland, NC (1980).

Education
California College of Arts and Crafts, M.F.A. (1976); California State University, Chico, CA, B.A. (1973).

Selected honors and awards
Fulbright Foundation Fellowship (2000, 1979); Architectural Foundation Design Award, Museum of Contemporary Art, Los Angeles, CA (1995); Pollock-Krasner Foundation Grant,

New York, NY (1995); Visionary Landscape Design Award, Landscape Architecture Magazine (1993); Design Excellence Award, General Services Administration, Washington, DC (1992); Visual Artist Fellowship, McKnight Foundation, Minneapolis, MN (1991); Dayton-Hudson Foundation Grant, Minneapolis, MN (1990); Jerome Foundation Grant, St. Paul, MN (1990); National Endowment for the Arts Fellowship (1989, 1977); Seattle Arts Commission Grant, Seattle, WA (1982); American-Scandinavian Foundation Grant, New York, NY (1978).

Selected museum collections
Corning Museum of Glass, Corning, NY; Glasmuseet Ebeltoft, Ebeltoft, Denmark; Metropolitan Museum of Art, New York, NY; Renwick Gallery, Smithsonian American Art Museum, Smithsonian Institution, Washington, DC; Victoria and Albert Museum, London, U.K.

Other object by this artist in the Corning Museum
Window, *The Crystal Pallets: deFence of Light*, 1983 (2000.4.52, gift of the artist).

For more information
Buechner 1979, pp. 183 and 266; Center on Contemporary Art, *COCA Folio: William T. Wiley/Richard Posner*, Seattle: the center, 1985; Charles A. Wustum Museum of Fine Arts, *Just Plane Screwy: Metaphysical and Metaphorical Tools by Artists*, Racine, WI: the museum, 1992; Lynn 2005, p. 107; Richard Posner, *Intervention and Alchemy: A Public Art Primer*, Minneapolis, MN: Division of Visual Arts, First Bank System, 1990; Richard Posner, *Windows of Vulnerability*, Seattle: the author, 1982; Stuhr and others 1997, pp. 73 and 108; David Willard, *Contemporary Glass: A Decade Apart*, Boise, ID: Boise Gallery of Art, 1984, pp. 26–27; Yelle 2000, p. 200.

Clifford Rainey
Born in 1948 in Whitehead, Northern Ireland. Lives in Oakland, CA.

Rainey is professor and chairman of the Glass Program, California College of the Arts, Oakland, CA (since 1991). He also taught at Pilchuck Glass School, Stanwood, WA (1993, 1991, 1989, 1988, 1985); Royal College of Art, London, U.K. (1977–1984); and the Hornsey College of Art, London, U.K. (1974–1975). He founded and headed the Worship Street Studio, London, U.K. (1985–1991), and he was co-founder of the Rainey-Cooper Partnership, London, U.K. (1982–1989).

Education
Royal College of Art, M.A. (1971–1973); North East London Polytechnic School of Sculpture, London, U.K. (1969–1971); Hornsey College of Art (1968–1969); Belfast College of Art, Belfast, Northern Ireland (1965–1968).

Selected museum collections
Art Gallery of Western Australia, Perth, WA, Australia; Corning Museum of Glass, Corning, NY; Detroit Institute of Arts, Detroit, MI; Kunstsammlungen der Veste Coburg, Coburg, Germany; Municipal Gallery, Dublin, Ireland; Musée de Design et d'Arts Appliqués Contemporains, Lausanne, Switzerland; Museum of

Modern Art, Dublin, Ireland; Toledo Museum of Art, Toledo, OH; Ulster Museum, Belfast, Northern Ireland; Victoria and Albert Museum, London, U.K.

Other objects by this artist in the Corning Museum
Sculpture, *Cu' Chulainn*, 1985 (2006.2.10, gift of the Ben W. Heineman Sr. Family); Sculpture, *Omagh*, 2001 (2006.4.60, gift of the Ben W. Heineman Sr. Family).

For more information
Austin and others 1993; Fox 2006, pp. 115–117 and 119; Dextra Frankel and Donald Kuspit, *Cast Glass Sculpture*, Fullerton, CA: California State University, 1986, pp. 34–37; Liam Kelly, *Clifford Rainey: Sculpture & Drawings, 1967–1987*, Belfast: Arts Council of Northern Ireland, and Dublin: Douglas Hyde Gallery, Trinity College, 1987; Lynn 2005, p. 101; Ricke 1990, pp. 90–91 and 305–306; Schack von Wittenau 2005, pp. 108–109; Stuhr and others 1997, pp. 74 and 109; Yelle 2000, pp. 206–207.

Robert Rauschenberg
Born in 1925 in Port Arthur, TX. Died in 2008 in Captiva Island, FL.

Rauschenberg was founder/director of the Robert Rauschenberg Foundation (since 1990); a Fellow of the Rhode Island School of Design, Providence, RI (since 1981); a member of the Royal Academy of Fine Arts, Stockholm, Sweden (since 1980); a member of the American Academy of Arts and Sciences, Boston, MA (since 1978); and founder/director of Change Inc., New York, NY (since 1970). He was president of the Trisha Brown Dance Company, New York, NY (1978), and he periodically worked as a set and costume designer for the dance companies of Trisha Brown, Merce Cunningham, Viola Farber, Steve Paxton, and Paul Taylor (since 1952). Rauschenberg served on the board of directors for AIDA-USA (1981) and P.S. 1, New York, NY (1977), and on the board of advisers of the Youth International Peace Prize Society, New York, NY (1981).

Education
Black Mountain College, Asheville, NC (1948–1952); Art Students' League, New York, NY (1949–1951); Académie Julian, Paris, France (1948); Kansas City Art Institute, Kansas City, MO (1947–1948); University of Texas at Austin, Austin, TX (1943).

Selected honors and awards
Medal Award, School of the Museum of Fine Arts, Boston, MA (2006); International Prize Julio Gonzalez for Lifetime Works, Institut Valencià d'Art Modern, Valencia, Spain (2005); Medal Award, School of the Museum of Fine Arts, Boston (2002); Eighth Wexner Prize, Wexner Center, Ohio State University, Columbus, OH (2000); Lifetime Achievement Award, International Sculpture Center, Washington, DC (1996); National Medal of Arts Award (1993); Commandeur, Ordre des Arts et des Lettres, Ministry of Culture and Communication, Paris, France (1992); Federal Design Achievement Award (1992); Art Award, International Center of Photography, New York, NY (1987); Golden Plate Award, American Academy of Achievement (1986); Grammy Award (Album Design for *Talking Heads*)

(1984); Honorary Doctorate, New York University, New York, NY (1984); Skowhegan Medal for Painting, Skowhegan School of Painting and Sculpture, Skowhegan, ME (1982); Officier, Ordre des Arts et des Lettres, Ministry of Culture and Communication, Paris, France (1981); Creative Arts Award, Brandeis University, Waltham, MA (1978); Honorary Doctorate, University of South Florida, Tampa, FL (1976); Honorary Doctorate, Grinnell College, Grinnell, IA (1967); Grand Prize (Painting), Venice Biennale, Venice, Italy (1964).

Selected museum collections

Albright-Knox Art Gallery, Buffalo, NY; Art Gallery of Ontario, Toronto, ON, Canada; Art Institute of Chicago, Chicago, IL; Baltimore Museum of Art, Baltimore, MD; Bayerisches Staatsgemäldesammlungen, Munich, Germany; Centro Cultural de Arte Contemporaneo, Mexico City, DF, Mexico; Cleveland Museum of Art, Cleveland OH; Corning Museum of Glass, Corning, NY; Dallas Museum of Art, Dallas, TX; Des Moines Art Center, Des Moines, IA; Detroit Institute of Arts, Detroit, MI; Hara Museum of Contemporary Art, Tokyo, Japan; High Museum of Art, Atlanta, GA; Hirshhorn Museum and Sculpture Garden, Smithsonian Institution, Washington, DC; Israel Museum, Jerusalem, Israel; Kunsthaus Zurich, Zurich, Switzerland; Kunstmuseum Basel, Basel, Switzerland; Kunstsammlung Nordrhein-Westfalen, Düsseldorf, Germany; Los Angeles County Museum of Art, Los Angeles, CA; Louisiana Museum of Modern Art, Humlebaek, Denmark; Menil Collection, Houston, TX; Minneapolis Institute of Arts, Minneapolis, MN; Moderna Museet, Stockholm, Sweden; Montreal Museum of Fine Arts, Montreal, QC, Canada; Musée National d'Art Moderne, Centre Georges Pompidou, Paris, France; Museum für Moderne Kunst, Frankfurt, Germany; Museum Ludwig, Cologne, Germany; Museum of Contemporary Art, Los Angeles, CA; Museum of Fine Arts, Boston, MA; Museum of Fine Arts, Houston, Houston, TX; Museum of Modern Art, New York, NY; National Gallery of Art, Washington, DC; National Gallery of Australia, Canberra, ACT, Australia; National Museum of Art, Osaka, Japan; Nelson-Atkins Museum of Art, Kansas City, MO; Neue Galerie Sammlung Ludwig, Aachen, Germany; New Orleans Museum of Art, New Orleans, LA; Philadelphia Museum of Art, Philadelphia, PA; San Francisco Museum of Modern Art, San Francisco, CA; Sogetsu Art Museum, Tokyo, Japan; Solomon R. Guggenheim Museum, New York, NY; Staatsgalerie Stuttgart, Stuttgart, Germany; Stedelijk Museum, Amsterdam, the Netherlands; Tate Gallery, London, U.K.; Toledo Museum of Art, Toledo, OH; Vancouver Art Gallery, Vancouver, BC, Canada; Wadsworth Atheneum Museum of Art, Hartford, CT; Walker Art Center, Minneapolis, MN; Wallraf-Richartz Museum, Cologne, Germany; Whitney Museum of American Art, New York, NY.

For more information

Dore Ashton, *Rauschenberg: XXXIV Drawings for Dante's Inferno*, New York: Harry N. Abrams, 1969; Heiner Bastian, *Beuys, Rauschenberg, Twombly, Warhol*, Düsseldorf: Te Neues Publishing, 1988; Yves-Alain Blois, *Robert Rauschenberg: Cardboards and Related Pieces*, Houston: Menil Foundation Inc., 2007; Thomas Crow and others, *Robert Rauschenberg: Combines*, Los Angeles: Museum of Contemporary Art, 2005; Jonathan Fineberg, *Art since 1940: Strategies of Being*, Englewood Cliffs,

NJ: Prentice Hall, 1995; Andrew Forge, *Rauschenberg*, New York: Harry N. Abrams, 1969; Walter Hopps and others, *Robert Rauschenberg: A Retrospective*, New York: Guggenheim Museum, 1997; Robert Hughes, *Epic Visions: The History of Art in America*, New York: Alfred A. Knopf, 1999; Hughes 1981, pp. 333–335 and 345–347; Sam Hunter, *Robert Rauschenberg*, New York: Rizzoli, 1999; Branden W. Joseph, *Random Order: Robert Rauschenberg and the Neo Avant-Garde*, Cambridge, MA, and London: MIT Press, 2003; Mary Lynn Kotz, *Robert Rauschenberg: Art and Life*, New York: Harry N. Abrams, 1990; Lucy Lippard, *Pop Art*, New York: Frederick R. Praeger, 1969; Lynn 2005, p. 27; Paul Mason, *Pop Artists*, Chicago: Heinemann Library, 2003; Robert S. Mattison, *Robert Rauschenberg: Breaking Boundaries*, New Haven, CT, and London: Yale University Press, 1995; Helen Molesworth, *Work Ethic*, State College, PA: Pennsylvania State University Press, 2003; Jed Perl, *New Art City*, New York: Alfred A. Knopf, 2005; John Perreault, "Don't Tread on Me: The Meanings of Rauschenberg's Glass Tires," *Glass* (UrbanGlass Art Quarterly), no. 70, Spring 1998, pp. 20–25; *Robert Rauschenberg: Inventive Genius*, American Masters Series, Educational Broadcasting Corporation, 1999, Film Odyssey and Wellspring Media, 2004; Nan Rosenthal, *Robert Rauschenberg*, New York: Abbeville Press, 1999; Leo Steinberg, *Encounters with Rauschenberg*, Chicago and London: University of Chicago Press, 2000; Kirk Varnedoe, *A Fine Disregard: What Makes Modern Art Modern*, New York: Harry N. Abrams, 1990; Kirk Varnedoe, *Pictures of Nothing: Abstract Art since Pollock*, Washington, DC: National Gallery of Art, 2006; Yelle 2000, p. 211; Smithsonian Interview.

Jill Reynolds

Born in 1956 in Chicago, IL. Lives in Beacon, NY.

Reynolds taught at the Penland School of Crafts, Penland, NC (2002); Rhode Island School of Design, Providence, RI (2000–2002); Pilchuck Glass School, Stanwood, WA (2001); Radcliffe Graduate Consortium in Women's Studies, Harvard University, Boston, MA (2001); Massachusetts College of Art, Boston, MA (1999–2000); Bard College, Annandale-on-Hudson, NY (1996); and Rutgers University, New Brunswick, NJ (1996, 1995, 1994). She was a graduate studio adviser at the Maine College of Art, Portland, ME (1999–2001), and print shop coordinator at Pilchuck Glass School, Stanwood, WA (1990–1995).

Reynolds was a visiting artist at the Pratt Fine Arts Center, Seattle, WA (1991), and at Centrum Foundation, Port Townsend, WA (1990). She was an emerging artist in residence at Pilchuck Glass School (1990).

Education

Mason Gross School of the Arts, Rutgers University, M.F.A. Sculpture (1996); Evergreen State College, Olympia, WA, B.A. Architecture (1979); Reed College, Portland, OR (1974–1975).

Selected honors and awards

Rakow Commission, Corning Museum of Glass, Corning, NY (2002); Artist Grant, Pollock-Krasner Foundation, New York, NY (2001); Sculpture Fellowship, Massachusetts Cultural Council, Boston, MA (2001); Associate, Radcliffe Institute for

Advanced Study, Harvard University, Boston, MA (1999–2000); Bunting Fellowship, Radcliffe Institute for Advanced Study, Harvard University (1998–1999); Pilchuck Glass School Scholarship (1989).

Selected museum collections
Cheney Cowles Museum, Spokane, WA; Corning Museum of Glass, Corning, NY; Seattle Art Museum, Seattle, WA; Tacoma Art Museum, Tacoma, WA.

For more information
Jan Garden Castro, *Threshold*, Tacoma, WA: Tacoma Art Museum, 2000; Fox 2006, pp. 131–134; Katy Kline and Steven Pinker, *Jill Reynolds: The Shape of Breath*, Cambridge, MA: List Visual Arts Center, Massachusetts Institute of Technology, 1997; Lynn 2005, p. 60; Sarah Nichols, *Well Hung: Chandeliers Revealed*, Pittsburgh: Pittsburgh Glass Center, 2006, pp. 22–23; Jill Reynolds, "In Context: Jill Reynolds," *Glass* (New York Experimental Glass Workshop), no. 54, Winter 1993, pp. 44–47; Rothschild Gallery, Radcliffe Institute, *Jill Reynolds: Nexus*, Cambridge, MA: Harvard University, 1999; Ruffner and others 1991, pp. 46–47 and 68; Patterson Sims and Vicki Halper, *Holding the Past: Historicism in Northwest Glass Sculpture*, Seattle: Seattle Art Museum, 1996.

Gerhard Ribka
Born in 1955 in Offenbach am Main, Germany. Lives in Irsee, Germany.

Ribka is lecturer and head of the glass department at the Staatliche Berufsfachschule für Glas und Schmuck, Kaufbeuern-Neugablonz, Germany (since 1993). He has taught at North Lands Creative Glass, Lybster, Caithness, U.K. (2002); Bild-Werk Frauenau, Frauenau, Germany (1999–2002, 1995–1997, 1989–1991); Pilchuck Glass School, Stanwood, WA (1998); Tama Art University, Tokyo, Japan (1998); and Staffordshire University, Stoke-on-Trent, U.K. (1991). He was head of stained glass restoration, Lincoln Cathedral, Lincoln, U.K. (1989–1993). Ribka was an artist in residence at Littleton Studios, Spruce Pine, NC (1998).

Education
Royal College of Art, London, U.K., M.F.A. Glass (1986–1988); apprenticeship in stained glass, Franz Mayer Studios, Munich, Germany (1980–1982); Würzburg University, Frankfurt, Germany, M.S. Chemistry (1974–1980).

Selected honors and awards
First Prize, Contributions to Art in Public Places Award, Munich, Germany (1992); Pilchuck Glass School Scholarship (1987).

Selected museum collections
Corning Museum of Glass, Corning, NY; Design Center, Ishikawa, Japan; Ernsting Stiftung Alter Hof Herding, Coesfeld, Germany; Glasmuseet Ebeltoft, Ebeltoft, Denmark; Glasmuseum Frauenau, Frauenau, Germany; Glasmuseum, Immenhausen, Germany.

For more information
Frantz 2003, pp. 28–31 and 53; *Gerhard Ribka: A Sad Life, Not Alone, the Skins*, London: Dan Klein Associates at Adrian Sassoon, Victoria and Albert Museum, 2006; *Gerhard Ribka. 3 Figures: Distant Doubts, but Spring, Fragile*, Irsee, Germany: the artist, 2007; Glasmuseet Ebeltoft, *The Visible Man*, Ebeltoft, Denmark: Glasmuseets Forlag, 2003; Oldknow 2005, p. 145.

Michael Rogers
Born in Wyoming, IL. Lives in Rochester, NY.

Rogers is professor and head of the Glass Program at the School of American Crafts, Rochester Institute of Technology, Rochester, NY (since 2002), and he was chairman of the school (2002–2005). He was associate professor and head of the glass program at the Aichi University of Education, Kariya, Japan (1991–2002). Rogers served on the board and as president of the Glass Art Society (1997–2004). He was an artist in residence at the Museum of Glass, Tacoma, WA (2007).

Education
University of Illinois, Urbana-Champaign, Champaign, IL, M.F.A. Sculpture (1981); Western Illinois University, Macomb, IL, M.A. (1978) and B.A. (1977).

Selected honors and awards
Honorary Lifetime Member, Glass Art Society (2007); Lillian Fairchild Award, University of Rochester, Rochester, NY (2007).

Selected museum collections
Corning Museum of Glass, Corning, NY; Glasmuseet Ebeltoft, Ebeltoft, Denmark; Grand Crystal Glass Museum, Taipei, Taiwan; Koganezaki Glass Museum, Shizuoka, Japan; L'viv National Museum, L'viv, Ukraine; Museo del Vidrio, Monterrey, Mexico; Muskegon Museum of Art, Muskegon, MI; Notojima Glass Museum, Notojima, Japan; Suntory Museum, Tokyo, Japan.

For more information
Frantz 2003, pp. 32–35 and 54.

René Roubíček
Born in 1922 in Prague, Czechoslovakia. Lives in Kamenický Šenov and Prague, Czech Republic.

Roubíček served as a consultant to the Academy of Fine Arts, Prague, Czechoslovakia (1966–1968); designer and then head designer at the Borské Sklo Glassworks, Nový Bor, Czechoslovakia (1953–1965); consultant to the Artistic Center for the Glass and Fine Ceramics Industry, Prague, Czechoslovakia (1952–1958); designer at the Železný Brod State Glassworks, Železný Brod, Czechoslovakia (1952–1953); and head of the department of glass cutting at the Specialized School of Glassmaking, Kamenický Šenov, Czechoslovakia (1945–1952).

Education
Academy of Applied Arts, Prague, Czechoslovakia (1949–1950); School of Decorative Arts, Prague (1940–1944).

Selected honors and awards
Central Switzerland Glass Prize, Lucerne, Switzerland (1980); Coburg Glass Prize, Kunstsammlungen der Veste Coburg, Coburg, Germany (1977); Bavarian National Prize and Gold Medal, Internationale Handwerksmesse, Munich, Germany (1970, 1969); State Prize, Prague, Czechoslovakia (1967); Grand Prize, Expo '58, Brussels, Belgium (1958).

Selected museum collections
Akademie der Künste, Berlin, Germany; Badisches Landesmuseum, Karlsruhe, Germany; Corning Museum of Glass, Corning, NY; East Bohemian Museum, Pardubice, Czech Republic; Glasmuseet Ebeltoft, Ebeltoft, Denmark; Glasmuseum Hentrich, Museum Kunst Palast, Düsseldorf, Germany; Glass Museum, Kamenický Šenov, Czech Republic; Glass Museum, Nový Bor, Czech Republic; Koganezaki Glass Museum, Shizuoka, Japan; Kunstsammlungen der Veste Coburg, Coburg, Germany; Moravian Gallery, Brno, Czech Republic; Musée de Design et d'Arts Appliqués Contemporains, Lausanne, Switzerland; Musée des Arts Décoratifs, Paris, France; Museum Bellerive, Zurich, Switzerland; Museum für Kunsthandwerk, Frankfurt am Main, Germany; Museum of Decorative Arts, Prague, Czech Republic; National Gallery, Prague, Czech Republic; North Bohemian Museum, Liberec, Czech Republic; Stedelijk Museum, Amsterdam, the Netherlands; Victoria and Albert Museum, London, U.K.

Other objects by this artist in the Corning Museum
Drinking Glasses with Bamboo Leaves (2), 1945–1946 (99.3.70, gift of The Steinberg Foundation); Spherical Vase, 1958 (68.3.45, gift of the National Gallery, Prague); Sculpture, Untitled, 1960 (83.3.239); Sculpture, Untitled, 1961 (99.3.48, gift of The Steinberg Foundation); Gourd-Shaped Vase, 1964 (99.3.42, gift of The Steinberg Foundation); Bottle-Shaped Vase, 1965 (99.3.43, gift of The Steinberg Foundation); Sculpture, Jazzparade, 1986 (90.3.29); Sculpture, Man, 1994 (95.4.358, gift of Mr. and Mrs. George B. Saxe).

For more information
Alena Adlerová and others, Sklo = Glass: Miluše Roubíčková, René Roubíček, London: Studio Glass Gallery, 1999; Oldknow 2005, pp. 196–197; Petrová 2001; Ricke 1990, pp. 122–123 and 306–308; Ricke 2005, pp. 284–296 and 394–396; Schack von Wittenau 2005, pp. 222–223.

Ginny Ruffner
Born in 1952 in Atlanta, GA. Lives in Seattle, WA.

Ruffner served as a consultant to the Product Design Department, Parsons the New School for Design, New York, NY (1994, 1993). She taught at Pilchuck Glass School, Stanwood, WA (1995, 1984–1990); Université d'Eté, Sars-Poteries, France (1990); New York Experimental Glass Workshop, New York, NY (1990, 1986, 1985); Penland School of Crafts, Penland, NC (1987); Pratt Fine Arts Center, Seattle, WA (1986, 1985); Tyler School of Art, Philadelphia, PA (1984); Summervail Craft School, Vail, CO (1983); California College of Arts and Crafts, Oakland, CA (1982); and DeKalb College, Atlanta, GA (1977).

Ruffner is a member of the advisory council, Achievement Advocates (since 2005), and the board of directors, On The Boards, Seattle, WA (since 2004). She was a board member of Artist Trust (Honorary), Seattle, WA (1998–2003); Arts Ballard, Seattle, WA (1997); James Renwick Alliance (Honorary), Smithsonian American Art Museum, Smithsonian Institution, Washington, DC (1993–1996); and UrbanGlass, Brooklyn, NY (1992–1994). She also served on the board of trustees, Pilchuck Glass School (1991–2001; vice president, 1994–2000), and the Glass Art Society, Seattle, WA (1988–1991; president, 1991), and as a commissioner, Seattle Art Commission, Seattle, WA (1991).

She was a visiting artist at the University of Hawaii, Honolulu, HI (2005); Waterford Crystal, Waterford, Ireland (2000); Pilchuck Glass School (1993, 1988); New Jersey State Arts Commission, Wheaton Village, Millville, NJ (1987); and the Penland School of Crafts (1983, 1979).

Education
University of Georgia, Athens, GA, M.F.A. Drawing and Painting (1975) and B.F.A. Drawing and Painting (1974).

Selected honors and awards
James Renwick Alliance (2007); King County Arts Commission, Seattle, WA (2003); Honorary Lifetime Member, Glass Art Society (2000); Woman of the Year, Palm Springs Desert Museum, Palm Springs, CA (1996); Award for Outstanding Achievement in Glass, UrbanGlass (1995); Visual Artist Fellowship, National Endowment for the Arts (1986); Georgia Business Committee for the Arts Award, Atlanta, GA (1985); National Endowment for the Arts/Southern Arts Federation Grant (1985).

Selected museum collections
Carnegie Museum of Art, Pittsburgh, PA; Cincinnati Art Museum, Cincinnati, OH; Cooper-Hewitt National Design Museum, Smithsonian Institution, New York, NY; Corning Museum of Glass, Corning, NY; Detroit Institute of Arts, Detroit, MI; Fine Arts Museums of San Francisco, San Francisco, CA; Glasmuseum Hentrich, Museum Kunst Palast, Düsseldorf, Germany; High Museum of Art, Atlanta, GA; Hokkaido Museum of Modern Art, Sapporo, Japan; Indianapolis Museum of Art, Indianapolis, IN; Koganezaki Glass Museum, Shizuoka, Japan; Los Angeles County Museum of Art, Los Angeles, CA; Metropolitan Museum of Art, New York, NY; Mint Museum of Craft + Design, Charlotte, NC; Montreal Museum of Fine Arts, Montreal, QC, Canada; Musée de Design et d'Arts Appliqués Contemporains, Lausanne, Switzerland; Museum of Arts and Design, New York, NY; Norton Museum of Art, West Palm Beach, FL; Queensland Art Gallery, South Brisbane, QLD, Australia; Racine Art Museum, Racine, WI; Renwick Gallery, Smithsonian American Art Museum, Smithsonian Institution, Washington, DC; Seattle Art Museum, Seattle, WA; Speed Art Museum, Louisville, KY; Tacoma Art Museum, Tacoma, WA; Toledo Museum of Art, Toledo, OH.

Other objects by this artist in the Corning Museum
Sculpture, Eat Your Hat, 1985 (85.4.32); Chandelier, 1989 (91.3.122, anonymous gift); Sculpture, Herman Nootics, 1989 (2007.4.203, gift of the Ben W. Heineman Sr. Family).

For more information
www.ginnyruffner.com; Fox 2006, pp. 95–99; Matthew Kangas, "Containing Space: Ginny Ruffner's Installations," in Kangas 2006, pp. 218–221; Lynn 2005, pp. 102, 156, and 169; Mann 1997, p. 13; Bonnie Miller, *Why Not?: The Art of Ginny Ruffner*, Seattle: Tacoma Art Museum in association with University of Washington Press, 1995; Tina Oldknow, "Il vetro e la musa: L'arte di Ginny Ruffner = Glass and the Muse: The Art of Ginny Ruffner," *Vetro* (Centro Studio Vetro, Murano), v. 4, no. 12, July–September 2001, pp. 14–18; Oldknow 2005, pp. 110–111; Ginny Ruffner, *Creativity: The Flowering Tornado*, Montgomery, AL: Montgomery Museum of Fine Arts, 2003; Watson 2002, pp. 24–25; Yelle 2000, pp. 224–227; Smithsonian Interview.

Gizela Šabóková
Born in 1952 in Nové Zámky, Czechoslovakia. Lives in Prague, Czech Republic.

Šabóková taught at the Musée-Atelier du Verre, Sars-Poteries, France (1998); Pilchuck Glass School, Stanwood, WA (1993); Fundació Centre del Vidre de Barcelona, Barcelona, Spain (1992); Espace Verre, Montreal, QC, Canada (1989); and Sheridan College, Oakville, Toronto, ON, Canada (1988).

Education
Academy of Applied Arts, Prague, Czechoslovakia (1973–1979); Specialized School for Glassmaking, Železný Brod, Czechoslovakia (1969–1973); Vocational School of Česky Kristal Works, Chlum u Trebone, Czechoslovakia (1967–1969).

Selected honors and awards
Grand Prize, Koganezaki Glass Museum, Shizuoka, Japan (2000); Salvador Dali Award, Prague, Czech Republic (1997); Masaryk Academy Prize, Prague, Czech Republic (1994); Jugendgestaltet, Munich, Germany (1982); 3rd Quadrienale, Erfurt, Germany (1982).

Selected museum collections
Carnegie Museum of Art, Pittsburgh, PA; Chrysler Museum of Art, Norfolk, VA; Corning Museum of Glass, Corning, NY; East Bohemian Museum, Pardubice, Czech Republic; Ernsting Stiftung Alter Hof Herding, Coesfeld, Germany; Glasmuseet Ebeltoft, Ebeltoft, Denmark; Glasmuseum, Immenhausen, Germany; Hokkaido Museum of Modern Art, Sapporo, Japan; Koganezaki Glass Museum, Shizuoka, Japan; Moravian Gallery, Brno, Czech Republic; Musée de Design et d'Arts Appliqués Contemporains, Lausanne, Switzerland; Musée des Arts Décoratifs, Paris, France; Musée des Arts Décoratifs de Gent, Ghent, Belgium; Musée-Atelier du Verre, Sars-Poteries, France; Museum Jan van der Togt, Amstelveen, the Netherlands; Museum of Arts and Design, New York, NY; Museum of Decorative Arts, Prague, Czech Republic; Museum of Fine Arts, Houston, Houston, TX; Museum of Glass and Jewelry, Jablonec, Czech Republic; National Museum, Wrocław, Poland; North Bohemian Museum, Liberec, Czech Republic; Ulster Museum, Belfast, Northern Ireland; Yokohama Museum of Art, Yokohama, Japan.

Other objects by this artist in the Corning Museum
Panel, *Figure*, 1988 (89.3.2); Sculpture, *The Sun*, 2003 (2004.3.3, gift of the artist).

For more information
www.gizelasabokova.com; Economist Gallery (London), *Contemporary Czech Glass Sculpture*, London: Rudolfinia Ltd., 1994, pp. 20–21; Oldknow 2005, p. 199; Sylva Petrová, *Gizela Šabóková*, Jablonec nad Nisou: the artist, Karel Bartoníček, and the Museum of Glass, 1995; Petrová 2001; Petrová 2004, pp. 62–63 and 91–92.

Judith Schaechter
Born in 1961 in Gainesville, FL. Lives in Philadelphia, PA.

Schaechter teaches at the University of the Arts, Philadelphia, PA (since 1994). She has taught at North Lands Creative Glass, Lybster, Caithness, U.K. (2007); UrbanGlass, Brooklyn, NY (2003, 2000, 1994); Pennsylvania Academy of Fine Arts, Philadelphia, PA (1995–1999); Pilchuck Glass School, Stanwood, WA (1996, 1993, 1992); Bild-Werk Frauenau, Frauenau, Germany (1994); and the Rhode Island School of Design, Providence, RI (1991, 1990).

Education
Rhode Island School of Design, B.F.A. Glass (1983).

Selected honors and awards
John Simon Guggenheim Fellowship (2005); Hauberg Fellowship, Pilchuck Glass School (2003); Innovation in Technique, UrbanGlass (2000); Leeway Foundation Award (1999); Joan Mitchell Foundation Award (1995); Pew Fellowship in the Arts (1992); Pennsylvania Council on the Arts (1990); Louis Comfort Tiffany Foundation Award (1989); National Endowment for the Arts (1988, 1986); Pennsylvania Council on the Arts (1985).

Selected museum collections
Carnegie Museum of Art, Pittsburgh, PA; Corning Museum of Glass, Corning, NY; Fine Arts Museums of San Francisco, San Francisco, CA; Metropolitan Museum of Art, New York, NY; Mint Museum of Craft + Design, Charlotte, NC; Montreal Museum of Fine Arts, Montreal, QC, Canada; Museum of Arts and Design, New York, NY; Philadelphia Museum of Art, Philadelphia, PA; Renwick Gallery, Smithsonian American Art Museum, Smithsonian Institution, Washington, DC; Speed Art Museum, Louisville, KY; Victoria and Albert Museum, London, U.K.

For more information
www.judithschaechter.com; Alex Baker, *Extra Virgin: The Stained Glass of Judith Schaechter*, Philadelphia: Free News Projects, 2006; Fox 2006, pp. 106 and 109–110; Frantz 2003, pp. 36–39 and 55; Oldknow 2005, pp. 146–147; Larry Rinder and others, *Whitney Biennial 2002*, New York: Whitney Museum of American Art, 2002, pp. 194–195; Darcey Steinke, *Judith Schaechter: Parables in Glass*, Philadelphia: Pennsylvania Academy of the Fine Arts, 1998; Judith Tannenbaum, *Judith Schaechter: Heart Attacks*, Philadelphia: Institute of Contemporary Art, University of Pennsylvania, 1995; Warmus 2003,

pp. 106 and 110–113; Watson and others 2007, p. 30; Yelle 2000, pp. 230–231.

Michael Scheiner

Born in 1956 in Philadelphia, PA. Lives in Central Falls, RI, and Aichi-Ken, Japan.

Scheiner teaches in and heads the glass program at the Nagoya University of Arts, Nagoya, Japan (since 2004). He has taught at the Rhode Island School of Design, Providence, RI (2001, 1998–1999, 1988–1996, 1983–1986); Pilchuck Glass School, Stanwood, WA (2001, 1993, 1990); Universidad de Los Andes, Bogotá, Colombia (2000); University of Hawaii at Manoa, Honolulu, HI (1996); and the Haystack Mountain School of Crafts, Deer Isle, ME (1995, 1987, 1985).

Scheiner was an artist in residence at the Canberra School of Art, Australian National University, Canberra, ACT, Australia (1998); EZRA Glass, Kanazu, Japan (1998); Illinois State University, Normal, IL (1997); Penland School of Crafts, Penland, NC (1996); Tokyo International School of Glass Art, Tokyo, Japan (1996); Toyama Institute of Glass Art, Toyama, Japan (1995); Niijima International Glass Arts Festival, Niijima, Japan (1992); and Alfred University, Alfred, NY (1991).

Education
Ohio State University, Columbus, OH, M.F.A. Sculpture and Glass (1982); Rhode Island School of Design, B.F.A. Sculpture and Glass (1980); European Honors Program, Rome, Italy (1978–1979).

Selected honors and awards
Fulbright Senior Scholar Fellowship, Universidad de Los Andes, Bogotá, Colombia (2000); Award for Innovative Use of Glass in Sculpture, UrbanGlass, Brooklyn, NY (2000, 1992); Faculty Development Grant, Rhode Island School of Design (1999); Rakow Commission, Corning Museum of Glass, Corning, NY (1998); National Endowment for the Arts Fellowship (1994, 1986); Artist Fellowship, New England Foundation for the Arts (1993); Louis Comfort Tiffany Biennial Competition Award (1993); Artist Fellowship, Rhode Island State Council on the Arts (1990); Ford Foundation Travel Grant, Murano, Italy (1980).

Selected museum collections
Arkansas Arts Center, Little Rock, AR; Brooklyn Museum, Brooklyn, NY; Carnegie Museum of Art, Pittsburgh, PA; Corning Museum of Glass, Corning, NY; Hokkaido Museum of Modern Art, Sapporo, Japan; Huntsville Museum of Art, Huntsville, AL; Mint Museum of Art, Charlotte, NC; Museum of American Glass, Wheaton Arts and Cultural Center, Millville, NJ; New Orleans Museum of Art, New Orleans, LA; Renwick Gallery, Smithsonian American Art Museum, Smithsonian Institution, Washington, DC; Rhode Island School of Design Museum, Providence, RI.

Other objects by this artist in the Corning Museum
Sculpture, *The Kiss*, 1989 (90.4.10); Sculpture, *Segmentation*, 1991 (92.4.109).

For more information
Susanne K. Frantz, *Clearly Thinking: The Sculpture of Peter Ivy and Michael Scheiner*, Phoenix, AZ: Phoenix Art Museum, 2002; Frantz, Ricke, and Mizuta 1998, pp. 94–97 and 144; Janet Koplos, "Michael Scheiner: By and Large," *Glass* (UrbanGlass Art Quarterly), no. 57, Fall 1994, pp. 22–29; Lynn 2005, p. 120; Oldknow 2005, p. 112; Yelle 2000, pp. 232–234.

Joyce J. Scott

Born in 1948 in Baltimore, MD. Lives in Baltimore, MD.

Scott was a visiting artist at the Museum of Glass, Tacoma, WA (2006); New School of the Arts, Miami, FL (2006); Roland Park Country School, Baltimore, MD (2006); University of Wisconsin, Milwaukee, WI (2006); Penland School of Crafts, Penland, NC (2003); Rhode Island School of Design, Providence, RI (1999); University of Akron, Akron, OH (1999); UrbanGlass, Brooklyn, NY (1999); Gaya-Girl Press, Baltimore, MD (1998); Iowa State University, Ames, IA (1998); Tennessee Technological University, Cookeville, TN (1998); Collaborative Print Workshop, Washington University, St. Louis, MO (1998, 1996); ArtPace, San Antonio, TX (1996); Moore College of Art and Design, Philadelphia, PA (1996); Skowhegan School of Painting and Sculpture, Skowhegan, ME (1996); University of Hawaii at Manoa, Honolulu, HI (1996); Anderson Ranch, Snowmass, CO (1995); Concordia University, Montreal, QC, Canada (1995); Pilchuck Glass School, Stanwood, WA (1992); Rutgers Center for Innovative Print and Paper, New Brunswick, NJ (1990); and the University of Delaware, Newark, DE (1990).

Education
Haystack Mountain School of Crafts, Deer Isle, ME (1976); Instituto Allende, San Miguel Allende, Guanajuato, Mexico, M.F.A. Crafts (1971); Maryland Institute, College of Art, Baltimore, MD, B.F.A. Education (1970).

Selected honors and awards
Masters of the Medium, James Renwick Alliance, Smithsonian American Art Museum, Smithsonian Institution, Washington, DC (2006); Governor's Arts Award at Artsalute: Maryland Citizens for the Arts Foundation, Walters Art Museum, Baltimore, MD (2002); Fellow, American Crafts Council, New York, NY (2001); National Living Treasure Award, Maryland Nominee (1996); Mid Atlantic Arts Foundation Award (1994); Pace Roberts Fellowship (1994); National Printing Fellowship (1992); Mid Atlantic Arts Consortium Award (1990); Maryland State Arts Council Fellowship (1987, 1981); Fellowship, National Endowment for the Arts (1980).

Selected museum collections
Baltimore Museum of Art, Baltimore, MD; Brooklyn Museum, Brooklyn, NY; Corning Museum of Glass, Corning, NY; Detroit Institute of Arts, Detroit, MI; Kruithuis Museum, Hertogenbosch, the Netherlands; Laumeier Sculpture Park, St. Louis, MO; Mint Museum of Craft + Design, Charlotte, NC; Montreal Museum of Fine Arts, Montreal, QC, Canada; Museum of Arts and Design, New York, NY; Museum of Fine Arts, Houston, Houston, TX; Philadelphia Museum of Art, Philadelphia, PA; Philbrook

Museum of Art, Tulsa, OK; Racine Art Museum, Racine, WI; Renwick Gallery, Smithsonian American Art Museum, Smithsonian Institution, Washington, DC; Rhode Island School of Design Museum, Providence, RI.

For more information
Joy James, *Spirit, Space and Survival: African American Women in (White) Academe*, New York and London: Routledge, 1993; Leslie King-Hammond and others, *Joyce J. Scott: Kickin' It with the Old Masters*, Baltimore: Baltimore Museum of Art and Maryland Institute, College of Art, 2000; Mann 1997, pp. 13 and 26; Kathlyn Moss and Alice Scherer, *The New Beadwork*, New York: Harry N. Abrams, 1992, pp. 81–82; Oldknow 2005, p. 50; Ruffner and others 1991, pp. 52–53 and 69–70; Joyce Scott, *Fearless Beadwork: . . . Handwritings & Drawings from Hell*, Rochester, NY: Visual Studies Workshop, 1994; Scott 1998.

Paul Seide
Born in 1949 in New York, NY. Lives in New York, NY.

Seide was co-founder of Milropa Studio, New York, NY, where he was design director (1975–1980).

Education
University of Wisconsin, Madison, WI, B.S. Fine Art (1974); Egani Neon Glassblowing School, New York, NY, Certificate (1971).

Selected museum collections
Chrysler Museum of Art, Norfolk, VA; Corning Museum of Glass, Corning, NY; Fine Arts Museum of the South, Mobile, AL; Musée de Design et d'Arts Appliqués Contemporains, Lausanne, Switzerland; Museum of American Glass, Wheaton Arts and Cultural Center, Millville, NJ; Museum of Fine Arts, St. Petersburg, FL; National Museum of Modern Art, Kyoto, Japan; Speed Art Museum, Louisville, KY; Toledo Museum of Art, Toledo, OH.

Other objects by this artist in the Corning Museum
Vase, 1975 (75.4.48, gift of the artist); Sculpture, Untitled Triple Loop, 1981 (91.4.61, gift of Harry Horvitz).

For more information
Sigrid Barten, *Licht und Transparenz*, Zurich: Museum Bellerive, 1988, pp. 46–55; Buechner 1979, pp. 205 and 269; David Donihue, *Luminosity*, New York: Alternative Museum, 1986; Duane Preble and Sarah Preble, *Artforms: An Introduction to the Visual Arts*, New York: HarperCollins, 1994, pp. 218–219; Yelle 2000, pp. 236–237.

Kiki Smith
Born in 1954 in Nuremberg, Germany. Lives in New York, NY.

Selected honors and awards
Medal Award, School of the Museum of Fine Arts, Boston, MA (2006); Athena Award for Excellence in Printmaking, Rhode Island School of Design, Providence, RI (2005); Member, American Academy of Arts and Letters (2005); Skowhegan Medal for Sculpture, Skowhegan School of Painting and Sculpture, Skowhegan, ME (2000).

Selected museum collections
Albright-Knox Art Gallery, Buffalo, NY; Art Institute of Chicago, Chicago, IL; Bonner Kunstverein, Bonn, Germany; Brooklyn Museum, Brooklyn, NY; Cincinnati Museum of Art, Cincinnati, OH; Cleveland Museum of Art, Cleveland, OH; Corcoran Gallery of Art, Washington, DC; Corning Museum of Glass, Corning, NY; Des Moines Art Center, Des Moines, IA; Detroit Institute of Arts, Detroit, MI; High Museum of Art, Atlanta, GA; Irish Museum of Modern Art, Dublin, Ireland; Israel Museum, Jerusalem, Israel; Los Angeles County Museum of Art, Los Angeles, CA; Louisiana Museum of Modern Art, Humlebaek, Denmark; Metropolitan Museum of Art, New York, NY; Milwaukee Art Museum, Milwaukee, WI; Moderna Museet, Stockholm, Sweden; Museum of Contemporary Art, Los Angeles, CA; Museum of Contemporary Art San Diego, La Jolla, CA; Museum of Fine Arts, Boston, MA; Museum of Fine Arts, Houston, Houston, TX; Museum of Modern Art, New York, NY; San Francisco Museum of Modern Art, San Francisco, CA; Speed Art Museum, Louisville, KY; Tate Gallery, London, U.K.; Toledo Museum of Art, Toledo, OH; Victoria and Albert Museum, London, U.K.; Virginia Museum of Fine Arts, Richmond, VA; Whitney Museum of American Art, New York, NY.

Other object by this artist in the Corning Museum
Sculpture, *Tail*, 1997 (2004.4.71).

For more information
Art21 Season Two: Art in the 21st Century, Alexandria, VA: Art21 Inc., distributed by PBS Home Video, 2003; Juli Cho Bailer, *Mining Glass*, Tacoma, WA: Museum of Glass, 2007; Jessica Bradley, *Kiki Smith*, Toronto: Power Plant, Contemporary Art Gallery at Harbourfront Centre, 1995; Siri Engberg and others, *Kiki Smith: A Gathering*, Minneapolis, MN: Walker Art Center, 2005; Fox 2006, pp. 118–120; Anneli Fuchs, *Kiki Smith*, Humlebaek, Denmark: Louisiana Museum of Modern Art, 1994; Mayo Graham and Christine Ross, *Kiki Smith*, Montreal: Montreal Museum of Fine Arts, 1996; Carl Haenlein, ed., and Carsten Ahrens, *Kiki Smith: All Creatures Great and Small*, Hanover, Germany: Kestner Gesellschaft, 1998; *Kiki Smith: New Work*, New York: PaceWildenstein, 2005; *Kiki Smith: Realms*, New York: PaceWildenstein, 2002; Olivia Lahs-Gonzalez, *My Nature: Works with Paper by Kiki Smith*, St. Louis: Saint Louis Art Museum, 1999; Lynn 2005, pp. 82–83 and 144–145; Mann 1997, p. 29; Peter Noever and R. A. Stein, *Kiki Smith: Silent Work*, Vienna: Österreichisches Museum für Angewandte Kunst, 1992; Helaine Posner, *Kiki Smith*, New York: Monacelli Press, 2005; Helaine Posner and Kiki Smith, *Kiki Smith: Telling Tales*, New York: International Center of Photography, 2001; Phyllis Rosenzweig, *Directions. Kiki Smith: Night*, Washington, DC: Hirshhorn Museum and Sculpture Garden, Smithsonian Institution, 1998; Ruffner and others 1991, pp. 56–57 and 71; Nancy Stapen, *Kiki Smith: Prints and Multiples*, Boston: Barbara Krakow Gallery, 1994; Wendy Weitman, *Kiki Smith: Prints, Books and Things*, New York: Museum of Modern Art, 2003; Yelle 2000, pp. 245–246.

Robert Sowers

Born in 1923 in Milwaukee, WI. Died in 1990 in Brooklyn, NY.

Sowers was an artist in residence at Dartmouth College, Hanover, NH (1971). He completed major commissions for St. George's Episcopal Church, Durham, NH; Temple Beth Emeth, Albany, NY; Holy Redeemer Church, West Lebanon, NH; All Saints Episcopal Church, Palo Alto, CA; and First Presbyterian Church, New Canaan, CT. His landmark commission for the American Airlines Terminal, Kennedy International Airport, New York, NY (completed 1960, dismantled 2008) was called "the longest window in the world." The window wall was made of 900 panels, and it was 317 feet long and 23 feet high.

Education
  Central School of Arts and Crafts, London, U.K., Stained Glass (1950–1953); independent study and travel in the U.K., France, Germany, and Italy (1950–1953); Columbia University, New York, NY, M.A. (1950); New School for Social Research, New York, NY, B.A. (1948).

Selected honors and awards
  Silver Medal, Architectural League of New York (1962, 1955); Certificate of Merit, Municipal Art Society of New York (1961); Tiffany Award (1956); Fulbright Foundation Fellowship (1950).

Selected museum collections
  Corning Museum of Glass, Corning, NY; Suermondt-Museum, Aachen, Germany.

Other objects by this artist in the Corning Museum (all gifts of Judi Jordan Sowers, unless otherwise noted)
  Panel, *Red One*, 1952 (92.2.6); Color Palettes (2) of Glass for American Airlines Terminal Window Wall, John F. Kennedy International Airport, New York, NY, about 1955–1958 (92.4.135); Panel, *Farewell to Franklin Street*, 1970s (90.4.122, bequest of the Robert Sowers Estate); Panel, *Tiffany Country*, 1971 (92.4.140); Panels, *Ginger* and *In-Forming*, 1972 (92.4.137, .139); Panel, *Green Alert*, 1973 (90.4.121, bequest of the Robert Sowers Estate); Panel, *In-Tense*, 1974 (92.4.138).

For more information
  Clarke 1979, pp. 55–59; Nordness 1970, p. 167; Robert Sowers, *The Language of Stained Glass*, Forest Grove, OR: Timber Press, 1981; Robert Sowers, *The Lost Art: A Survey of One Thousand Years of Stained Glass*, New York: G. Wittenborn, 1954; Robert Sowers, *Rethinking the Forms of Visual Expression*, Berkeley: University of California Press, 1990; Robert Sowers, *Stained Glass: An Architectural Art*, New York: Universe Books, 1965.

Therman Statom

Born in 1953 in Winter Haven, FL. Lives in Omaha, NE.

Statom taught at the Penland School of Crafts, Penland, NC (2003, 2001, 1999, 1995, 1994); Glass Furnace, Istanbul, Turkey (2002); Tampa Museum of Art, Tampa, FL (2002); Bild-Werk Frauenau, Frauenau, Germany (2001); Wheaton Village, Millville, NJ (2001);

Lowe Art Museum, University of Miami, Coral Gables, FL (2000); California College of Arts and Crafts, Oakland, CA (2000, 1999); Pilchuck Glass School, Stanwood, WA (2000, 1993–1997, 1983–1986); Kent State University, Kent, OH (1997); and the Rhode Island School of Design, Providence, RI (1997).

Education
  Pratt Institute, Brooklyn, NY, M.F.A. Sculpture (1978); Rhode Island School of Design, B.F.A. Sculpture (1974); Pilchuck Glass School (1971).

Selected honors and awards
  American Craft Council Award (1999); National Endowment for the Arts Fellowship (1998, 1982); City of Los Angeles 1997/98 Cultural Grant (1997); Brody Arts Foundation Fellowship (1985); Pratt Institute Fellowship (1978); Ford Foundation Fellowship (1977).

Selected museum collections
  California African-American Museum, Los Angeles, CA; Corning Museum of Glass, Corning, NY; Craft and Folk Art Museum, Los Angeles, CA; Detroit Institute of Arts, Detroit, MI; High Museum of Art, Atlanta, GA; Los Angeles County Museum of Art, Los Angeles, CA; Milwaukee Art Museum, Milwaukee, WI; Mint Museum of Craft + Design, Charlotte, NC; Musée de Design et d'Arts Appliqués Contemporains, Lausanne, Switzerland; Musée des Arts Décoratifs, Paris, France; Renwick Gallery, Smithsonian American Art Museum, Smithsonian Institution, Washington, DC; Toledo Museum of Art, Toledo, OH.

Other object by this artist in the Corning Museum
  Sculpture, *Chair*, 1986 (2001.4.237, gift of Mike and Annie Belkin).

For more information
  www.thermanstatom.com; Fox 2006, pp. 123–125; Frantz 1999, pp. 30–33; Matthew Kangas, "Therman Statom: Installing Space," *Glass* (UrbanGlass Art Quarterly), no. 65, Winter 1996, pp. 28–35; Lynn 2005, pp. 48, 54, 117, and 201; Oldknow 2005, p. 116; Maria Porges, "Therman Statom: Northern Tide," *American Craft*, v. 55, no. 3, June/July 1995, pp. 39–41; Scott 1998, pp. 55–56; Warmus 2003, pp. 71 and 92–93; Yelle 2000, pp. 257–259.

Lino Tagliapietra

Born in 1934 in Murano, Italy. Lives in Murano, Italy, and Seattle, WA.

Since 1980, Tagliapietra has periodically taught at C.E.R.F.A.V., Vannes-le-Châtel, France; Centre International de Recherche sur le Verre, Marseilles, France; Haystack Mountain School of Crafts, Deer Isle, ME; JamFactory, Adelaide, SA, Australia; Pratt Fine Arts Center, Seattle, WA; Rhode Island School of Design, Providence, RI; California State University, San Jose, CA; The Studio of The Corning Museum of Glass, Corning, NY; Toyama Institute of Glass Art, Toyama, Japan; University of Sydney, Sydney, NSW, Australia; and UrbanGlass, Brooklyn, NY. He has taught at Pilchuck Glass School, Stanwood, WA (since 1979), and he taught at the Scuola

Internazionale del Vetro, Murano, Italy (1981, 1978, 1976). Tagliapietra was artistic and technical director at Effetre International, Murano, Italy (1976–1989); co-founder and chief maestro of La Murrina, Murano, Italy (1968–1976); and glassblower and designer for Venini & C., Murano, Italy (1966–1968) and Vetreria Galliano Ferro, Murano, Italy (1955–1965).

He is a Fellow of The Corning Museum of Glass (since 1993).

Education
Began apprenticeship with Archimede Seguso, Vetreria Archimede Seguso, Murano, Italy (1946); achieved title of maestro, Murano, Italy (1956).

Selected honors and awards
Cristal Award, Museo del Vidrio, Monterrey, Mexico (2007); Distinguished Educator Award, James Renwick Alliance, Smithsonian American Art Museum, Smithsonian Institution, Washington, DC (2006); Artist Visionaries! Lifetime Achievement Award, Museum of Arts and Design, New York, NY (2004); Honorary Doctorate, Centre College, Danville, KY (2004); President's Distinguished Artist Award, University of the Arts, Philadelphia, PA (2004); Medal for Excellence in Craft Award, Society of Arts and Crafts, Boston, MA (2001); Lifetime Achievement Award, Glass Art Society (1997); Urkunde Goldmedaille, Germany (1997); Award for Preservation of Glassworking Techniques, UrbanGlass (1996); Rakow Commission, Corning Museum of Glass (1996); Grand Prize for Lighting, Barcelona Trade Fair, Barcelona, Spain (1972); Borsella d'Oro Award, Murano, Italy (1968).

Selected museum collections
Bellevue Art Museum, Bellevue, WA; Carnegie Museum of Art, Pittsburgh, PA; Chrysler Museum of Art, Norfolk, VA; Columbus Museum of Art, Columbus, OH; Corning Museum of Glass, Corning, NY; Dayton Art Institute, Dayton, OH; Detroit Institute of Arts, Detroit, MI; Fine Arts Museums of San Francisco, San Francisco, CA; Glasmuseet Ebeltoft, Ebeltoft, Denmark; Hokkaido Museum of Modern Art, Sapporo, Japan; Kestner Museum, Hanover, Germany; Metropolitan Museum of Art, New York, NY; Mint Museum of Craft + Design, Charlotte, NC; Montgomery Museum of Fine Arts, Montgomery, AL; Musée de Design et d'Arts Appliqués Contemporains, Lausanne, Switzerland; Musée des Arts Décoratifs, Paris, France; Museum Boymans van Beuningen, Rotterdam, the Netherlands; Museum Het Paleis, The Hague, the Netherlands; Museum of Fine Arts, Houston, Houston, TX; Museum of Glass, Tacoma, WA; National Museum of Modern Art, Tokyo, Japan; Norton Museum of Art, West Palm Beach, FL; Palazzo Grassi, Venice, Italy; Racine Art Museum, Racine, WI; Scottsdale Museum of Contemporary Art, Scottsdale, AZ; Seattle Art Museum, Seattle, WA; Statens Museum for Kunst, Copenhagen, Denmark; Toledo Museum of Art, Toledo, OH; Victoria and Albert Museum, London, U.K.

Other objects by this artist in the Corning Museum (all gifts of the Ben W. Heineman Sr. Family, unless otherwise noted)
Vessel, *Lacrima I*, 1991 (2006.4.282); Sculpture, *Spirale*, 1994 (2007.4.237); Vessels, *Hopi*, 1996 (96.4.166, the 11th Rakow Commission); Sculpture, *Spirale*, 1996 (2006.4.283); Vessel,

Pamplona, 1997 (2006.4.284); Vessel, *Venere in seta* (Venus in silk), 1997 (2006.4.285); Vessel, *Eve*, 1998 (2007.3.93); Vessel, *Stromboli HG921*, 2002 (2006.4.286).

Design (for Effetre International, Italy): "Psycho" Vase, designed in 1983 and made in 1984 (84.3.213); *Filigrana Incalmo* Plate, 1986 (88.3.25, gift of Emanuel and Phyllis Lacher); "Tessuto" Vase, 1986 (88.3.26, gift of Emanuel and Phyllis Lacher).

Design (for Steuben Glass, United States): Sculpture, *Fenice II*, 1998 (2000.4.8, gift of Royal & Sun Alliance and Christina Rifkin); Sculpture, *Saturno I*, 1998 (2000.4.54, gift of Steuben Glass).

For more information
www.linotagliapietra.com; Marino Barovier, ed., *Tagliapietra: A Venetian Glass Maestro*, Dublin: Links for Publishing, 1998; Titus M. Eliens, *A. D. Copier & Lino Tagliapietra: Inspiration in Glass*, The Hague: Gemeentemuseum, 2000; Fox 2006, pp. 26–27; Susanne K. Frantz, *Lino Tagliapietra in Retrospect: A Modern Renaissance in Italian Glass*, Seattle: University of Washington Press, 2008; Beth Ann Girstein and Jennifer L. Atkinson, eds., *Lino Tagliapietra*, Brockton, MA: Fuller Museum of Art, and Boston: Society of Arts and Crafts, 2001; Lynn 2005, p. 43; Oldknow 2005, p. 237; Giovanni Sarpellon, *Lino Tagliapietra*, Venice: Arsenale Editrice, 1994; Warmus 2003, pp. 13, 19, and 34–35.

Pavel Trnka
Born in 1948 in Poděbrady, Czechoslovakia. Lives in Prague, Czech Republic.

Education
Academy of Applied Arts, Prague, Czechoslovakia (1967–1973); Specialized School for Glassmaking, Železný Brod, Czechoslovakia (1963–1967).

Selected honors and awards
First Prize, National Theater subway station, Prague, Czechoslovakia (1983); Third Prize, International Year of Women, Prague (1976); Applied Arts Award, Ministry of Culture, Prague (1975).

Selected museum collections
Corning Museum of Glass, Corning, NY; East Bohemian Museum, Pardubice, Czech Republic; Glasmuseet Ebeltoft, Ebeltoft, Denmark; Moravian Gallery, Brno, Czech Republic; Musée des Arts Décoratifs, Paris, France; Museum of Decorative Arts, Prague, Czech Republic; Museum of Glass and Jewelry, Jablonec, Czech Republic; North Bohemian Museum, Liberec, Czech Republic; Ulster Museum, Belfast, Northern Ireland; Yokohama Museum of Art, Yokohama, Japan.

For more information
Muzeum Skla a Bižutérie 1995; Oldknow 2005, p. 120; Oldřich Palata, *Stanislav Libenský a jeho škola = Stanislav Libenský and His School*, Salzburg: Galerie Prager Kabinett, 2001; Petrová 2001; Petrová 2004, pp. 66–67 and 92–93; Ricke 1990, pp.

194–196 and 313–314; Jiří Urban, *Světlo stín čas: Pavel Trnka = Light, Shadow, Time: Pavel Trnka*, Prague: Galerie Bratří Čapků, 1997.

Dana Vachtová
Born in 1937 in Prague, Czechoslovakia. Lives in Prague, Czech Republic.

Education
Academy of Applied Arts, Prague, Czechoslovakia (1956–1963); Secondary Art School, Prague (1952–1956).

Selected honors and awards
Silver Award, "Kristallnacht Project," American Interfaith Institute, Philadelphia, PA (1992); Coburg Glass Prize '77, Kunstsammlungen der Veste Coburg, Coburg, Germany (1977).

Selected museum collections
Corning Museum of Glass, Corning, NY; East Bohemian Museum, Pardubice, Czech Republic; Kunstsammlungen der Veste Coburg, Coburg, Germany; Moravian Gallery, Brno, Czech Republic; Musée de Design et d'Arts Appliqués Contemporains, Lausanne, Switzerland; Musées Royaux d'Art et d'Histoire, Brussels, Belgium; Museum of Decorative Arts, Prague, Czech Republic; Museum of Glass and Jewelry, Jablonec, Czech Republic; Museum Jan van der Togt, Amstelveen, the Netherlands; National Gallery, Prague, Czech Republic; North Bohemian Museum, Liberec, Czech Republic.

Other objects by this artist in the Corning Museum
Plate with Abstract Decoration, 1961 (2006.3.68); Sculpture, *Girder*, 1991 (95.3.1).

For more information
www.vachtova.com; Muzeum Skla a Bižutérie 1995, pp. 43 and 54; Petrová 2001; Petrová 2004, pp. 68–69 and 93; Ricke 2005, pp. 324–333 and 401–402; Weschenfelder 2006, pp. 285 and 370.

Bertil Vallien
Born in 1938 in Stockholm, Sweden. Lives in Eriksmala, Sweden.

Vallien is a designer for Kosta Boda, Kosta, Sweden (since 1963). He taught at North Lands Creative Glass, Lybster, Caithness, U.K. (1997, 1996); University of Hawaii at Manoa, Honolulu, HI (1994, 1992); New York Experimental Glass Workshop, New York, NY (1993); Pratt Fine Arts Center, Seattle, WA (1993); Pilchuck Glass School, Stanwood, WA (1980–1992); and the National College of Arts, Crafts, and Design, Stockholm, Sweden (1967–1984). He was an artist in residence at Pilchuck Glass School (1984–1986), and at the Rhode Island School of Design, Providence, RI (1985).

Education
Royal scholarship to study in the United States and Mexico (1961–1963); National College of Arts, Crafts, and Design (1957–1961).

Selected honors and awards
Gold Medal, Royal Academy of Science, Stockholm, Sweden (2005); Visionaries! Award, Museum of Arts and Design, New York, NY (2001); Kalmar Cultural Award, Kalmar, Sweden (1999); Millennium Award, Swedish Crystal Manufacturers Association (1999); Outstanding Achievement in Glass Award, UrbanGlass, Brooklyn, NY (1995); Formland Prize, Copenhagen, Denmark (1991, 1988); Diploma, Nordform-90, Malmö, Sweden (1990); Coburg Glass Prize '85, Kunstsammlungen der Veste Coburg, Coburg, Germany (1985); Silver Medal, International Juried Art Competition, New York, NY (1985); First Prize, Swedish Design, Nationalmuseum, Stockholm, Sweden (1983); Illum Prize, Copenhagen, Denmark (1967); Östersund Cultural Scholarship, Östersund, Sweden (1965); Royal Scholarship, Stockholm, Sweden (1961).

Selected museum collections
Art Gallery of Western Australia, Perth, WA, Australia; Art Institute of Chicago, Chicago, IL; Corning Museum of Glass, Corning, NY; Detroit Institute of Arts, Detroit, MI; Glasmuseet Ebeltoft, Ebeltoft, Denmark; Glasmuseum Hentrich, Museum Kunst Palast, Düsseldorf, Germany; Hokkaido Museum of Modern Art, Sapporo, Japan; Indianapolis Museum of Art, Indianapolis, IN; Metropolitan Museum of Art, New York, NY; Musée de Design et d'Arts Appliqués Contemporains, Lausanne, Switzerland; Musée des Arts Décoratifs, Paris, France; Museum of Arts and Design, New York, NY; National Museum of Modern Art, Kyoto, Japan; National Museum of Modern Art, Tokyo, Japan; Nationalmuseum, Stockholm, Sweden; Neue Sammlung, Munich, Germany; Röhsska Museum of Design and Decorative Arts, Gothenburg, Sweden; Smålands Museum, Växjö, Sweden; Speed Art Museum, Louisville, KY; Toledo Museum of Art, Toledo, OH; Trondheim Art Museum, Trondheim, Norway; Victoria and Albert Museum, London, U.K; Yokohama Museum of Art, Yokohama, Japan.

Other objects by this artist in the Corning Museum
Sculpture, *Staircase*, 1983 (83.3.186); Sculptures, *Cargo Seed* and Untitled, 1988 (2007.3.94, .95, gifts of the Ben W. Heineman Sr. Family).

Design (for Åfors Glasbruk, Sweden): Bottle-Shaped Vase, 1968 (74.3.153); Vases, 1974 (74.3.147, .148, gifts of Åforsgruppen AB).

Design (for Kosta Boda, Sweden): Vessel, *Captivity*, 1978 (78.3.72); Bottle (Atelje 306), 1978 (79.3.53); Bottle, *Trumpet Blower in Sand* (Unik 4201), 1978 (83.3.250); Vase (Atelje 335), about 1978 (79.3.55); Two Bottles (Atelje 334), about 1978 (79.3.68); Vase (Unik 2897), 1979 (79.3.46); Bottle (Unik 3338), 1979 (79.3.47); *Pokals* (Unik 3764, 3772), 1979 (79.3.48, .49); Vase (Unik 3996), 1979 (79.3.50); Bottle (Atelje 240/3), 1979 (79.3.51); Bottle (Atelje 273), 1979 (79.3.52); Bottle (Atelje 325/400), 1979 (79.3.54); Bowl, 1980s (99.3.19, gift of Mr. and Mrs. Dwight P. Lanmon); Bottle (Atelje 520), 1984 (84.3.252, gift of Hans Werner).

For more information
www.bertilvallien.se; Angela Adegren, *Bertil Vallien/Gunnar*

Lindqvist, Stockholm: Carlssons, 1994; Monica Boman, *Faces of Swedish Design*, Stockholm: Swedish Society of Crafts and Design, 1988, pp. 26–27; Buechner 1979, pp. 225–226 and 271; Fox 2006, pp. 87 and 89–90; Frantz 1999, pp. 34–37; William L. Geary, *Scandinavian Glass: Creative Energies*, Atglen, PA: Schiffer, 2003, pp. 65–68; Ilse-Neuman 1997, pp. 74–93; Börge Kamras and Barbro Kamras, *Bertil Vallien: Kraków, Warszawa*, Borgholm, Sweden: Galleri Kamras, 1999; Matthew Kangas, "Bertil Vallien: Somna Vakna," in Kangas 2006, pp. 260–265; Lynn 2005, p. 92; Mann 1997, p. 14; Tara McDonnell, *Bertil Vallien: Glass Eats Light*, Tacoma, WA: Museum of Glass: International Center for Contemporary Art, 2003; Oldknow 2005, p. 121; Ricke 1990, pp. 84–89 and 314–316; Charlotte Sahl-Madsen and Sandra Blach, eds., *Den nordiske åre = The Nordic Spirit*, Ebeltoft, Denmark: Glasmuseet Ebeltoft, 1999, pp. 50–51; Statens Historiska Museet, *Bertil Vallien*, Stockholm: the museum, 1998; Warmus 2003, pp. 70 and 94–97; Yelle 2000, pp. 272–275.

Jack Wax

Born in 1954 in Tarrytown, NY. Lives in Richmond, VA.

Wax is glass area leader and professor at the School of the Arts, Virginia Commonwealth University, Richmond, VA (since 2002). He taught at Illinois State University, Normal, IL (1997–2002); Haystack Mountain School of Crafts, Deer Isle, ME (2002, 1997); The Studio of The Corning Museum of Glass, Corning, NY (1997, 1996); Penland School of Crafts, Penland, NC (1997, 1996, 1991); Pilchuck Glass School, Stanwood, WA (1996); Toyama Institute of Glass Art, Toyama, Japan (1991–1996); Cleveland Institute of Art, Cleveland, OH (1990–1991); University of the Arts, Philadelphia College of Art and Design, Philadelphia, PA (1988–1990); Rhode Island School of Design, Providence, RI (1990, 1987, 1981–1985); Tyler School of Art, Temple University, Philadelphia, PA (1987–1990); and Ohio State University, Columbus, OH (1986).

Education
 Rhode Island School of Design, M.F.A. Sculpture/Glass (1981–1983); Pilchuck Glass School (1979, 1974–1976); Tyler School of Art, Temple University, B.F.A. Ceramics/Glass (1975–1978); Haystack Mountain School of Crafts (1977); Penland School of Crafts (1977, 1974); Archie Bray Foundation, Helena, MT (1975, 1974); Goddard College, Plainfield, VT (1972–1975); Northwestern University, Archaeological Field School, Kampsville, IL (1973).

Selected honors and awards
 Pollack Award (2007); Reynolds Fellowship (2007); Virginia Museum of Fine Arts Professional Artist Fellowship (2007); Illinois State University Research Grant (2002, 2000); Illinois Artists' Fellowship (1997); National Endowment for the Arts Individual Artists Fellowship (1988–1989); National Endowment for the Arts Fellowship (1986–1987); Scholarship, Graduate Studies, Rhode Island School of Design (1981–1983); Teaching and Technical Assistantship, Pilchuck Glass School (1976–1979); Special Technical Assistantship, Penland School of Crafts (1977); Teaching and Technical Assistantship, Haystack Mountain School of Crafts (1977).

Selected museum collections
 Corning Museum of Glass, Corning, NY; Glasmuseet Ebeltoft, Ebeltoft, Denmark; Los Angeles County Museum of Art, Los Angeles, CA; Renwick Gallery, Smithsonian American Art Museum, Smithsonian Institution, Washington, DC; Speed Art Museum, Louisville, KY; Tang Museum, Taipei, Taiwan.

Other object by this artist in the Corning Museum
 Sculpture, *Circus Lights*, 1986 (87.4.3).

For more information
 Fox 2006, pp. 70 and 79; Frantz, Ricke, and Mizuta 1998, pp. 108–113 and 147; Oldknow 2005, p. 123; Stuhr and others 1997, pp. 92 and 112; Weiss 1998, pp. 17 and 20.

Robert Willson

Born in 1912 in Mertzon, TX. Died in 2000 in San Antonio, TX.

Willson taught at the University of Miami, Coral Gables, FL (1952–1977); Ozarka College, Melbourne, AR (1948–1952); Nob Hill Pottery, Mountainburg, AR (1948–1950); Texas Wesleyan University, Fort Worth, TX (1940–1948); Trinity University, San Antonio, TX (1946–1947); and the University of Mexico, Mexico City, Mexico (1935).
 He was founder/director of the Council of Ozark Artists and Craftsmen; president/director of Florida Craftsmen; consultant/director of the Peoria Art Museum, Peoria, IL (1969); director of the Nob Hill Art Gallery, Melbourne, AR (1948–1952); and director of the Texas Wesleyan University Art Gallery (1940–1948).

Education
 U.S. Marine School, Quantico, VA, and U.S. Navy School, Washington, DC (1942); University de Bellas Artes, San Miguel de Allende, Mexico, M.F.A. (1941); San Carlos Academy of Art, Mexico City, Mexico (1935); University of Texas, Austin, TX, B.F.A. (1934); Southern Methodist University, Dallas, TX (1930–1931).

Selected honors and awards
 Academician with Gold Medal, Italian Academy of Arts and Labor, Salsomaggiore Terme, Italy (1980); Feldman Foundation Research Grant to Venice (1976); College Grants for Glass, Shell Co. Foundation (1973, 1971); Member, Istituto Veneto per il Lavoro, Venice, Italy (1968); International Research Grant in Glass, U.S. Office of Education (1966–1968); University of Miami Research Grants in Glass to Italy (1966, 1964); Merit Prize, San Francisco Museum of Modern Art Annual Exhibition (1957); National Study Grant, Corning Museum of Glass, Corning, NY (1956); Farmer International Foreign Exchange Fellowship, University of Texas, Austin, TX (1935).

Selected museum collections
 Auckland War Memorial Museum, Auckland, New Zealand; Chrysler Museum of Art, Norfolk, VA; Corning Museum of Glass, Corning, NY; Correr Museum, Venice, Italy; Los Angeles County Museum of Art, Los Angeles, CA; Marion Koogler McNay Art Museum, San Antonio, TX; Metropolitan Museum of Art, New York, NY; Mint Museum of Craft + Design, Charlotte, NC; Museo del Vetro (Musei Civici Veneziani), Murano, Italy; Museum

of Arts and Design, New York, NY; Museum of Fine Arts, Houston, Houston, TX; Museum of New Mexico, Santa Fe, NM; New Orleans Museum of Art, New Orleans, LA; Philbrook Museum of Art, Tulsa, OK; Racine Art Museum, Racine, WI; Renwick Gallery, Smithsonian American Art Museum, Smithsonian Institution, Washington, DC; Ringling Museum of Art, Sarasota, FL; San Antonio Museum of Art, San Antonio, TX; Toledo Museum of Art, Toledo, OH; Victoria and Albert Museum, London, U.K.

Other objects by this artist in the Corning Museum (all gifts of Margaret Pace Willson, unless otherwise noted)
Sculpture, *King and Queen*, 1974 (2001.3.19); Sculpture, *Architectural Symbol*, 1975 (2007.3.73, gift of Elmerina and Paul Parkman); Sculpture, *Family Totem*, 1976 (2001.3.20); Paperweight with Horse and Rider, about 1980 (2001.4.261); Orange and White Paperweight, about 1980 (2001.4.263); Paperweight with Colored Canes, about 1980 (2001.4.264); Small Sphere, about 1980 (2001.4.265); Sculptures, *Love Letter*, *Tree Altar*, and *Navajo Man*, 1983 (2001.3.21–.23); Sculpture, *Tree Symbol*, 1984 (86.3.107, gift of the artist); Sculpture, *Ranch Doll*, 1984 (2001.3.34); Sculpture, *Night Watch (with Herd)*, 1985 (2001.3.24); Sculpture, *Sun and Moon*, 1986 (2001.3.25); Sculptures, *In the Cosmos* and *Mesa at Sunset*, 1988 (2003.3.61, .63); Sculptures, *Blue Chisel* and *Counting*, 1990 (2001.3.26, .40); Sculpture, *Red Nile (People)*, 1991 (2001.3.27); Sculptures, *Mirage* and *Lady of Character* (2001.3.28, .29); Sculpture, *Ranch Horse (Wild One)*, 1992 (2003.3.62); Sculpture, *Old Wave (Harbor Wave)*, about 1992 (2001.3.35); Sculpture, *Vineyard*, about 1993 (2003.3.64); Sculptures, *The Textures*, *Builder's Cube V*, and *The New Doors of Life* (2001.3.30, .31, .41); Sculpture, *Rites of Stonehenge*, 1996 (2003.3.57); Sculptures, *Builder's Cube II, III*, and *IV*, 1996 (2003.3.58–.60); Sculptures, *Ocean Music* and *Roman Wall*, 1997 (2001.3.32, .33).

For more information
www.robertwillson.com; Renato Borsato and others, *A Story in Glass: Robert Willson*, San Antonio, TX: Tejas Art Press, 1984; Fox 2006, pp. 87–88; Matthew Kangas, *Robert Willson: Image-Maker*, San Antonio, TX: Pace-Willson Foundation in association with University of Washington Press, 2001; Matthew Kangas, "Robert Willson: Image Maker," in Kangas 2006, pp. 254–259; Lynn 2005, pp. 38–39; Daniel Piersol, *Trail of the Maverick: Watercolors and Drawings by Robert Willson, 1975–1998*, New Orleans: New Orleans Museum of Art, 1999.

Christopher Wilmarth
Born in 1943 in Sonoma, CA. Died in 1987 in Brooklyn, NY.

Wilmarth taught at Columbia University, New York, NY (1986), and at the Cooper Union for the Advancement of Science and Art, New York, NY (1969). He was an artist in residence at the University of California, Berkeley, CA (1979).

Education
Cooper Union for the Advancement of Science and Art, B.F.A. (1965).

Selected museum collections
Albright-Knox Art Gallery, Buffalo, NY; Art Institute of Chicago, Chicago, IL; Carnegie Museum of Art, Pittsburgh, PA; Chrysler Museum of Art, Norfolk, VA; Cleveland Museum of Art, Cleveland, OH; Corning Museum of Glass, Corning, NY; Dallas Museum of Art, Dallas, TX; Denver Art Museum, Denver, CO; Des Moines Art Center, Des Moines, IA; Fine Arts Museums of San Francisco, San Francisco, CA; Hirshhorn Museum and Sculpture Garden, Smithsonian Institution, Washington, DC; Metropolitan Museum of Art, New York, NY; Museum of Fine Arts, Houston, Houston, TX; Museum of Modern Art, New York, NY; National Gallery of Art, Washington, DC; New Orleans Museum of Art, New Orleans, LA; Philadelphia Museum of Art, Philadelphia, PA; Phoenix Art Museum, Phoenix, AZ; Saint Louis Art Museum, St. Louis, MO; San Francisco Museum of Modern Art, San Francisco, CA; Seattle Art Museum, Seattle, WA; Toledo Museum of Art, Toledo, OH; Virginia Museum of Fine Arts, Richmond, VA; Wadsworth Atheneum Museum of Art, Hartford, CT; Walker Art Center, Minneapolis, MN; Whitney Museum of American Art, New York, NY.

Other object by this artist in the Corning Museum
Sculpture, *Left Stream*, 1974 (2001.4.257, gift of Ronnie Greenberg and John Van Doren).

For more information
Brooklyn Museum 1985, pp. 26–27; Fox 2006, pp. 26–28; Hughes 1981, pp. 393 and 396; Brett Littman, "Christopher Wilmarth's Glass Poems," *Glass* (UrbanGlass Art Quarterly), no. 71, Summer 1998, pp. 44–47; Lynn 2005, p. 181; Steven Henry Madoff and others, *Christopher Wilmarth: Light and Gravity*, Princeton, NJ: Princeton University Press, 2004; Mann 1997, p. 13; Joseph Masheck, *Christopher Wilmarth: Nine Clearings for a Standing Man*, Hartford, CT: Wadsworth Atheneum, 1974; Laura Rosenstock, *Christopher Wilmarth*, New York: Museum of Modern Art, 1989; Edward Saywell, *Christopher Wilmarth: Drawing into Sculpture*, New Haven, CT: Yale University Press, 2003; Miles Unger, "Christopher Wilmarth: Layers, Clearing, Breath," *Sculpture*, v. 17, no. 9, November 1998, pp. 70–71; Christopher Wilmarth and Dore Ashton, *Breath: Inspired by Seven Poems of Stéphane Mallarmé*, trans. Frederick Morgan, New York: Christopher Wilmarth, 1982; Yelle 2000, pp. 292–294.

Ann Wolff (also known as Ann Wärff)
Born in 1937 in Lübeck, Germany. Lives in Gotland, Sweden, and Berlin, Germany.

Wolff taught at the Hochschule für Bildende Künste, Hamburg, Germany (1993–1998), and at Pilchuck Glass School, Stanwood, WA (1995, 1986, 1984, 1979, 1977). She was a designer for Kosta Boda, Sweden (1964–1978), and for Pukebergs Glasbruk, Sweden (1960–1964).

Education
Ulm School of Design (Hochschule für Gestaltung), Ulm, Germany (1956–1959).

Selected honors and awards
Jurors Award, Toledo Museum of Art, Toledo, OH (2005); Rakow Commission, Corning Museum of Glass, Corning, NY (1997); Gold Medal, Bayerischer Staatspreis, Munich, Germany (1988); WCC Glass Prize, Bratislava, Czechoslovakia (1984); Lessebo Kommuns Kulturpris, Lessebo, Sweden (1982); Special Prize, Internationale Glaskunst, Kassel, Germany (1981); First Prize, Zentralschweizer Glaspreis Kunst, Switzerland (1980); First Prize, Coburg Glass Prize '77, Kunstsammlungen der Veste Coburg, Coburg, Germany (1977); Special Libraries Association Award, Western Canada Chapter (1974); Lunning Prize, New York, NY (1968).

Selected museum collections
Alexander-Tutsek-Stiftung, Munich, Germany; Badisches Landesmuseum, Karlsruhe, Germany; Corning Museum of Glass, Corning, NY; Dansk Kunstindustrimuseum, Copenhagen, Denmark; Dresdner Kunstgewerbemuseum, Dresden, Germany; Ernsting Stiftung Alter Hof Herding, Coesfeld, Germany; Glasmuseet Ebeltoft, Ebeltoft, Denmark; Glasmuseum Hentrich, Museum Kunst Palast, Düsseldorf, Germany; Hoganäs Museum, Hoganäs, Sweden; Hokkaido Museum of Modern Art, Sapporo, Japan; Kestner Museum, Hanover, Germany; Kunstsammlungen der Veste Coburg, Coburg, Germany; Malmö Museum, Malmö, Sweden; Metropolitan Museum of Art, New York, NY; Mint Museum of Craft + Design, Charlotte, NC; Musée de Design et d'Arts Appliqués Contemporains, Lausanne, Switzerland; Musée des Arts Décoratifs, Paris, France; Museum Bellerive, Zurich, Switzerland; Museum für Kunst und Gewerbe, Hamburg, Germany; Museum of Arts and Design, New York, NY; National Museum of Modern Art, Tokyo, Japan; Nationalmuseum, Stockholm, Sweden; Röhsska Museum of Design and Decorative Arts, Gothenburg, Sweden; Stedelijk Museum, Amsterdam, the Netherlands; Toledo Museum of Art, Toledo, OH; Smålands Museum, Växjö, Sweden; Victoria and Albert Museum, London, U.K.; Württembergisches Landesmuseum, Stuttgart, Germany.

Other objects by this artist in the Corning Museum
Vessel, *Plate Scenery*, 1978 (78.3.74); Vessel, *The Milky Way*, 1979 (79.3.42); Bowl, about 1982–1984 (92.3.38, bequest of David Brokars); Sculpture, *Lilith*, 1986 (2006.3.24, gift of the Ben W. Heineman Sr. Family); Vessel, *Stay at Home*, 1986 (2006.3.25, gift of the Ben W. Heineman Sr. Family); Vessel, *Cup and Cup*, 1986 (2006.3.26, gift of the Ben W. Heineman Sr. Family); Sculpture, *The Silent*, 1997 (97.3.38, the 12th Rakow Commission).

Design (for Kosta Boda, Sweden): Decorative Sculpture (96740), about 1970 (70.3.73); Sculpture, Untitled, 1979 (79.3.36).

With Goran Wärff (Swedish, b. 1933): Bowl, 1969 (70.3.72).

For more information
www.annwolff.se; *Ann Wolff*, Zurich: Sanske Galerie, and Kalmar, Sweden: Arch Gallery, 2000; Pauline Asingh, *Ann Wolff: Observations*, Ebeltoft, Denmark: Glasmuseet Ebeltoft, 2005; Buechner 1979, pp. 237–238 and 273; Heike Issaias and others, *Ann Wolff*, Stockholm: Raster Förlag, 2002; Jordana Pomeroy, *Nordic Cool: Hot Women Designers*, Washington, DC: National Museum of Women in the Arts, 2004, p. 5; Schack von Wittenau 2005, pp. 190–191.

Bibliography

Works that are cited more than once in the "Artists' Biographies" are listed below by author(s)/editor(s) and date.

Austin and others 1993
Carole Austin and others, *Nine Decades: The Northern California Craft Movement, 1907 to Present*, San Francisco: San Francisco Craft & Folk Art Museum, 1993.
Brooklyn Museum 1985
Brooklyn Museum, *Working in Brooklyn: Sculpture*, Brooklyn, NY: the museum, 1985.
Buechner 1979
Thomas S. Buechner, ed., *New Glass: A Worldwide Survey*, Corning: Corning Museum of Glass, 1979.
Clarke 1979
Brian Clarke, ed., *Architectural Stained Glass*, New York: Architectural Record Books, 1979.
Dorigato and Klein 1996
Attilia Dorigato and Dan Klein, eds., *Venezia Aperto Vetro: International New Glass*, Venice: Arsenale Editrice, 1996.
Fox 2006
Howard N. Fox, *Glass: Material Matters*, Los Angeles: Los Angeles County Museum of Art, 2006.
Frantz 1989
Susanne K. Frantz, *Contemporary Glass: A World Survey from The Corning Museum of Glass*, New York: Harry N. Abrams, 1989.
Frantz 1999
Susanne K. Frantz, *Eleven Glass Sculptures*, Corning: Corning Incorporated, 1999.
Frantz 2003
Susanne K. Frantz, *The Other Side of the Looking Glass: The Glass Body and Its Metaphors*, Redding, CA: Turtle Bay Exploration Park, 2003.
Frantz, Ricke, and Mizuta 1998
Susanne K. Frantz, Helmut Ricke, and Yoriko Mizuta, *The Glass Skin*, Düsseldorf: Kunstmuseum, Sapporo: Hokkaido Museum of Art, and Corning: Corning Museum of Glass, 1998.
Graham 1999
Jean Graham, *Holding Light: Contemporary Glass Sculpture*, Austin, TX: Austin Museum of Art, 1999.
Hughes 1981
Robert Hughes, *The Shock of the New*, New York: Alfred A. Knopf, 1981.
Ilse-Neuman 1997
Ursula Ilse-Neuman, *Four Acts in Glass: Installations by Chihuly, Morris, Powers, and Vallien*, Seattle: Bryan Ohno Gallery, 1997.

Kangas 2006
    Matthew Kangas, *Craft and Concept: The Rematerialization of the Art Object*, New York: Midmarch Arts Press, 2006.
Kehlmann 1992
    Robert Kehlmann, *20th-Century Stained Glass: A New Definition*, Kyoto: Kyoto Shoin, 1992.
Lynggaard 1998
    Finn Lynggaard, ed., *The Story of Studio Glass*, Copenhagen: Rhodos, 1998.
Lynn 2004
    Martha Drexler Lynn, *American Studio Glass, 1960–1990: An Interpretive Study*, New York: Hudson Hills Press, 2004.
Lynn 2005
    Martha Drexler Lynn, *Sculpture, Glass and American Museums*, Philadelphia: University of Pennsylvania Press, 2005.
Mann 1997
    Audrey Mann, *Recent Glass Sculpture: A Union of Ideas*, Milwaukee: Milwaukee Art Museum, 1997.
Moor 1997
    Andrew Moor, *Architectural Glass Art*, New York: Rizzoli, 1997.
Muzeum Skla a Bižutérie 1995
    Muzeum Skla a Bižutérie, *Česká tavená skleněná plastika '95 = Czech Mould-Melted Glass Objects '95*, Jablonec nad Nisou, Czech Republic: the museum, 1995.
Nordness 1970
    Lee Nordness, *Objects: U.S.A.*, New York: Viking Press, 1970.
Oldknow 2005
    Tina Oldknow, *25 Years of New Glass Review*, Corning: Corning Museum of Glass, 2005.
Opie 2004
    Jennifer Hawkins Opie, *Contemporary International Glass*, London: V&A Publications, 2004.
Petrová 2001
    Sylva Petrová, *Czech Glass*, Prague: Gallery Praha, 2001.
Petrová 2004
    Sylva Petrová, *Captured Light and Space: Czech Contemporary Glass = Hikari to kūkan no hosoku: Cheko gendai garasu*, Prague: Commissioner General Office for the Participation of the Czech Republic in the World Exposition EXPO 2005, 2004.
Ricke 1990
    Helmut Ricke, *Neues Glas in Europa = New Glass in Europe*, Düsseldorf: Verlagsanstalt Handwerk, 1990.
Ricke 2005
    Helmut Ricke, ed., *Czech Glass, 1945–1980: Design in an Age of Adversity*, Stuttgart: Arnoldsche Art Publishers, 2005.
Ruffner and others 1991
    Ginny Ruffner and others, *Glass: Material in the Service of Meaning*, Tacoma, WA: Tacoma Art Museum, 1991.
Schack von Wittenau 2005
    Clementine Schack von Wittenau, *Neues Glas und Studioglas = New Glass and Studio Glass*, Coburg, Germany: Kunstsammlungen der Veste Coburg, 2005.
Scott 1998
    Joyce Scott, *Stop Asking/We Exist: 25 African-American Craft Artists*, Pittsburgh: Society for Contemporary Crafts, 1998.
Sekera and Šetlík 1998
    Jan Sekera and Jiří Šetlík, *Sklo a prostor = Glass and Space*, Prague: Czech Museum of Fine Arts, 1998.

Smithsonian Interview
    Oral History Interview, Nanette L. Laitman Documentation Project for Craft and Decorative Arts in America, Archives of American Art, Smithsonian Institution, Washington, DC (http://www.aaa.si.edu/collections/oralhistories).
Stuhr and others 1997
    Joanne Stuhr and others, *Cálido! Contemporary Warm Glass*, Tucson, AZ: Tucson Museum of Art, 1997.
Warmus 2003
    William Warmus, *Fire and Form: The Art of Contemporary Glass*, West Palm Beach, FL: Norton Museum of Art, 2003.
Watson 2002
    Neil Watson, *Some Assembly Required*, Tacoma, WA: Museum of Glass: International Center for Contemporary Art, 2002.
Watson and others 2007
    Neil Watson and others, *Shattering Glass: New Perspectives*, Katonah, NY: Katonah Museum of Art, 2007.
Weiss 1998
    Dick Weiss, *Telling Compelling Tales: Narration in Contemporary Glass*, Helena, MT: Holter Museum, 1998.
Weschenfelder 2006
    Klaus Weschenfelder, ed., *Coburger Glaspreis für zeitgenössische Glaskunst in Europa 2006 = Coburg Glass Prize for Contemporary Glass in Europe 2006*, Coburg, Germany: Kunstsammlungen der Veste Coburg, 2006.
Yelle 2000
    Richard W. Yelle, *Glass Art from UrbanGlass*, Atglen, PA: Schiffer, 2000.

Index of Artists

Numbers in boldface indicate pages on which illustrations appear.